Issue | 135

RADICAL *Review*
HISTORY

T0339232

Radical Histories of Sanctuary
Issue Editors: A. Naomi Paik, Jason Ruiz, and Rebecca M. Schreiber

TEACHING RADICAL HISTORY

CURATED SPACES

Sanctuary's Radical Networks

A. Naomi Paik, Jason Ruiz, and Rebecca M. Schreiber

On the cover of this issue is a photograph from an installation and performance work by artist Caleb Duarte in collaboration with five Guatemalan refugee youths who were part of Fremont High School's Newcomer Education Support and Transition (NEST) program in Oakland. This artwork, titled *Walking the Beast*, was displayed as part of Bay Area Now 8 held at the Yerba Buena Center for the Arts (YBCA) in San Francisco in the summer of 2018. The installation included a 20′ × 10′ × 18′ structure resembling a partially built church or house, secured by a cement foundation filled with dirt. During the three-hour performance on September 7, 2018, these students dug into the dirt "stage" in order to bury themselves. One of the main themes of this work, which builds on Duarte's previous collaborative artworks, draws from his questioning of the role of institutions that offer sanctuary or protection for immigrants and refugees.[1] Similarly, *Walking the Beast* serves as an intervention into the space of YBCA, an arts center that is located in San Francisco, one of the first sanctuary cities in the United States.[2]

This installation at YBCA emerged out of Duarte's "Urgente Arte" ("Urgent Art") workshops with refugee youth involved with the NEST program and held at La Peña Cultural Center in Oakland between 2016 and 2018. As part of these workshops, students created a fictional "Embassy of the Central American Refugee," imagining an autonomous form of sanctuary that can be distinguished from those created by or within state and religious institutions.[3] The performances that they created, including *Walking the Beast*, emerged out of a context in which Central American refugees are "left with only their bodies to resist" to "draw attention to

Radical History Review
Issue 135 (October 2019)   DOI 10.1215/01636545-7607797
© 2019 by MARHO: The Radical Historians' Organization, Inc.

the true crises," which include "U.S. intervention and nation-states' long-term unwillingness to enforce human rights protections in the region," as Leisy Abrego has argued.[4] In their collaborations with Duarte, the Central American youth created performances in which they used their bodies to stage a response to the structural conditions that compelled them to move and that have shaped their everyday lives.

Like Duarte, this special issue responds to our contemporary moment and context. We began assembling this collection from the United States not long after the presidential election of Donald Trump. The forty-fifth president fueled his rise to power with anti-immigrant attacks, which he has enacted on a policy level ever since taking office. He authorized a so-called Muslim ban that has now been affirmed as fully constitutional by the Supreme Court; made any undocumented or otherwise deportable noncitizen a priority for deportation; signed off on a "zero tolerance" policy at the southern border, leading to the separations of migrant children from their families; and has constantly demanded a wall along the US–Mexico border that, at the time of this writing, has led to the longest government shutdown in US history. As immigration scholars know well, the past few decades of immigration legislation and policy have given the current administration a robust arsenal of policies, funding, and enforcement tools to deploy against noncitizens.

In response to these intensified attacks, social movements operating under the sign of sanctuary have become emboldened. The number of sanctuary churches and temples, as well as sanctuary jurisdictions in cities, counties, and states, has increased, while new types of sanctuary spaces have emerged in schools, campuses, restaurants, and homes. Immigrant empowerment organizations have mobilized self-defense committees, know-your-rights teach-ins, ICE- and cop-watching trainings, and other forms of community-based resistance.

These contemporary movements draw on and extend a rich history in the United States. The sanctuary movement for migrants and refugees arose in the 1980s in response to the US-backed political violence in Central America that forced tens of thousands to flee their homes for their lives, only to be denied asylum by the US government. Faith communities across the nation came together to house these asylum seekers in their churches and temples, using their positions of moral leadership to expose the violent ruptures of US foreign policy and immigration restrictions. The New Sanctuary Movement (NSM) emerged in the early 2000s to defend immigrants, particularly long-term residents, from the escalating deportation regimes instigated by the post-9/11 creation of the Department of Homeland Security (DHS), Immigration and Customs Enforcement (ICE), and Customs and Border Protection (CBP). Churches and local communities once again stepped up to defend their neighbors from forced removal. Thus, while some have been galvanized into social justice work for the first time in response to the Trump regime, foundations for the energized sanctuary movements were built not only on the past few decades but also on longue durée histories of community self-defense and on already existing organizing by multiple affected communities.

While US sanctuary movements in recent history have focused on noncitizens under duress, sectors of the current movement are necessarily expanding their purview to grapple with the collusions of the state and capital that target ever more people and places. Indeed, the current administration's attacks are not isolated to racially outcast noncitizens, and the undercurrents that gave rise to Trump are not isolated to the United States, as seen in the concomitant ascendance of right-wing populist movements worldwide—in countries like Brazil, Hungary, Germany, the Philippines, Britain (Brexit), and others. These movements draw on the common strategy of scapegoating and targeting outcasts—whether noncitizens; racial, ethnic, or religious minorities; or queer, poor, disabled, or Indigenous people. This global phenomenon means that the foundations of these troubling political trends are structural, which also means strategies for contesting them must understand these deep roots.

This issue grapples with these structural roots to elucidate how the multiple subjugations they engender are connected to each other. We believe that sanctuary's expansive conceptual range facilitates this analysis. While we do include multiple contributions that focus on migrants, this issue also considers forms of sanctuary developed by and for other targeted groups. It aims to highlight how multiply-constituted forms of subjugation link up struggles in conjunction—for example, for gay rights and policing reform; migrant rights in relation to housing and urban displacement; and migration in the context of settler colonialism and Indigenous sovereignty. Sanctuary, we argue, provides an expansive archive of social movements that we might not otherwise see as being connected.

Histories and Genealogies

Sanctuary offers a capacious concept with roots in religious and ethical genealogies that it carries with it, even in secular contexts. Defined as "a holy place," "a place that offers refuge," and even, since 2018, a "city of refuge," *sanctuary* denotes a spatial notion, a place of protection or safe harbor. It also includes the practices "of protection beyond the law," signaling its fraught relationship to the state. Its religious roots speak to a higher or ultimate authority beyond secular, civil government.[5] In medieval ecclesiastical law, fugitives from justice found refuge in churches that provided a space of mediation between the accused person and the government institution they fled. These fugitives were not always sympathetic figures, such as debtors, but also included people who had committed serious offenses like murder. But these alternatives to government punishment were brought to an end with the rise of the modern, sovereign nation-state.[6] Sanctuary, at its core, provided an alternative, and ultimate, source of authority, rooted in the divine; it thereby challenged the sovereignty essential to the very definition of a nation-state. Put differently, the existence of sanctuary practices and spaces stood as a reminder that the nation-state does not have exclusive sovereign control over what happens within its territory.

This antagonistic relationship between spaces and practices of sanctuary and the sovereign nation-state carries over from sanctuary's religious foundations to secular contexts and contestations over justice and power. Subnational jurisdictions draw on localized sources of authority in city, county, and state governments to contest federal-level policies. Supranational formations like human rights regimes and international law also provide subjugated peoples an alternative venue to demand justice and recognition beyond the nation-state. We can see claims to such supranational formations in the We Charge Genocide campaigns that went to the United Nations in 1951, to charge the US government of committing genocide against its Black citizens, and in 2014, to protest the criminalization and lethal hyperpolicing of Chicago youth of color.[7] However, the fact that international human rights institutions and laws exist, yet fail to rein in violations committed by nation-states like the United States, Israel, or Russia, for example, points to the limits of looking to institutional powers for protection or recognition.

Indeed, as Rachel Ida Buff notes in her article "Sanctuary Everywhere: Some Key Words, 1945–Present," institutions, even when operating beyond the state, can form part of the problem. The human rights regime, Buff explains, codified distinctions between refugees deserving of protection by the international community and migrants deserving of far less. This original distinction, grounded in the tension between national sovereignty and internationalism, continues to plague how states and international institutions deal with issues of migration today. She and our other authors illumine the limits of looking to institutional forms of power to defend people made vulnerable by the violence of the state and capital.

Buff, however, also highlights other supra- or transnational solidarity movements that did not look to state sovereigns or other institutions of power for recognition or protection. Movements in the mid-twentieth century that brought together labor, immigrant, anti-imperial, and ethnic organizations struggling for universal rights not yet in existence, she argues, anticipate contemporary sanctuary movements that center intersectional approaches to social justice. Similarly, Jason Ezell's analysis of the Short Mountain Sanctuary in "'Returning Forest Darlings'" provides a concrete example of a community that "looked away from the state" and "relied on decentralized organization, obscurantist networking practices, and politically strategic affect to defy state surveillance."

As Ezell shows, sanctuary often involves not just carving out spaces of refuge but also creating networks of community that extend beyond spatial boundaries. Put differently, as he and other contributors show, sanctuary is defined not solely by spatial arrangements but also by mobile practices. The contributors thus converse with histories of sanctuary that illustrate how movement away from a site of danger was sometimes required to provide refuge at all. US sanctuary activists in the 1980s transported refugees across national borders into and within the US territory; abolitionists led slaves from the southern states to freedom in defiance of the Fugitive Slave Acts and, we must remember, the US Constitution, which protected the rights of slave owners to claim their human "property," who had no rights at all.

Contemporary sanctuary movements, then, draw on this rich genealogy of breaking what St. Augustine and Martin Luther King, Jr. described as immoral, "unjust law," which, as King explained in his "Letter from a Birmingham Jail," is "no law at all."[8] Elliott Young grappled with this genealogy and the necessity to violate unjust law in a collaborative workshop he and his colleagues and students organized at Lewis & Clark College in the wake of the 2016 presidential election. In his *Teaching Radical History* essay "From Sanctuary to Civil Disobedience: History and Praxis," Young describes how efforts to designate the school a sanctuary campus gave birth to this workshop, which focused on civil disobedience in response to the administration's refusal of sanctuary and, more broadly, to the Trump administration. The open workshop fed into and worked alongside campus protests and direct actions by Portland activists; this, Young argues, indicates how sanctuary practices can create spaces for civil disobedience and movement-building.

Sanctuary as Oppositional Practice

This issue demonstrates how sanctuary at times requires defying the law, precisely because its practices seek to defend and empower those targeted by the state. Some sanctuary movement leaders, such as John Fife, who appears in Sunaina Maira's roundtable, explicitly embraced their defiance of unjust law and were criminalized and convicted because of it. They understood that is not possible to both affirm the power of the state and work within its permissible boundaries while also standing for the people the state targets for exclusion, expulsion, and removal. Efforts to do both cannot succeed.

For example, sanctuary and immigrant rights activists have at times affirmed the "felons, not families" rhetoric of the Barack Obama administration. They ultimately agreed with the government they criticize—propping up good, law-abiding undocumented immigrants by explicitly casting out "bad," law-breaking immigrants, who, they conceded, the state rightfully detains and deports. This strategy of accepting the demands of the nation-state and its sovereign right to decide who gets to be here and who does not has not only proven its consistent failure, but it has also led us to the dilemmas we face today. Many of us have become accustomed to the presence of militarized borders, forced removals, seemingly permanent refugee camps, metastasizing surveillance systems, and so on.

Further, by giving credence to the state, we have at times missed critical opportunities to see the connections among seemingly disparate struggles and work in solidarity. Treva Ellison, in "From Sanctuary to Safe Space," shows such wasted opportunities in their analysis of gay and lesbian police reform efforts in

Los Angeles, some of which worked with the police department to decriminalize gay social life, while failing to work with Black and Latinx communities to contest the police as an agent of violence and inequity. Ellison's analysis elucidates how identity-based politics limited these efforts, while simultaneously inviting us to consider the more radical gay and lesbian organizations that refused to grant legitimacy to the LAPD, the city, or reformist nonprofit organizations. Ellison further invites us to consider what sort of nonreformist reform of policing—one that brought together issues of race, sexuality, class, gender, and urban space—might emerge from our understanding of this history.

Alongside Ellison, the following essays critique efforts at liberal reform that would pit differently oppressed groups against one another, foreclose solidarity, or shore up the authority of the state that lies at the root of shared struggles. They highlight not only the pitfalls of liberal approaches to sanctuary but also historical and contemporary examples of organizers and affected communities taking an abolitionist approach to sanctuary. As one of us (Paik) has argued, such an abolitionist sanctuary movement focuses both on tearing down the forms of state violence and capitalist dispossession that affect broad swaths of ordinary people, and on envisioning and building up the world we want in its place. An abolitionist sanctuary movement is by necessity intersectional in its analyses and strategies.[9] It understands that the many branches of subjugation grow from shared roots in extractive and settler colonialism, capitalist exploitation, and a world divided by borders into nation-states. As feminist scholar Nadine Naber argues, these forces that target so many people based on race, gender, relations to capital, geography, sexuality, ability, health, and so on "make the connections for us."[10]

Even while some of the movements and histories examined here focus on specific sites, these local struggles articulate with transnational movements and frames of analysis. The necessity to think transnationally emerges from the fact that migration and migrant rights, by definition, cannot be contained by any single nation-state. But more important, the structural conditions leading to rising autocratic, right-wing regimes across the globe both signal and emerge from the growing contradiction of a post-Westphalian world organized into nation-states in an increasingly globalized economy and society. Put another way, the increasing globalization of capital and the displacements and disruptions to social and economic life they induce pull against the lockdown of borders at national edges and the increased policing within them. These structural roots and connections in the predicaments we face today means that struggles by and for subjugated peoples are shared across borders.

These shared roots also mean that organizers can trade inspiration, strategies, and tactics with each other, as seen in the roundtable assembled by Sunaina Maira. In "Freedom to Move, Freedom to Stay, Freedom to Return," Maira stages a transnational conversation among migrant solidarity activists in the United States,

Europe, and Australia. While confronting particular national regimes that thwart the movement and freedom of migrants, these organizers share an intersectional, transnational framework of analysis, and exchange the strategies they deploy in solidarity with migrants. They ground the unruly connections they make among varied oppressed people in the histories of state and capitalist violence that make the struggles for migrants inseparable from those for prisoners, Indigenous people, workers, Arab and Muslim people, queer folks, and those displaced by gentrification and by settler states like Israel, Australia, and the United States.

Autonomous Sanctuary Spaces and Practices

While contemporary scholarly work tends to examine either religious or state forms of sanctuary, this issue emphasizes the ways that members of affected communities, both historically and in the present, have provided autonomous, noninstitutional sanctuary spaces for each other, while also engaging in ongoing practices of solidarity.

This issue contributes to contemporary scholarship by including sanctuary traditions that developed in relation to Indigenous sovereignties. In contexts where Indigenous peoples were at times refugees in their own homelands (such as in the Americas), this issue examines notions of sanctuary in relation to the self-determination of Indigenous nations. In her essay "Sanctuaryscapes in the North American Southwest," Aimee Villarreal researches intertribal forms of sanctuary place-making and notions of radical hospitality that existed previous to the formation of the United States as a nation-state. Her essay provides a longer history of the ways in which Indigenous peoples had spatial autonomy and created autonomous, nonstate forms of sanctuary. Further, according to Villarreal, recovering the specific local histories of sanctuary enables us to imagine and "build alternative spaces of belonging" in the present. Situating sanctuary in relation to Indigenous sovereignties thus changes how we view sanctuary traditions in the past, which also has significance for the present, a period characterized by heightened forms of nationalism and restrictive immigration policies.

This issue also examines the intersections of sanctuary and Indigenous sovereignties in the work of contemporary activist groups, while illuminating the ways that activists' strategies travel across national borders. Maira's transnational round-table examines migrant solidarity activism in various locations around the world, including the work of Rise: Refugees, Survivors and Ex-detainees, a refugee-led group in Australia that has a "Sovereignty and Sanctuary" campaign. Through their organizing efforts, groups such as Rise, and No One Is Illegal in Canada, aim to decenter nation-states' assertion of sovereignty over and against Indigenous peoples as part of a larger struggle against border imperialism across the globe.[11] Indigenous activists thus challenge the ability of nation-states to define citizenship and instead provide a means to imagine those who had been deemed "noncitizens" as members of communities.

In focusing on affected communities' production of sanctuary practices, this issue also emphasizes "everyday enactments of sanctuary" that go beyond what Maurice Stierl refers to as "humanitarian approaches and hierarchy of care."[12] These efforts include migrants' creative organizing against anti-immigrant laws on the local, state, and federal levels, such as that discussed in "Sanctuary in a Small Southern City," Kyle Lambelet's interview with Anton Flores-Maisonet, who elaborates on his work with Casa Alterna, a community organization that offers sanctuary and accompaniment to immigrants living in LaGrange, Georgia. Many of these everyday acts of sanctuary occur on the local level, addressing the needs of immigrant and refugee communities, such as educating members of these communities to protect themselves rather than contacting the police. Ezell further examines how gay liberationists and back-to-the-land movements converged to create gay sanctuaries in the rural southeastern United States. Members of this sanctuary movement not only carved out spaces of liberation and refuge for themselves but also made their own media to connect people who remained spatially separated but linked to a wider community.

Carla Hung's essay, "Sanctuary Squats," describes how Eritrean migrants and refugees helped to provide autonomous housing for one another by squatting in abandoned buildings, only to be violently evicted by the state. Arriving to Rome in the contexts of "fortress Europe," rising xenophobic nationalism in Italy and elsewhere on the continent, and the history of Italian colonialism in East Africa, these refugee communities created sanctuary and care in the practices of providing food, shelter, and self-defense against state violence with and for each other. Further, their predicament compelled them to advocate for housing rights in the context of gentrification and displacements of urban housing in Rome. Some of this organizing relates to challenging policies, including those around housing, that may not be specifically anti-immigrant but that were created to keep out migrants.

This work is key even in US cities where politicians and residents support sanctuary policies, like those where real estate developers' interests lie in constructing high-end housing projects that displace low-income residents. In *Embassy of the Refugee*, Caleb Duarte and students from NEST imagine autonomous spaces not only for refugees and migrants but also for those who need a place to live in cities—such as Oakland—where there is a lack of affordable housing.[13] In these and other contexts, everyday acts of sanctuary involve a more expansive view of what sanctuary means in places where low-income residents can't afford to live. In *Embassy of the Refugee*, the artists thus draw connections between the "freedom of movement and the freedom to inhabit," providing a vision of sanctuary practices that emphasize shared experiences and solidarity between refugees, immigrants, and members of other displaced populations, including those who are unhoused.[14] The creation of this artwork parallels practices by community institutions that fight for the right to housing, health care, and education for all.

Queer Interventions

Along with our emphasis on self-made sanctuary practices and communities, we aim to put sanctuary—with all of its varied meanings and iterations—in conversation with queer studies and GLBTQ history. Most explicitly, Treva Ellison's and Jason Ezell's essays build on previous work in queer studies, especially queer history, that has asked how GLBT and other queer-identified people have formed communities of tolerance, protection, and care in hostile environments. In doing so, they speak to arguments established in Christina Hanhardt's research on the politics of violence, safety, and space in US cities (some of which appeared in issue 100 of this journal), which in just a few years has already proven instrumental in challenging readers to see narratives of "safety" as menacingly more complex than they first appear.[15] In considering how queer people created safe spaces for themselves in North American cities over the course of the twentieth century, Hanhardt argues that "the quest for safety that is collective rather than individualized requires an analysis of who or what constitutes a threat and why, and a recognition that those forces maintain their might by being in flux. And among the most transformative visions are those driven less by a fixed goal of safety than by the admittedly abstract concept of freedom."[16] As urban neighborhoods become construed and marketed as "safe," Hanhardt asks us to consider the question, "Safe for whom?" Ellison and Ezell take up this question through particularly fascinating case studies, taking readers to urban Los Angeles in the 1960s and 1970s and queer communes and living experiments in the US Southeast in the late 1970s and beyond. These cases illuminate some important ways in which queer people have long been following the practices and principles of sanctuary, even if they rarely labeled it as such.

We do not mean to imply that queer sanctuary practices and those seeking to protect transnational migrants easily map onto one another. Ellison and Ezell examine identity categories that have inched closer to the dominant culture in the United States and other national contexts since the mid to late twentieth century. Although there are many places in the world where queer people, practices, and communities would benefit from sanctuary (Chechnya comes to mind at the time of this writing), we must also acknowledge that the politics of homonormativity mean that the politics of safety have changed since the decades that are the subject of Ellison's and Ezell's research.[17]

Neither do we mean to imply that "queer" and "migrant" are mutually exclusive categories of analysis or political praxis. A sizable body of scholarship, some of which is cited by authors in this issue, examines the queerness of migration and the migratory history of queer subjectivities.[18] News images of same-sex weddings between members of the so-called migrant caravan in late 2018, as well as the presence of transgender asylum seekers in many national contexts, attest to the fact that queer people are bound to be a part of any given migrant stream, even when they are made invisible by how the public—or historians—see and understand that population. Homophobia *within* migrant communities is also a reminder that "queer" and "migrant" are not separate categories of analysis. We encourage the reader to look for the queer potentiality in all of the disparate histories provided throughout this issue.

When we, the editors, embarked upon making this issue, we could not have predicted that a significant portion of it would focus on the politics and practices of queer sanctuary, but we came to see that there is much to explore in the critical terrain where queer studies and sanctuary intersect. The works described above attest to that. Although we see the need for much further research in this arena, we have included essays that we hope will spark conversation and debate. We especially hope that scholars will continue to explore this terrain in non-US contexts.

Conclusion

As we write this introduction, these points of connection between the "freedom of movement and the freedom to inhabit" couldn't be more relevant. While refugees and migrants, as well as people without housing, can create sanctuary spaces and alternative forms of community, they are still at risk of being displaced by state agents. In December 2018, police evicted members of the Housing and Dignity Village, a women-of-color-led encampment of unhoused women and children in Oakland (a sanctuary city). Meanwhile, during the first few days of the new year

Figure 1. *Floating Ladder* was part of a collaborative art project by Caleb Duarte and Central American asylum seekers living at El Barretal, a refugee camp in Tijuana, Mexico. Photo by Marilyn Flores.

in January 2019, Mexican police armed with tear gas evicted a group of Central American refugees at Benito Juárez, the only self-organized Caravana Migrante camp in Tijuana. Prior to the eviction, Caleb Duarte went to Tijuana to visit El Barretal, a temporary refugee camp, and create art with those who were living there. One of the three collaborative projects that he organized involved the creation of a fabric ladder, which they tied to helium balloons that lifted it above the encampment. As part of a project in another shelter, refugees built small houses, and in a third they built sculptures. As Duarte noted on social media a few days later: "We created and lifted a ladder towards the sky to take us to another planet, another land or another home. We saw a miniature wall from above as we imagined alternative worlds. We created small dwellings and imagined the color of carpets and number of rooms. We talked and created sculptures."[19]

In creating this artwork, Duarte and his collaborators imagined other ways of looking at the Mexico–US border, and one image, that of the fabric ladder, sticks with us as we offer this issue to readers (fig. 1). We were not fortunate to witness the sight of their ladder lifting off of the ground and floating skyward over a refugee encampment, but we are inspired by the symbolism of their work. By envisioning their movement and mobility, they orient us toward other possibilities.

A. Naomi Paik, Jason Ruiz, Rebecca M. Schreiber

A. Naomi Paik is an assistant professor of Asian American studies at the University of Illinois, Urbana-Champaign. Her book, *Rightlessness: Testimony and Redress in U.S. Prison Camps since World War II* (2016; winner, Best Book in History, AAAS 2018; runner-up, John Hope Franklin Prize for best book in American Studies, ASA, 2017) reads testimonial narratives of subjects rendered rightless by the US state through their imprisonment in camps. She has published articles in *Social Text, Radical History Review, Cultural Dynamics, Race and Class, E-misférica, Humanity*, and the collection *Guantánamo and American Empire*. She is currently writing *Bans, Walls, Raids, Sanctuary*, a short book on the criminalization of migrants in the United States and radical sanctuary movements. She is coediting three special issues of *Radical History Review* —"Militarism and Capitalism" (Winter 2019), "Radical Histories of Sanctuary" (Fall 2019), and "Policing, Justice, and the Radical Imagination" (Spring 2020).

Jason Ruiz is associate professor of American studies at the University of Notre Dame, where he is affiliated faculty with the Program in Gender Studies and the Institute for Latino Studies. Ruiz's research focuses on American perceptions of Latin America with emphases on race, cultural and economic imperialism, tourism, gender, and sexuality. His first book, *Americans in the Treasure House: Travel to Porfirian Mexico and the Cultural Politics of Empire* was published in 2014. Ruiz has also published in *American Studies, Journal of Transnational American Studies, Oral History Review, Aztlán*, and elsewhere. In addition, he is the coeditor of four special issues and two books: *Radical History Review*, nos. 100 (Winter 2007), 123 (Fall 2015), and 129 (Fall 2017); *Queer Twin Cities* (2010); and *The Routledge History of American Sexualities* (forthcoming). He is the principal investigator of *Latinx Murals of Pilsen*, a digital research project devoted to public art in Chicago. Ruiz is currently a 2019–20 Whiting Foundation Public Engagement Fellow.

Rebecca M. Schreiber is a professor in the American Studies Department at the University of New Mexico. Her research focuses on issues of migration between the United States and Mexico and considers relations to place, identity, and dislocation through forms of visual culture. Her most recent book, *The Undocumented Everyday: Migrant Lives and the Politics of Visibility* (2018; winner of the College Art Association's Frank Jewett Mather Award for Art Criticism, 2019), examines how Mexican and Central American migrants have depicted themselves and members of their communities in documentary photography, film, video, and audio projects since 9/11. She has published in edited collections including *Border Spaces: Visualizing the U.S.-Mexico Frontera*, *Remaking Reality: U.S. Documentary Culture after 1945*, *The Latina/o Midwest Reader*, and *Imagining Our Americas: Towards a Transnational Frame*, as well as in *American Quarterly*, *Radical History Review*, *Chiricú Journal: Latina/o Literatures, Arts, and Cultures*, *Journal of American Studies*, and *Afterimage*. She is also the author of *Cold War Exiles in Mexico: U.S. Dissidents and the Culture of Critical Resistance* (2008).

Notes

1. Jiménez, "Chicano's Collaborative Art Projects."
2. See Ridgely, "Cities of Refuge."
3. Schreiber, "Performing Sanctuary."
4. Abrego, "Central American Refugees Reveal the Crisis of the State," 14.
5. *Oxford English Dictionary Online*, "Sanctuary, n. 1." www.oed.com/view/Entry/170516 (accessed 15 January 2019).
6. See, for example, Shoemaker, *Sanctuary and Crime in the Middle Ages*.
7. See Civil Rights Congress, *We Charge Genocide*; We Charge Genocide, "Police Violence against Chicago's Youth of Color."
8. King, "Letter from a Birmingham Jail."
9. Paik, "Abolitionist Futures." See also Davis, *Abolition Democracy*.
10. Naber, "'The U.S. and Israel Make the Connections for Us.'"
11. For more on No One Is Illegal, see Walia, *Undoing Border Imperialism*. Other scholarly work that positions sanctuary in relation to Indigenous sovereignties includes Ellis, "The Border(s) Crossed Us Too," and Martínez and Schreiber, "Sovereignty and Sanctuary."
12. Darling and Squire, "Everyday Enactments of Sanctuary," 191. See Maira, this issue, 149.
13. Schreiber, "Performing Sanctuary."
14. Loyd, Mitchelson, and Burridge, introduction, 10.
15. See Hanhardt, *Safe Space*.
16. Hanhardt, *Safe Space*, 30.
17. At the time of this writing, in January 2019, news agencies and nongovernmental organizations are reporting a resurgence in homophobic purges in Chechnya, which first captured global attention the previous year and include the alleged detention, torture, and disappearance of GLBTQ people at the hands of governmental agents.
18. Among many others, see Luibhéid and Cantú, *Queer Migrations*; Luibhéid, *Entry Denied*; and Chávez, *Queer Migration Politics*.
19. Caleb Duarte, Facebook post, January 13, 2019.

References

Abrego, Leisy J. "Central American Refugees Reveal the Crisis of the State." In *The Oxford Handbook of Migration Crises*, edited by Cecilia Menjívar et al., 213–28. Oxford: Oxford University Press, 2018.

Chávez, Karma R. *Queer Migration Politics: Activist Rhetoric and Coalitional Possibilities.* Urbana: University of Illinois Press, 2013.

Civil Rights Congress. *We Charge Genocide: The Historic Petition to the United Nations for Relief from a Crime of the United States Government against the Negro People.* New York: Civil Rights Congress, 1951.

Darling, Jonathan, and Vicki Squire. "Everyday Enactments of Sanctuary: The UK City of Sanctuary Movement." In *Sanctuary Practices in International Perspectives: Migration, Citizenship, and Social Movements*, edited by Randy K. Lippert and Sean Rehaag, 191–204. New York: Routledge, 2013.

Davis, Angela. *Abolition Democracy: Beyond Empire, Prisons, and Torture.* New York: Seven Stories Press, 2005.

Ellis, Elizabeth. "The Border(s) Crossed Us Too: The Intersections of Native American and Immigrant Fights for Justice." *E-misférica* 14, no. 1 (2018). http://beta.hemisphericinstitute .org/en/emisferica-14-1-expulsion/14-1-essays/the-border-s-crossed-us-too-the -intersections-of-native-american-and-immigrant-fights-for-justice-2.html/.

Hanhardt, Christina. *Safe Space: Gay Neighborhood History and the Politics of Violence.* Durham, NC: Duke University Press, 2013.

Jiménez, Elissa. "Chicano's Collaborative Art Projects Challenge Institutions That Claim to Offer Sanctuary." *El Tecolote*, October 4, 2018. http://eltecolote.org/content/en/arts_ culture/chicanos-collaborative-art-projects-challenge-institutions-that-claim-to-offer -sanctuary/.

King, Martin Luther, Jr. "Letter from a Birmingham Jail." April 16, 1963. The Martin Luther King Jr. Research and Education Institute. http://okra.stanford.edu/transcription /document_images/undecided/630416-019.pdf (accessed January 26, 2019).

Loyd, Jenna M., Matt Mitchelson, and Andrew Burridge. Introduction to *Beyond Walls and Cages: Prisons, Borders, and Global Crisis.* Athens: University of Georgia Press, 2012.

Luibhéid, Eithne. *Entry Denied: Controlling Sexuality at the Border.* Minneapolis: University of Minnesota Press, 2002.

Luibhéid, Eithne, and Lionel Cantú, eds. *Queer Migrations: Sexuality, U.S. Citizenship, and Border Crossings.* Minneapolis: University of Minnesota Press, 2005.

Martínez, Rafael A., and Rebecca M. Schreiber. "Sovereignty and Sanctuary: A Roundtable." In "Brown Spaces: Latinx Memory, Meanings, Stories of (Be)Longing." Special issue, *Chiricú Journal: Latina/o Literatures, Arts and Cultures* 3, no. 1 (Fall 2018): 141–54.

Naber, Nadine. "'The U.S. and Israel Make the Connections for Us': Anti-Imperialism and Black-Palestinian Solidarity." *Critical Ethnic Studies* 3, no. 2 (Fall 2017): 15–30.

Paik, A. Naomi. "Abolitionist Futures and the US Sanctuary Movement." *Race and Class* 59, no. 2 (2017): 3–25.

Ridgely, Jennifer. "Cities of Refuge: Immigration Enforcement, Police, and the Insurgent Genealogies of Citizenship in U.S. Sanctuary Cities." *Urban Geography* 29, no. 1 (2008): 53–77.

Schreiber, Rebecca M. "Performing Sanctuary: 'Urgent Art' and the 'Embassy of the Central American Refugee.'" Manuscript.

Shoemaker, Karl. *Sanctuary and Crime in the Middle Ages, 400–1500.* New York: Fordham University Press, 2011.

Walia, Harsha. *Undoing Border Imperialism.* Chico, CA: AK Press, 2013.

We Charge Genocide. "Police Violence against Chicago's Youth of Color." September 2014. http://report.wechargegenocide.org/.

Figure 1. The artwork is a print by Emily Cohane-Mann and is used by permission of the American Friends Service Committee, whose "Sanctuary Everywhere" campaign aims to create safe, inclusive spaces for all people, especially those communities targeted by state violence. Learn more at afsc.org /sanctuaryeverywhere.

Sanctuary Everywhere

Some Key Words, 1945–Present

Rachel Ida Buff

During the spring of 2018, a caravan of Central Americans assembled on the Mexico–Guatemala border and began walking toward the United States. The caravan was one of a series organized by the Pueblo Sin Fronteras collective, which is based in California and Tijuana. The collective stated that its purpose is to accompany "migrants and refugees in their journey of hope and together demand *our human rights*" (emphasis in original). Invoking the human rights of migrants and refugees together, the collective implicitly challenged sixty years of international and state policy toward itinerant peoples.[1]

Pueblo Sin Fronteras promoted the status of the caravan as a matter of international law. Describing itself as "refugee-led," the organization invoked the historic 1951 Convention on the Status of Refugees of the United Nations High Commissioner for Refugees (UNHCR) and its 1967 Protocol to claim human rights and status for its members as asylum seekers.

Calling itself Via Crucis Migrantes, or the Migrants' Way of the Cross, the caravan walked from Central America to the United States. Like the 2017 caravan by the same name, the march was timed to coincide with the Christian Holy Week. Its name echoed the title of a 2006 book by liberation theologian Gioacchino Campese, *The Way of the Cross of the Migrant Jesus*. Campese derives a notion of "crucified peoples" from Central American liberation theology and applies it to contemporary undocumented migrants.[2]

Radical History Review

Issue 135 (October 2019) DOI 10.1215/01636545-7607809

© 2019 by MARHO: The Radical Historians' Organization, Inc.

Pueblo Sin Fronteras links the global struggles of migrants and refugees, citizens and denizens, against militarized immigration and policing. A letter from the Palestinian Stop the Wall Campaign to the caravan connects the flight of Central Americans from violence and poverty to the situation in Gaza and the West Bank. Both, the letter asserts, are the fallout of repressive imperial practices, including decades of US military intervention and exploitative trade policies, which Israel has consistently supported. The campaign's offering of solidarity also imagines a world without walls as an internationalist project, one that simultaneously refuses state-enforced distinctions between migrants and refugees. The letter hailed the caravan: "We salute your March of the over 1500 migrants that challenge US racist and exclusivist migration policies that stop the people from crossing borders, depriving them of their basic rights to freedom of movement and rights as refugees."[3]

Caravan participants defy distinctions between migrants and refugees. They do this implicitly through their collective migration and presence at the border as well as explicitly through their public statements. In their March 23 statement, caravan members identified themselves as "citizens" and demanded that international refugee rights protocols be recognized:

To Mexico and the United States we demand:
Respect our rights as refugees and our right to dignified work to be able to support our families.
Open the borders to us because we are citizens, just like the people of the countries where we are or travel to.
That the rights the nations of the world have signed, including the right to freedom of expression, be respected.
That the conventions on refugee rights are not empty rhetoric.
The borders are stained red because there, the working class is killed![4]

By broadcasting their status as refugees *and* migrants, Pueblo Sin Fronteras and caravan members upend legal distinctions separating those deserving and not deserving of refuge. The statement explicitly invokes an internationalist class critique and attributes the state violence taking place at the border to the inequities of global capitalism.

Despite the caravan's rhetoric about human rights, the Trump administration treated the migrant caravan as an aggressive invasion of "criminal aliens." They proceeded as if migrants carried the very instability they fled in Central America, as if it were a contagious social disease instead of a historically created condition. This rhetorical strategy deployed the xenophobia mobilized during the 2016 presidential election to defend "national sovereignty" against an imagined horde of hostile invaders and potential terrorists. This strategy continued throughout the spring and summer of 2018, demonizing the second caravan just in time for the midterm elections in November. Rarely using the term "refugee," this rhetorical strategy tended to use the term "migrants," "criminal aliens," or "illegal aliens."[5]

In response to the approach of the Via Crucis Migrantes, Attorney General Jefferson Beauregard Sessions III directed the Department of Homeland Security (DHS) to implement an enhanced, "zero tolerance," policy of criminally prosecuting undocumented entry. The criminalization of migration has long separated families. But stricter enforcement under "zero tolerance" dictated that adults entering with children be immediately taken into the criminal court system and separated from each other, stoking international scandal during the summer of 2018. Further, US officials threatened to prosecute undocumented parents for "endangering" their children by "smuggling" them into the country. None of these official responses used the word "refugee." Premising its response on a long-standing discourse of "invasion" by undocumented immigrants, the DHS ignored human rights claims, treating asylum seekers as unauthorized entrants. By refusing the caravan's language of refugee human rights, the zero tolerance policy effectively conflated asylum seeking and undocumented entry.[6]

The arrival of the Via Crucis Migrantes caravan at the US–Mexico border and the subsequent mustering of zero tolerance against them highlight the ongoing erosion of distinctions between refugees and migrants recognized by international law since 1951. As this distinction withers, conditions for asylum seekers degrade. At the same time, this erosion creates space for emergent definitions created by social movements.

Migrant caravans challenge the walls built by global racial capitalism by demanding safe harbor, or sanctuary, for Central Americans fleeing the depredations of empire. Groups of migrants travel together for protection and solidarity. Their rhetoric, a grassroots semantic jujitsu that insists on defining citizenship and refuge from below, is part of a broad practice which some advocates have begun to call "sanctuary everywhere."[7] While the depredations of this historical moment are widespread, "sanctuary everywhere" articulates its possibilities of solidarity and refuge.[8]

Sanctuary can denote both broad aspiration and specific practices; it draws on religious roots as well as internationalist imaginings. Meanings and practices of sanctuary change in relation to the dynamics of international and national law. The broad, emancipatory conceptualization of sanctuary that has evolved since 2016 represents a resurgence of internationalist possibilities repressed by discourses and practices purporting to advance "human rights." "Sanctuary" becomes not only a specific place in a church or other building but a set of practices by which people come into relations of accompaniment and solidarity.

This essay examines the historical relationship between practices of sanctuary and the juridical terms "refugee" and "migrant." I argue that these three terms shape and transform one another. As an emergent practice, sanctuary sometimes occupies the space just beyond what is possible to articulate in legal terms. At other times, it exists between juridical possibilities of refuge and deportation, adapting to the exigencies of conditions on the ground. I return to the freighted possibilities of the current moment at the end of the essay.

To trace a history of sanctuary practices, I begin with the "human rights moment" of the immediate post–World War II era, using the term "sanctuary" as a heuristic to examine foundational discourses of displaced persons and refugee rights, as well as the function of established nations and new nations like Israel in delimiting them. The essay then proceeds to examine the historical context of the founding of the US sanctuary movement at another moment of imperial formation: the revival of Cold War foreign policy imperatives during the US-backed "dirty wars" in Central America during the 1980s. Finally, I return to the present to attend the broadcasts of the contemporary sanctuary movement, monitoring the potential for harbor and solidarity they might portend.

Between Sovereignty and Sanctuary: Refugees, Migrants, and Citizens, 1945–55

In 1949, German Jewish émigré philosopher Hannah Arendt addressed a crisis in the post–World War II European landscape: "The problem of statelessness on so large a scale had the effect of confronting the nations of the world with an inescapable and perplexing question: whether there exist such 'human rights' independent of all specific political status and deriving solely from the facts of being human?"[9]

Arendt referred to the question of the "last million" gravely impacted by World War II—"displaced persons," in the term newly coined by the US military. Debate about displaced persons animated controversy during the Allied powers' occupation of Germany and the founding of the United Nations. Despite resettlement campaigns by the United Nations Relief and Rehabilitation Administration (UNRRA), one million people remained unwilling or unable to be returned to their nations of origin by 1946. Many of those officially designated as displaced persons, or DPs, wandered the countryside. Globally, millions of people who, because they were not direct victims of Hitler or Stalin, did not qualify for the term lacked the ability to return safely home as a result of the war.

The emergence of the juridical figure of the refugee represented a limited response to the European displaced persons crisis. Given traction by the newly formed United Nations, international human rights law wrestled with the displacements of the Holocaust and war. Through the framework of sanctuary and sovereignty, we might say that emergent liberal human rights internationalism attempted to institute safe harbor for displaced persons outside the arena of national law. But this emergent refugee regime met limits in the militarization of the early Cold War, which promoted strong national borders over human rights. Concerned with national security, individual nations deployed the developing distinction between migrants and refugees to exclude the former and delimit the latter.

The harbor created by postwar human rights law occupied a key contradiction between national sovereignty and internationalism. UN refugee policy underwrote the right to seek asylum but deliberately stopped short of any potential infringement of national sovereignty, declining to guarantee the right to be granted asylum in any specific country. Therefore, the "right to have rights," in Arendt's framing, affirmed by the United Nations Declaration on Human Rights, remained subordinate to the political interests of individual nations. Because signatory nations were left to define refugee admissions as well as citizenship requirements, refugees were guaranteed neither entrance nor ongoing rights to safe harbor. Individual nations retained the freedom to redefine people who saw themselves as asylum seekers. When Tijuana mayor Juan Manuel Gastelum asserted his opposition to Central Americans arriving in November 2018, claiming that "human rights should be reserved for righteous humans," he gave voice to this enduring contradiction.[10]

In the context of an ascendant Cold War global order that emphasized national security against the threat posed by internationalism, particular nations carefully inspected refugees as prospective citizens. Screening them for entry fell outside of international jurisdiction because it was considered to be an aspect of national sovereignty. Human rights, as conceptualized by postwar theorists like Arendt as well as by emerging international law, came to rely on the shelter of national citizenship.[11]

The United Nations carefully defined the conditions that entitled individuals to claim asylum and set up protocols to determine who could be considered a refugee. The UN Convention and Protocol on the Status of Refugees (1951) defined refugees as those displaced

> owing to well-founded fear of being persecuted for reasons of race, religion, nationality, membership of a particular social group or political opinion, is outside the country of his nationality and is unable or, owing to such fear, is unwilling to avail himself of the protection of that country; or who, not having a nationality and being outside the country of his former habitual residence as a result of such events, is unable or, owing to such fear, is unwilling to return to it.[12]

The creation of the juridical figure of the refugee as potential rights-bearing citizen in international law also implicitly engendered the emergence of the category of migrant, entitled to far less. As the postwar refugee regime humanized particular categories of displaced persons, it excluded others, creating potentially violent hierarchies of belonging.[13]

The devastation of the European Holocaust made Jews symbolic figures in the emergence of the postwar refugee regime. The founding of the state of Israel—"a country without a people for a people without a country," in Jewish Zionist Israel Zangwill's paraphrase of nineteenth-century Christian Zionists—

represented, to the former Allies, a strategic solution to the problem of Jewish displaced persons after the war. But locating refuge for one population in the founding of a sovereign, ethnically delimited nation resulted in further displacement and the loss of the Palestinian "right of return" to long-held ancestral lands. Establishment of the state of Israel in 1948, and the resulting *nakba* (Arabic for "disaster") of Palestinian displacement resulted in the founding of the United Nations Relief and Works Agency for Palestine Refugees in the Near East (UNRWA) in 1949. Although it was intended as a temporary response to the crisis of 1948, UNRWA continues to respond to the ongoing exigencies of Palestinian displacement into the present day. Just as the emergence of the refugee in international law also resulted in the displacement of those deemed "migrants," the founding of the state of Israel as a safe harbor for Jews displaced by the violence of World War II occasioned violent dispossession of Palestinians.[14]

In the United States, the McCarran-Walter (Immigration and Nationality) Act of 1952 constituted a limited response to the emergence of the global refugee regime. The law allowed for the admission of refugees, in particular those fleeing communist regimes, at the same time as it reinstated national-origin quotas designed to curtail the arrival of migrants from Asia, Africa, and southern and eastern Europe. It established legal grounds for the admission of refugees at the same time as it certified a key distinction in US law between "political" refugees seeking freedom and "economic" migrants driven by personal gain. Articulating this division between deserving and undeserving immigrants, the McCarran-Walter Act drew on a long, racialized history of nativist public policy distinguishing between what historian Mae Ngai calls "impossible subjects" and potential citizens. After the passage of the McCarran-Walter legislation, the Immigration and Naturalization Service (INS), the predecessor of ICE (US Immigration and Customs Enforcement), wasted no time in inaugurating Operation Wetback, a massive, militarized operation at the US–Mexico border and in Mexican American communities in the Southwest and California intended to deport migrants racialized as "illegal aliens."[15]

The collision of international law with the displacements caused by immigration enforcement and national borders indicates the freighted semantic emerging between "refugees" and "migrants." As Palestinians became refugees, Jewish refugees became Israeli citizens. While Operation Wetback failed to "clean up" the problem of undocumented border crossing, the INS public relations campaign surrounding it succeeded in broadcasting the term "illegal alien" into mass media coverage of migrants at the US–Mexico border, which persists in its deleterious effects on foreign-born communities into the present era. The terms "refugee" and "migrant," then, are both historically created and interdependent.[16]

The post–World War II refugee regime was not the first articulation of an internationalist rights discourse, nor was it the only one extant at the time. Postwar hopes for the United Nations coexisted with alternative internationalist models that represented decades of struggle across continents. Historian Gerald Cohen explains that many liberal internationalists like Arendt heralded the creation of the UNRRA in 1943 as "the first blueprint of the postwar order": a more humanitarian, internationally cooperative world. Imagining worlds based on international solidarity instead of national security, such blueprints propose alternate outlines of sanctuary for all.[17]

Like Pueblo Sin Fronteras, internationalist advocates for worker rights after 1945 recognized the emergent regime of global border control as an imperial project, serving the interests of settler-colonial nation-states and the ascendant global power of the United States. Instead of distinguishing between refugees and migrants, these internationalists promoted an idea of universal rights that did not depend on national borders. While they did not use the word "sanctuary," these advocates envisioned categories of belonging beyond the purview of national security regimes. As the pseudonymous Jewish writer L. Rock wrote in opposition to British policy in Palestine in the late 1930s, the solution was "struggle against Zionism, against Arab national exclusivism and anti-Jewish actions, against imperialism, for the democratization of the country and its political independence."[18] In the immediate postwar period, such internationalist imaginings provided antic alternatives to locating refuge within securitized national borders.

The postwar ascendance of Zionism after the war foreclosed a long, many-stranded Jewish tradition: what Jacob Plitman describes as "diasporism." Throughout the Jewish diaspora, many theorized a collective Jewish identity that would ensure safety but not depend on the formation of an ethnically specific nation. The international socialist labor bunds, in another example, envisioned international worker rights that paralleled the coalition work of the American Committee for the Protection of the Foreign Born (ACPFB) described below. The founding of the state of Israel in 1948 affixed Jewish safety to citizenship in the nation-state, at the expense of Palestinian sovereignty as well as alternative internationalisms.[19] At the same time as the founding of Israel foreclosed alternate ideas about Jewish safety, US Cold War political formations displaced insurgent, internationalist ideas of rights.

In November 1945, 217 Indonesian maritime laborers articulated their criticism of borders as mechanism of imperial control. They left their British and Dutch ships in New York Harbor, because, as a spokesman explained to the media, "the ships were carrying munitions and supplies to murder their families in Indonesia." Refusing to stay in midtown Manhattan because of their awareness of white supremacy in the United States, the sailors found harbor in Harlem, where they received a hero's welcome. When their shore leaves expired, many were detained at Ellis Island, because Asian-exclusion immigration laws precluded their legal entry.

Effectively stateless in New York City, these Indonesian sailors allied themselves with African Americans against white supremacy, relying on international solidarity to protect them and guide them to safe harbor.

Around the world, ship and dock workers protested the detention of Indonesian sailors in New York and Australia. A coalition of labor, immigrant rights, and national organizations fought their deportations. Because of this international advocacy, the sailors were eventually able to return to the Indonesian Republican authorities through the Red Cross station at Batavia three years before the Dutch conceded defeat by Indonesian National Revolution in 1949. International solidarity kept them out of immigration detention at Ellis Island and allowed for their return to a homeland emerging from centuries of colonial domination.[20]

Many Greek maritime laborers found themselves in a position similar to the Indonesian sailors after the war. While they did not experience the racial barriers to entry that faced Asian sailors, many left-leaning Greek sailors feared returning to their country after the end of the Greek Civil War resulted in the rise of the right-wing, US-backed Alexandros Papagos regime. This regime detained, exiled, and executed many former partisans who had fought the Nazi occupation of Greece. Like the Indonesians, Greek sailors found support from a coalition coordinated by the ACPFB. This coalition lobbied for the rights of Greek, Indonesian, and other displaced sailors as global workers. As Joseph Curran of the National Maritime Union put it in 1946, "the alien brother's problem is not a separate problem. It is a union problem."[21]

Drawn from a combination of labor unions as well as anti-imperialist, immigrant rights, and ethnic organizations, the coalition representing displaced maritime laborers anticipated contemporary sanctuary formations. Advocates proposed an anti-imperial, internationalist idea of universal rights. Significantly, these internationalist advocates argued for the extension of US labor law to cover "the alien brother," effectively extending US labor rights to all workers on US ships, regardless of their citizenship status. The maritime labor coalition embraced a labor internationalism that would provide national labor protections to noncitizens, regardless of their status as refugees or migrants.

The coalition supporting maritime labor rights gained some traction in mainstream US politics, although it was eventually defeated by the rise of the "flag of convenience" system, which effectively offshored shipping ownership. As a component of international maritime capitalism, the flag-of-convenience system deployed US imperial influence in Panama, Liberia, and Honduras to shelter US-owned ships from national labor laws. Shipping interests then invoked the national sovereignty of these countries in defense of this system. Just as human rights law was delimited by UN recognition of the imperatives of national security, shipping interests used imperial maneuvers to defeat the insurgent internationalism of universal worker rights.

The newly inaugurated refugee regime after World War II succeeded in gaining international recognition of refugee status. But these efforts found their limits at the borders of national sovereignty and an emergent imperial, Cold War order dominated by the United States and the Soviet Union. This postwar refugee regime elevated one cohort of displaced persons to the newly created status of refugee. But because national sovereignty limited the power of insurgent international law, the status of refugee did not ensure safe harbor. Further, acknowledging the vulnerable position of refugees indirectly resulted in the widespread degradation of migrants' rights, as the refugee regime assumed that nonrefugee migrants were not justified in leaving their homelands and therefore lacked entitlement to rights and protections. The semantic divide between migrants and refugees in US public discourse and policy eventually necessitated the creation of alternate terms and practices creating safe harbor for those displaced from their homelands.[22]

Dirty Wars: Refugees, "Aliens," and the Sanctuary Movement, 1980–87

"Counterrevolutionary repression has led to vast refugee populations. . . . To grant Salvadorans or Guatemalans political asylum would be to admit that repressive systems are in effect in their homelands—systems funded by U.S. tax dollars."
—Rosemary Radford Reuther[23]

"What the campesinos are doing is only just,
and you should always be at their side.
What the National Guard is likely to do is unjust.
If they attack, you should be there next to the campesinos.
Accompany them. Take the same risks they do."
—Archbishop Oscar Romero[24]

"You shall treat the alien who resides with you no differently than the natives born among you; have the same love for them as for yourself; for you too were once aliens in the land of Egypt."
—Leviticus 19:33–34[25]

The United States delayed ratification of the 1951 Convention on the Status of Refugees, finally signing off on the subsequent United Nations Protocol in 1967. Between 1945 and 1980, US refugee policy did not align fully with the lofty, yet limited, ambitions proposed by international law. Instead, domestic refugee admissions operated through a disparate series of congressional actions and presidential initiatives that responded to particular situations, such as the displaced persons crisis immediately after World War II or the Cuban Revolution of 1959. The watershed Refugee Act of 1980 articulated "a permanent and systematic procedure for the admission to this country of refugees of special humanitarian concern." It created a refugee track in INS admissions, which relied on congressional consultation as well as annual presidential determination of the number of refugees to be admitted. For the first time, the Refugee Act implemented provision for migrants already in the country to claim asylum.[26]

Promoted by the Carter administration as a humanitarian program, the Refugee Act of 1980 took effect at a time of renewed Cold War polarization. Under the Reagan Doctrine, national security operatives fomented and aided forces they deemed "counterinsurgent" around the world, from Afghanistan to Angola to Cambodia. Like the previous Truman and Eisenhower Doctrines, the Reagan Doctrine understood national liberation and socialist reform movements as exclusively coordinated by and beneficial to the Soviet Union. Proponents of this Cold War distinction were able to draw on an antecedent distinction between political refugees and economic migrants. Those fleeing despotic regimes friendly to the United States in Haiti or El Salvador were categorized as "economic migrants," while those fleeing communist adversaries in Cuba or Czechoslovakia had far greater chances of receiving asylum.[27]

Under the Reagan Doctrine, the United States poured money and matériel into fighting both elected regimes and popular insurgencies in Central America through counterinsurgency strategies, including torture and domestic repression. This period is often described as the "dirty wars," a term originating in French counterinsurgency campaigns in Vietnam and Algeria but applied specifically to Latin America starting with Argentina in the 1970s. The term describes a counterinsurgency campaign carried out by secret police and military security forces against a popular uprising. These campaigns often entail the torture and murder of noncombatants, precipitating displacements that also engender new forms of counterinsurgency.[28]

As agrarian labor organizing provoked extreme repression in El Salvador and precipitated civil war in 1979, the United States backed the counterinsurgency campaigns of successive right-wing dictators against a coalition of popular organizations known as the Farabundo Martí National Liberation Front (FMLN). With the aid of US money and advisors, the regimes of Roberto D'Aubuisson and José Napoleón Duarte waged war on popular organizations, including the Catholic Church. Rural "pacification" campaigns featured the bombing of the countryside and the deaths of thousands of civilians. US aid to El Salvador depended on congressional recertification of human rights practices every six months. Somehow, the regime managed to pass this scrutiny each time. Under Secretary of State Alexander Haig, diplomats red-baited US nuns murdered in 1980, lied about military brutality and civilian casualties, or suffered the consequences of testifying to the truth by being fired and discredited. Elliott Abrams, the State Department's designated Central American expert, repeatedly welcomed death squad leader Roberto D'Aubuisson to Washington, disavowing his crimes.[29]

In Guatemala, the Central Intelligence Agency (CIA) deployed the newly devised tactic of fomenting political coups. Fresh from the overthrow of Mohammad Mossadegh in Iran in 1953, agents worked to replace the popularly elected Jacobo Árbenz with the despot Carlos Castillo Armas in 1954, precipitating a decades-long civil war. Powerful American politicians, such as Allen Dulles, the first civilian head of the CIA (1953–61) and his brother, presidential advisor John Foster Dulles, had vested interests in the United Fruit Company, which owned vast banana plantations in Guatemala. With CIA assistance, authoritarian regimes maintained the inequitable land distribution favorable to United Fruit, repressing indigenous and trade union resistance. Although the Carter administration cut off aid to Guatemala, military and counterinsurgency officers continued to train in the United States. And once Carter left office, the Reagan administration funneled money to the regime for covert operations.[30]

When US support for the dirty wars encountered domestic opposition in the form of congressional inquiries and popular protests, Israel worked as a proxy in the region, providing arms and advisors. Despite the state of Israel's history as a refuge for Jewish displaced persons, the nation played a key role in the creation of Central American refugee migration. Proxy support for right-wing regimes in Central America was a component of its long-standing alliance with the United States. Further, these activities assuaged an Israeli sense of political isolation resulting from the United Nations resolution equating Zionism with racism, operative from 1975 to 1991. Israel also responded to allegations of global terrorist networks linking left-wing insurgencies in the region to the Palestine Liberation Organization (PLO). Accordingly, Israeli strategists shared counterinsurgency tactics designed for Palestine.

Guatemalan military leaders like Efraín Ríos Montt spoke openly about the "Palestinianization" of Mayan Indians in the Guatemalan highlands. Israel offered Latin American right-wing regimes arms confiscated from the PLO for the cost of shipping. Israeli advisors helped craft a Salvadoran and Guatemalan rural pacification plan aimed at destroying the power of indigenous and peasant cooperatives that used the model of the kibbutz to relocate and remodel rural life there. Colonel Eduardo Wohlers directed the Guatemalan "Plan of Assistance to Conflict Areas," described by researcher George Black as follows: "Agriculture holds the key to Israel's current role. In it [there is] an interlocking mosaic of assistance programs—weapons to help the Guatemalan Army crush the opposition and lay waste to the countryside, security and intelligence advice to control the local population, and agrarian development models to construct on the ashes of the highlands."[31]

Supported by the United States and Israel, the dirty wars in Central American resulted in massive civilian casualties as well as the displacement of hundreds of thousands of refugees. As Rosemary Radford Reuther explains above, escalating migration from Central America was a consequence of US foreign policy. But the Reagan administration's interpretation of refugee policy allowed few Central Americans to qualify for refugee status. In 1983, the enduring policy distinction between migrants departing supposedly friendly regimes and refugees fleeing totalitarianism resulted in 2 percent of Salvadorans who applied receiving asylum, in contrast to 82 percent of Afghan, 74 percent of Iranian, and 30 percent of Polish applications. In 1984, 97.5 percent of Salvadorans who applied for asylum were rejected. Central American refugees were caught between the imperatives of international humanitarianism toward refugees, partially ratified in the Refugee Act of 1980, and the exigencies of Reagan Doctrine foreign policy, which described the regimes they fled as democratic.[32]

While it recognized the humanitarian importance of refugee admissions, the Refugee Act of 1980 maintained the Cold War prerogatives of the McCarran-Walter Act. Asylum seekers had to prove "credible fear" to an administration charged with believing that particular regimes were compliant with human rights standards. Those who could not pass muster were considered mere migrants to be deported for undocumented crossing or detained on reaching ports of entry. Typically, those fleeing regimes backed by or friendly to the United States are rarely recognized as refugees. They are classified instead as "economic migrants," seeking to better themselves, but not experiencing the "credible fear" of persecution if returned to their nations of origin. The historical distinction between the reception of Cuban and Haitian refugees illuminates this contradiction: Cubans fleeing the Castro regime have been welcomed as freedom seekers escaping communism, whereas Afro-diasporic Haitians leaving the US-backed despotism of François "Papa Doc" and Jean Claude "Baby Doc" Duvalier have been termed "economic migrants" and returned to face their fates in Haiti. In addition to being freighted by US alliances with particular regimes, the contrast between the national welcome of predominantly light-skinned Cubans and the deep ambivalence and punitive response to darker-skinned Marielitos and Haitians illuminate how access to the refugee process is determined by race and class.[33]

This distinction also corresponds with the long history of white supremacist immigration policy that originates in late nineteenth-century Asian exclusion, evolving into national-origin quotas and restrictive border policies throughout the twentieth century. As they crossed the US–Mexico border, Central Americans were subject to being categorized as "Mexican" or "Hispanic." These categories linked them to existing discourses about "wetbacks" and "illegal aliens," making it seem more logical that their petitions for asylum should be denied, despite conditions in their nations of origin. A contemporary congressional policy study further linked undocumented migrants to crime, warning of the potential for the formation of a "fugitive underground class."[34]

As conflict in Central America intensified, sending thousands into exile, the Organization of American States responded by revising the UNHCR's definition of refugee status. Adopted in 1984, the Cartagena Declaration added to the 1951 and 1967 definitions "persons who have fled their country because their lives, safety or freedom have been threatened by generalized violence, foreign aggression, internal conflicts, massive violation of human rights or other circumstances which have seriously disturbed public order." This modification amplified the significance of Article 3 of the Geneva Convention of 1949, which prohibited wartime violence to civilian "life or person," to include the ongoing dirty wars.[35]

This expanded human rights definition had limited traction in the United States. Ambassador H. Eugene Douglas, US Coordinator for Refugee Affairs, pushed back against of the Cartagena Declaration, emphasizing the importance of the distinction between migrants and refugees: "By confusing the distinction between migrants and refugees, the concept of political asylum that Congress placed in the Refugee Act of 1980 will be progressively eroded. . . . If everyone is a refugee, then no one is a refugee."[36]

By 1980, the INS was deporting between five hundred and one thousand Salvadorans and Guatemalans per month. In March of that year, Salvadoran archbishop Oscar Romero, a liberation theologian and widely beloved advocate for the poor, was assassinated while saying Mass. His death brought the issue of human rights in El Salvador to the attention of churches around the world. In the United States, Romero's exhortations to "accompany" El Salvador's poor, cited above, inspired faith-based activist solidarity with Central American migrants.[37]

Responding to this crisis, activist churches in the United States and Central America inaugurated a sanctuary movement to help migrants leave their homes and locate safe harbor after crossing into the United States. Religious delegations to Central America during the late 1970s returned with descriptions of the violence taking place there. Lay participants in Witness for Peace in Nicaragua and El Salvador reported on the increasing activism of churches there at the same time that the writings of liberation theologians percolated north. The roots of the sanctuary movement, then, were both ecclesiastic and international.[38]

In the United States, sanctuary workers crossed the border to help undocumented Central Americans enter. Others traveled to observe conditions in refugee camps in Honduras and El Salvador. The movement drew on the Old Testament notion that religious institutions should shelter "the stranger," cited above. Sanctuary congregations became places of refuge, sheltering those who fled the dirty wars but were not recognized by the US government as refugees. Sanctuary workers invoked Archbishop Romero's invocation that "accompanying" the struggles of the poor constituted holy work, asserting the moral necessity of international solidarity across borders of nation, race, and class.[39]

Initially, sanctuary movement advocates focused on obtaining legal asylum for the thousands of Central American refugees denied it. As migrants made US sanctuary workers increasingly aware of the violence taking place in Central America, the internationalist strand of the movement emphasized the root causes of migration in US imperial foreign policy. As the sanctuary movement spread to religious congregations as well as social movement spaces throughout the nation, an "underground railroad" involving over 160 places of worship and community organizations, as well as sympathetic journalists, moved several thousand asylum seekers around the nation and offered haven as well as a podium to broadcast their situations.[40]

An anonymous article in the professional journal *Social Work* described the "early days" of the sanctuary movement, when advocates focused on raising monies to release migrants from prison. Gradually, sanctuary workers and migrants realized that even when they were successful in freeing prisoners, Central American migrants were still considered undocumented, with few rights or economic prospects. This realization led to bolder actions, like a "freedom train" in which undocumented Central Americans traveled from city to city, publicizing their situations.[41]

As the anonymous attribution suggests, advocates recognized the threat they faced by aiding undocumented migrants. Section 274 of the McCarran-Walter Act criminalized transporting "illegal aliens" across the border or within the country, as well as "concealing, harboring, sheltering," or even "encouraging" undocumented individuals. Sanctuary workers faced penalties: fines of $2,000 and up to five years of incarceration for each individual assisted. The *Social Work* article articulates the early sanctuary movement's emphasis on distinguishing between what the author calls "political" and "economic refugees," emphasizing that the majority of undocumented migrants arrive for economic reasons. Highlighting the difference between the needs of refugees and those of migrants, it explains that sanctuary workers "believe that sending political refugees back to persecution in their homeland violates the law in that political refugees are protected by the U.S. Refugee Act of 1980, the UN Protocol on Refugees, and the Geneva Convention."[42]

The distinction between "political refugees" and "economic migrants" was central as long as sanctuary workers labored only to help Central Americans with the legal processes leading to asylum. But as the movement developed, migrant testimonies emphasized the origins of the crisis in US foreign policy, rather than in the allegiances or motivations of those fleeing the dirty wars. Increasingly, awareness of the violence of imperial policies in Central America overwhelmed movement confidence in policies distinguishing between refugees and migrants. As the Center for Constitutional Rights explained in 1985: "'declaring sanctuary' is a moral, political, and legal decision—an act to communicate to legislative bodies their dissatisfaction with current United States Central American policies."[43]

Through the sanctuary movement, progressive congregations and some secular organizations criticized Reagan Doctrine foreign policy as well as administrative machinations around refugee policy. With some notable exceptions, US media coverage of the dirty wars portrayed Central American popular movements as threatening guerilla insurgencies. The popular 1984 film *Red Dawn* broadcast the possibility of invasion from the south, depicting a menacing coalition of Sandinistas and Soviet apparatchiks. As the accounts of Central Americans fleeing the dirty wars exposed the falsity of this official line and motivated sanctuary workers to subvert federal law, the movement was targeted for federal surveillance.[44]

The 1985–86 trial of eleven sanctuary workers, half of them clergy, highlighted the protracted political conflict over refugees from the dirty wars. The evidence against the defendants had been gathered by the FBI, which utilized paid informants to infiltrate churches and movement meetings. The prosecution depicted their crimes as "alien smuggling" and attempted to have the word "refugee" banned from the trial, referring to Central Americans involved in the sanctuary movement as "alien co-conspirators." When eight of the eleven were convicted, and their appeal subsequently denied by the Supreme Court, the trial provided a context for sanctuary workers to explain their conviction that US foreign policy interfered with the rights to asylum laid out by the Refugee Act of 1980. Susan Bibler Coutin explains, "Paradoxically, prosecution and surveillance both criminalized and exonerated sanctuary workers."[45]

In its critique of US foreign policy, the sanctuary movement drew on an anti-imperialist, internationalist tradition that persisted in the United States, despite repression throughout the Cold War. This residual anti-imperialism was reignited by liberation theology penned by Central American intellectuals like Ignacio Ellacuría and Jon Sobrino, traveling both in ecclesiastical circles and on the journeys of thousands of Central Americans fleeing their homelands. The emergent form of the 1980s sanctuary movement found articulation in the three thousand faith groups and dozens of cities that declared themselves sanctuaries. Six hundred African American organizers in Operation PUSH declared sanctuary in Chicago, as Jesse Jackson compared the movement to the antebellum Underground Railroad to liberate enslaved Black people. The Akwesasne Nation declared its land spanning the boundary of New York State and Canada as a sanctuary and provided legal counsel to Guatemalan Mayan Indians as they sheltered on traditional Seminole lands in Florida.[46]

Central Americans' testimonies about human rights abuses in their homelands also infused anti-imperialist movements like the Committee in Solidarity with the People of El Salvador (CISPES) and Witness for Peace. Through these organizations, North Americans traveled to Central America, returning to affirm stories told by refugees from the region and to pressure the media to cover the dirty wars more extensively and equitably. Historian Bradford Martin credits the international connections forged in these movements with precipitating public disclosure of the "Iran-Contra affair" in 1987.[47]

Confronting the limits of US policy toward refugees and migrants, the sanctuary movement of the 1980s reimagined universal rights outside of the Cold War framework reinvigorated by the Reagan Doctrine. The movement violated laws it considered unjust to provide asylum for Central Americans outside the tight limits set by national policy and created a transnational network which facilitated the flow of information about the dirty wars beyond the exceedingly truncated coverage prevalent in US mass media. Importantly, the sanctuary movement brought the term "sanctuary" into public consciousness as an emergent answer to the practical shortcomings of human rights law. While the movement dwindled by the early 1990s, the idea of sanctuary persisted as an imaginative principle.

Sanctuary Everywhere

When I look out at you, each and every one here, this is a sea of love. This is
like the Katrina that is going to overtake any wall that is going to be built
because this sea of love is going to make that change.
—Ravi Ragbir, director, New Sanctuary Coalition, in "Let My People Stay"

Every Thursday morning a group of people walk seven times in silence around 26 Federal Plaza in New York City, which holds the immigration courthouse. The New York New Sanctuary Coalition has been holding these Jericho Walks since 2011, as part of their ongoing attempt to "carve out some hope where there is hopelessness," in the words of the Reverend Juan Carlos Ruiz, cofounder and organizer of the New Sanctuary Coalition. Modeled on the Old Testament story of Joshua, who, as the song goes, "fit the battle of Jericho, and the walls came tumbling down," the Jericho Walk poses the power of the assembled immigrant rights advocates against the edifices of power and deportation.[49]

Founded in 2007, the contemporary New Sanctuary Movement (NSM) responds to the enhanced immigration enforcement that is a vital component of post-9/11 securitization. In using Old Testament tropes to illuminate moral might against state power, the New Sanctuary Movement draws on an arsenal familiar from the strategies of the 1980s sanctuary movement. But advocates stand on ground radically transformed by the past twenty years.

Federal Plaza is blocks away from the site of the World Trade Center felled on September 11, 2001. The work of the New Sanctuary Movement takes place in context of the homeland securitization of immigration enforcement. As a result, contemporary sanctuary is an emergent and fast-changing cultural form. The New Sanctuary Coalition of New York modifies the accompaniment practices of the sanctuary movement of the 1980s to fill immigration courts with crowds of "documented" US citizens on behalf of "friends" undergoing check-in visits. This version of accompaniment brings visibility to the ever-present threat of deportation, sometimes changing the outcomes of immigration court visits.[50]

No new federal immigration policy has passed Congress since the Illegal Immigration Reform and Individual Responsibility Act (IIRIRA) of 1996 provided grounds for the enhanced criminalization and policing of migrant communities, for example, by instituting 287(g) programs that authorize local police collaboration with federal immigration enforcement. But "homeland security" laws like the USA PATRIOT Act of 2001 and the Real ID Act of 2005 have had devastating effects on foreign-born communities, depriving noncitizens of access to legal identification and providing expansive grounds for the detention and deportation of undocumented residents, particularly those suspected of links to terrorism. A host of subfederal laws at the state level, along with the rise of xenophobia in public discourse, erodes the rights of the foreign born. Such subfederal laws are most notoriously represented by the controversial Senate Bill 1070 in Arizona authorizing law-enforcement personnel to ask for identification papers from people they suspect of being undocumented.[51]

After 9/11, an emergent grammar of homeland security drew on residual nativism and Islamophobia to conflate Muslim and Arab Americans with both terrorism and out-of-control migration. This discourse deployed the Cold War semantic division between deserving refugees and threatening migrants during almost two decades of refugee-generating conflicts waged by US forces, allies, munitions, and drones in Iraq, Afghanistan, Pakistan, Israel/Palestine, Yemen, and more. At this moment of increased US international engagement, a nationalist language of borders and securitization that perceived refugees as potential terrorists gained traction. As refugees became associated in this discourse with "terror," it eroded the post-1951 distinction between "deserving" refugees and suspect migrants.[52]

This rhetoric of counterterrorism advanced further in the Trump administration's rapid implementation of Executive Order 13769, a controversial ban on travelers, refugees, and migrants from seven mostly Muslim nations. Like past restrictive immigration laws, this policy draws on xenophobia, white supremacy, and Islamophobia. But in a departure from Cold War immigration policy, the order also conflates migrants with refugees as equally threatening and undesirable, upending prior distinctions between these two terms. Mandating a temporary ban on refugee admissions, the order asserted the criminal proclivities of immigrants as well as those "who entered through the United States refugee resettlement program."[53]

Public discourse in both nativist and immigrant rights circles increasingly uses the words "migrants" and "refugees" interchangeably: Pueblo Sin Fronteras says "refugees and migrants," and the Trump administration responds by treating asylum seekers as undocumented entrants. Anyone wanting to cross the border confronts the xenophobic rage of public policy, as evidenced by the troops deployed to "defend" the US–Mexico border against the migrant caravan. As the distinctions between refugees and migrants erodes, it creates a space to assert the right to freedom of movement for all.[54]

Responding to the amplified xenophobia present since the 2016 election, the New Sanctuary Movement includes broad advocacy and organizing around immigrant rights and community empowerment. Contemporary immigrant rights formations are influenced by the emergent activism of "DREAMers," or "undocumented youth activists," to use visual culture scholar Rebecca Schreiber's term. "Undocumented and unafraid" activists worked against federal as well as state and local anti-immigration policies. Courageous and innovative, they organized civil disobediences and infiltrated detention centers to monitor conditions there.[55]

With the collapse of long-standing definitions of refugees and migrants in this era of zero tolerance, sanctuary rearticulates the grounds for collective refuge. Like the sanctuary movement of the 1980s, the New Sanctuary Movement provides shelter while raising awareness of the issues faced by foreign-born communities. It publicizes cases like that of Salvadoran-American Araceli Vasquez, who went into sanctuary in Denver during the summer of 2017. The publicity drawn by those who go into sanctuary allows the immigrant rights movement to gain the much-needed visibility that has been obscured, in large part by the homeland security state's deployment of images of criminality and deviance to define migration.[56]

Just as 1980s advocates deployed the word "sanctuary" to respond to a gap in rights at the junction of national and international laws, the contemporary New Sanctuary Movement has begun to invent new forms: sanctuary cities, communities, and campuses. These innovations have occasioned opposition in the form of state and federal "anti-sanctuary" bills, which threaten to cut off public funds to sanctuary communities.[57]

Contemporary sanctuary practices are emergent forms, requiring imagination as well as organizing. For example, a "Sanctuary Campus Toolkit" produced collaboratively by the immigrant rights organization Cosecha and the Harvard University Law Clinic provides extensive legal resources for campus organizations seeking to protect foreign-born students, faculty, and staff. This text cites historical antecedents, such as Oberlin College's defiance of the Fugitive Slave Law and its welcome of Japanese American students during the 1940s internment, universities and colleges that harbored students seeking to evade the Vietnam-era draft, and institutions which refused to allow ROTC on campus because of its discriminatory policies against gay, lesbian, and transgender students. The authors explain: "As universities now decide to move forward, they should know that they carry forward an important tradition of colleges and universities as sites of courageous resistance and protection."[58]

As a social movement, sanctuary is born in and responds to emergency. The zero tolerance policy adopted in the spring of 2017 made family separation in detention facilities a consequence of undocumented crossing.[59] In the spring of 2018, the issue gained traction as photographs and videos emerged that depicted children crying behind chain-link fences. Widespread protests took place in cities and towns across the country, proclaiming "families belong together." As Lisa Cacho points out, this framing can narrow much broader claims by immigrant rights advocates. However, during the summer of 2018, the broad, abolitionist phrase, #abolishICE, caught fire.[60]

As an aspiration, #abolishICE echoes the internationalist claims of Pueblo Sin Fronteras, conjuring an alternate history of global rights suppressed by the Cold War and subsequent political formations. The use of the word "abolition" echoes the work of Black and white antebellum activists who sheltered, advocated for, and accompanied African Americans to court, working against their deportations from free to slave states. The critique of the securitized Immigration and Customs Enforcement agency suggests the possibility of a world in which national sovereignty is not an impediment to creating refuge for the most precarious in all nations. As a slogan, #abolishICE parallels the Palestinian Stop the Wall Campaign as it recognizes the depredations of walls and borders.

Like the #abolishICE hashtag, international organizations like Pueblo Sin Fronteras and the Palestinian Stop the Wall Campaign link the global struggles of migrants, refugees, citizens, and denizens against militarized immigration and policing. These groups represent an international movement, #worldwithoutwalls, which recognizes the depredations of internal walls, like those built around Brazilian favelas and those maintaining the Israeli occupation of Palestinian lands, as similar in kind to the international borders that cut across indigenous lands and deter people fleeing Central America from seeking shelter in the United States. Enhanced securitization of these walls and fences maintains repressive orders and secures the borders of neighborhoods as well as imperial nation-states.[61]

Importantly, these organizations acknowledge the depredations of walls within as well as between sovereign nations. They recognize that to work against such walls is to work against a global system of empire, which includes the brutal legacies that have created the contemporary map of nations as well as ongoing imperial practices. Imagining a world without walls is an alternative internationalist project, connecting struggles for indigenous sovereignty and migrant justice to those against state violence.

As Judith Butler has recently written, sanctuary is a term we might deploy to describe broad struggles for freedom, against securitization: "Sanctuary is a vanishing ideal within the new security state, one worth reanimating not only for scholars at risk but also for the undocumented and those who engage in political dissent—in other words, for all those who have reason to fear the state by virtue of their precarious position."[62]

At the time of this writing, the contemporary sanctuary movement mobilizes to greet the most recent caravans from Central America at the border in January 2019. Inaugurating a "Sanctuary Caravan" that intends to meet the Fall 2018 migrant caravan at the US–Mexico border, the New Sanctuary Coalition asserts the existence of "fundamental human rights" that transcend national citizenship. The coalition writes: "We reaffirm our conviction that every member of the Central American Caravan has an inalienable human right to flee from violence and poverty and toward better economic and political conditions elsewhere, regardless of national boundaries. We submit that they possess a right to enter and remain in the U.S. equal to anyone born there."[63]

This convergence is one of many. As juridical categories of "refugee" and "migrant" succumb to the deluge of US as well as worldwide xenophobia, sanctuary presents an alternative. Practices of sanctuary proliferate everywhere, within and beyond the scope of a juridical regime compromised by the limits of international law. Contemporary sanctuary formations draw on past practices as well as innovating new ones, creating a rising tide: the "sea of love" that Ragbir imagines in the quote cited above. Like the sea, they are everywhere.

Sanctuary everywhere: The weekly Jericho Walks in New York City take place on hallowed land: the African cemetery partially paved over by construction of the federal buildings in lower Manhattan. Sometimes the walks have concluded with participants taking a knee, in homage to the gesture of athletes in solidarity with the Movement for Black Lives.[64]

Sanctuary everywhere: In Milwaukee, since 2017, local mobilizations against 287(g) bills have drawn a new coalition of Muslim-Arab and Black Lives Matter organizers into immigrant rights work. A May 2018 demonstration against Israeli Defense Forces killings of protesters in Gaza brought leaders from the predominantly Latinx immigrant rights organization, Voces de la Frontera, together with Palestine solidarity activists.

Sanctuary everywhere: The word exceeds its category. It stands in for what became unsayable during the Cold War; what was articulated by survivors of the genocidal dirty wars. It becomes a banner for what is still possible, even in the bleakest of times.

Rachel Ida Buff teaches history and comparative ethnic studies at the University of Wisconsin–Milwaukee. She is author, most recently, of *Against the Deportation Terror: Organizing for Immigrant Rights in the Twentieth Century* (2017), and writes frequently for popular outlets such as *Truthout* and *The Nation*. Currently, she is working on a project entitled "Terms of Occupancy: What We Talk about When We Talk about Migration."

Notes

My thanks to Joe Austin, Benjamin Balthaser, Nan Enstad, Wendy Kozol, and S. Ani Mukherji for their comments on prior drafts. The Center for 21st Century Studies at University of Wisconsin-Milwaukee provided crucial space and time for the writing of this piece. Timely interventions by two anonymous reviewers as well as the editors of this issue helped me figure out what I was trying to say in the first place.

1.   Pueblo Sin Fronteras, "Refugee Caravan 2018."
2.   Campese, "¿Cuantos Más?," 284.
3.   Palestinian Stop the Wall Campaign, "Letter."
4.   Palestinian Stop the Wall Campaign, "Letter."
5.   U.S. Citizenship and Immigration Services, "Obtaining Asylum"; Whitfield, "The Immigrant Caravan Lays Bare the Conflict between Jesus and Power"; Semple and Jordan, "Migrant Caravan of Asylum Seekers Reaches U.S. Border"; Ahmed, Rodgers, and Ernst, "How the Migrant Caravan Became a Trump Election Strategy."
6.   These protests were organized by the National Domestic Workers Alliance, the Leadership Conference on Civil Rights, the ACLU, the Women's March, and MoveOn. Arnold, "Everything to Know about the Nationwide Immigration Separation Protest on June 30." In 1997, the Supreme Court ruled in *Flores v. Reno* that unaccompanied minors detained at the border should either be released to adult guardians or relatives, or held in the "least restrictive environment" possible. A subsequent ruling by a federal judge in California dictated the release of children and parents traveling together. Because they cannot be released without an adult guardian, children separated from the adults with whom they travel often wind up in federal detention centers and prisons. See National Center for Youth Law, "Flores v. Reno"; Cillizza, "The Remarkable History of the Family Separation Crisis"; and Hernández, "Habitual Punishment." For rhetorical connections between smuggling and family separation, see Hennessey-Fiske, "Migrants, Young and Old, Are Not Always Related"; Jordan, "Breaking Up Families"; "Absent a Border Wall, Trump Opts to Punish Migrant Parents by Seizing Their Kids"; National Public Radio, "Border Patrol Union Official Discusses Family Separation Policy"; Valverde, "What You Need to Know about the Trump Administration's Zero Tolerance Policy."
7.   Buff, "Refugee Planet: Sanctuary Everywhere." "Sanctuary Everywhere" is also a current campaign of the American Friends' Service Committee. See www.afsc.org /sanctuaryeverywhere (accessed May 30, 2018).
8.   Naomi Paik writes of the capacity-building work of sanctuary practices: "Beyond its grounded intervention of non-cooperation and safe harbor, sanctuary already performs conceptual work that can undermine the criminalization of migrants and other vulnerable people." Paik, "Abolitionist Futures and the New Sanctuary Movement," 17.
9.   Cohen, "The 'Human Rights Revolution' at Work," 47–48.
10. Quoted in Romero, "Migrants Meet with Fear, Disdain, in Tijuana, Mexico." Goodwin Gill, "Introductory Note"; DeGooyer, "Nothing but Human"; Cohen, *In War's Wake*, 4–5.
11. Benhabib, *The Reluctant Modernism of Hannah Arendt*, 62–102.
12. For the UNHCR definition of refugees, see United Nations High Commissioner for Refugees, *Convention and Protocol Relating to the Status of Refugees*, especially pages 14–16.

13. Esmeir, *Juridical Humanity*, 2–8.

14. Garfinkle traces the history of the phrase, more commonly attributed to Theodor Herzl as "a land without a people for a people without a land," in "On the Origin, Meaning, Use and Abuse of a Phrase," 540, 543. See also Said, *The Question of Palestine*, especially pages 3–55. On UNRWA, see United Nations Relief and Works Agency for Palestine, "Who We Are."

15. See Ngai, *Impossible Subjects*.

16. On Operation Wetback, see Hernandez, *Migra!*, 169–218; Buff, *Against the Deportation Terror*, 108–37. On the McCarran-Walter (Immigration and Nationality) Act, see García, *The Refugee Challenge in Post-Cold War America*, 162; Buff, *Immigration and the Political Economy of Home*, 45–76.

17. See Brick, *Daniel Bell and the Decline of Intellectual Radicalism*, 154–60. Cohen, *In War's Wake*, 60.

18. Quoted in Greenstein, *Zionism and Its Discontents*, 155.

19. Plitman, "On an Emerging Diasporism." For more on "diaspora nationalism," see Karlip, *The Tragedy of a Generation*, reviewed by Dynner, 2014; Pianko, *Zionism and the Roads Not Taken*.

20. *The Lamp*, no. 36, June 1947; see also Buff, *Against the Deportation Terror*, 78–80.

21. "Passing the Word"; Buff, *Against the Deportation Terror*, 89–92.

22. Hester, *Deportation*, 35–60; on camps and international human rights discourse, see also Paik, *Rightlessness*, especially pages 9–13.

23. Golden and McConnell, *Sanctuary*, viii.

24. Romero, "on Accompaniment."

25. "Havens of Refuge," 2.

26. Public Law 92-212; "States Parties to the 1951 Convention on the Status of Refugees and the 1967 Protocol"; Golden and McConnell, *Sanctuary*, 67; Coutin, *The Culture of Protest*, 93; García, *The Refugee Challenge in Post-Cold War America*, 5–6.

27. Carl Lindskoog argues that Reagan Administration impetus to stop Haitian refugee migration, through interdiction as well as deportation, coincided with implementation of the Refugee Act, undermining it in practice. See Lindskoog, *Detain and Punish*, especially pages 51–71.

28. For a definition of the term "dirty war," see Smith and Roberts, "War in the Gray." On the Salvadoran civil war, see Bonner, "Time for a U.S. Apology to El Salvador."

29. Golden and McConnell, *Sanctuary*, 19–24; Bonner, "Time for a U.S. Apology to El Salvador."

30. Golden and McConnell, *Sanctuary*, 24–27. On Iran, see Kinzer, *All the Shah's Men*, and Kinzer, *Overthrow*.

31. Black, "Israeli Connection Not Just Guns for Guatemala"; Rubenberg, "Israel and Guatemala"; "The UN Resolution on Zionism."

32. According to María Christina García, "both geopolitical and domestic considerations have played a role in determining the numerical quota [of refugees] and how it will be allocated" (*The Refugee Challenge in Post-Cold War America*, 6). Statistics: Golden and McConnell, *Sanctuary*, 44 and 77.

33. "Marielitos" refers to the 135,000 Cubans who left the Cuban port of Mariel in 1980. Many had served time in Cuban prisons. Racialized by the US media, they did not receive the warm reception enjoyed by early cohorts of Cuban migrants. See Robles, "Marielitos Face Long Delayed Reckoning: Expulsion to Cuba"; Lindskoog, *Detain and Punish*.

34. Harwood, *In Liberty's Shadow*, 20, cited in Coutin, *The Culture of Protest*, 95.

35. Cartagena Document, www.oas.org/dil/1984_cartagena_declaration_on_refugees.pdf (accessed June 7, 2018); the Cartagena document is discussed in García, *The Refugee Challenge in Post-Cold War America*, 46. On the Geneva Convention see "Havens of Refuge," 8.

36. Quoted in Golden and McConnell, *Sanctuary*, 41.

37. Bonner, "Time for a U.S. Apology to El Salvador."

38. Martin, *The Other Eighties*, 25–44; Maier, "Archbishop Romero and Liberation Theology."

39. Coutin, *The Culture of Protest*, 23–50. On accompaniment, see also Tomlinson and Lipsitz, "American Studies as Accompaniment," 8–10.

40. Statistic on 1980 deportations from Golden and McConnell, *Sanctuary*, 1.

41. "Social Work in the Sanctuary Movement," 74–76.

42. Quote from "Social Work in the Sanctuary Movement," 74; McCarran Walter Act referenced in "Havens of Refuge," 8.

43. "Havens of Refuge," 5.

44. Journalists Alma Guillermoprieto and Raymond Bonner, for example, consistently covered the depredations of the US-backed regime in El Salvador. See Bonner's more recent "Time for a U.S. Apology to El Salvador." On criminalization of sanctuary, see Golden and McConnell, *Sanctuary*, 1–2.

45. On trial were Jim Corbett; Rev. John Fife; Wayne King; Sister Darlene Nicgorski; Phillip Willis-Conger, a seminary student; Rev. Ramon Dagoberto Quinones, a Catholic priest; Maria del Socorro Pardo Viuda de Aguilar; Wendy LeWin; Rev. Anthony Clark, 37, of Nogales, Ariz.; and Peggy Hutchison, 31, a Tucson missionary. Espinoza, MacDonald, and Witt, "Sanctuary Activists Lose Conspiracy Trial"; King, "Trial Opening in Arizona"; Coutin, "Smugglers or Samaritans in Tucson, Arizona," 549; Golden and McConnell, *Sanctuary*, 75–76.

46. Golden and McConnell, *Sanctuary*, 53–61; Camposeco, introduction; Martin, *The Other Eighties*, 25–44.

47. Martin, *The Other Eighties*, 27.

48. "Let My People Stay."

49. Juan Carlos Ruiz, interview with author, February 20, 2018.

50. This strategy has had some success in the deportation case of Ravi Ragbir, as well as in lesser-known cases. On Ragbir's case, see Hawkins, "Federal Judge Blasts ICE for 'Cruel' Tactics, Frees Immigrant Rights Activist Ravi Ragbir."

51. Arizona Immigration Law (SB 1070). Gulasekaram and Ramakrishnan, "Immigration Federalism." Under the rubric of "effective counter-terrorism," the regime of enhanced immigration enforcement undermines foreign-born communities. The 2002 implementation of the National Security Exit-Entry Registration System (NSEERS) required nonimmigrant Muslim and Arab men and boys to register with the DHS. Of the 84,000 who complied, 13,000 faced removal proceedings, mostly on grounds of minor immigration infractions such as visa overstay. None were charged with actual terrorist activities.

52. "The National Security Entrance-Exit Registry"; Gladstone and Sugiyama, "Trump's Travel Ban." Legal scholar Noura Erakat argues that the August 2018 move of the Trump administration to defund the United Nations Relief and Works Agency moves to redefine the nature and number of Palestinian refugees. Settler-colonial projects physically

displace people and then rhetorically erase even the incidence of displacement, at the cost of even the limited humanitarianism permitted by the emergence of liberal human rights after 1945. Erakat explains: "The United States and Israel want to resolve the Palestinian refugee issue not by allowing refugees to return but by changing the legal definition so that they cease to exist" (Erakat, "Trump Has No Right to Define Who Is a Palestinian Refugee").

53. "Executive Order Protecting the Nation from Foreign Terrorist Entry into the United State."
54. See, for example, Giatarelli, "Border Police, Troops Brace for Caravan Surge in Arizona."
55. Schreiber, *The Undocumented Everyday*, 238–67.
56. Schwartz, "Searching for a New Sanctuary Movement"; "Araceli Vasquez in Sanctuary."
57. In 2015 organizing by the workers' center/immigrant rights organization Voces de la Frontera defeated an "anti-sanctuary cities" bill in the state. See Stein and Marley, "State Senate Unlikely to Take Up Sanctuary Cities Bill."
58. Harvard Law Clinic and Cosecha, "Sanctuary Campus."
59. Madrigal, "The Making of an On-Line Moral Crisis."
60. Cacho, *Social Death*.
61. Stop the Wall, "Call for Global Day of Action."
62. Butler, "The Criminalization of Knowledge."
63. New Sanctuary Coalition, "Sanctuary Caravan."
64. Juan Carlos Ruiz, interview with author, February 20, 2018.

References

"Absent a Border Wall, Trump Opts to Punish Migrant Parents by Seizing Their Kids." *St. Louis Post-Dispatch*, May 13, 2018. www.stltoday.com/opinion/editorial/editorial-absent-a-border -wall-trump-opts-to-punish-migrant/article_c6ea8e98-6576-537d-bf5a-285c689fbf8d .html.

Ahmed, Azam, Katie Rodgers, and Jeff Ernst. "How the Migrant Caravan Became a Trump Election Strategy." *New York Times*, October 24, 2018. www.nytimes.com/2018/10/24 /world/americas/migrant-caravan-trump.html.

"Araceli Vasquez in Sanctuary." American Friends Service Committee. www.afsc.org/araceli (accessed June 8, 2018).

Arizona Immigration Law (SB 1070). immigration.findlaw.com/immigration-laws-and-resources /arizona-immigration-law-s-b-1070.html (accessed November 19, 2018).

Arnold, Amanda. "Everything to Know about the Nationwide Immigration Separation Protest on June 30." *The Cut*, June 28, 2018. www.thecut.com/2018/06/families-belong-together -immigrant-separation-protest.html.

Benhabib, Seyla. *The Reluctant Modernism of Hannah Arendt*. New York: Rowman and Littlefield, 2003.

Black, George. "Israeli Connection Not Just Guns for Guatemala." *NACLA Report*, September 25, 2007.

Bonner, Raymond. "Time for a U.S. Apology to El Salvador." *The Nation*, April 15, 2016. www .thenation.com/article/time-for-a-us-apology-to-el-salvador/.

Brick, Howard. *Daniel Bell and the Decline of Intellectual Radicalism: Social Theory and Political Reconciliation in the 1940s*. Madison: University of Wisconsin Press, 1986.

Buff, Rachel Ida. *Against the Deportation Terror: Organizing for Immigrant Rights in the Twentieth Century*. Philadelphia: Temple University Press, 2017.

Buff, Rachel Ida. *Immigration and the Political Economy of Home: Caribbean Brooklyn and American Indian Minneapolis, 1945–1992.* Berkeley: University of California Press, 2001.

Buff, Rachel Ida. "Refugee Planet: Sanctuary Everywhere." *Deadly Exchange,* November 2017. deadlyexchange.org/planet-refugee-sanctuary-everywhere/.

Butler, Judith. "The Criminalization of Knowledge: Why the Struggle for Academic Freedom Is the Struggle for Democracy." *Chronicle of Higher Education,* May 27, 2018. www.chronicle .com/article/The-Criminalization-of/243501?cid=wcontentgrid_41_2.

Cacho, Lisa Marie. *Social Death: Racialized Rightlessness and the Criminalization of the Unprotected.* New York: New York University Press, 2012.

Campese, Gioacchino. "¿Cuantos Más? The Crucified Peoples at the U.S.-Mexico Border." In *A Promised Land, a Perilous Journey: Theological Perspectives on Migration,* edited by Daniel Groody and Gioacchino Campese, 271–98. South Bend, IN: University of Notre Dame, 2008.

Camposeco, Jerónimo. Introduction to *Maya in Exile: Guatemalans in Florida,* by Allen F. Burns. Philadelphia: Temple University Press, 1993.

"Cartagena Document." www.oas.org/dil/1984_cartagena_declaration_on_refugees.pdf (accessed June 7, 2018).

Cillizza, Chris. "The Remarkable History of the Family Separation Crisis." June 18, 2018. www .cnn.com/2018/06/18/politics/donald-trump-immigration-policies-q-and-a/index.html.

Cohen, G. Daniel. "The 'Human Rights Revolution' at Work: Displaced Persons in Postwar Europe." In *Human Rights in the Twentieth Century,* edited by Stefan Ludwig Hoffman, 45–68. New York: Cambridge University Press, 2011.

Cohen, G. Daniel. *In War's Wake: Europe's Displaced Persons in the Postwar Order.* New York: Oxford University Press, 2011.

Coutin, Susan Bibler. *The Culture of Protest: Religious Activism and the U.S. Sanctuary Movement.* Boulder: Westview Press, 1993.

Coutin, Susan Bibler. "Smugglers or Samaritans in Tucson, Arizona: Producing and Contesting Legal Truth." *American Ethnologist* 22, no. 3 (August 1995): 549–71.

DeGooyer, Stephanie. "Nothing but Human: On 'The Right to Have Rights.'" www.versobooks .com/blogs/3663-nothing-but-human-on-the-right-to-have-rights (accessed May 25, 2018).

Dynner, Glenn. "Review of *The Tragedy of a Generation.*" *American Historical Review* (December 2014): 1810–11.

Erakat, Noura. "Trump Has No Right to Define Who Is a Palestinian Refugee." *Middle East Eye,* September 5, 2018. www.middleeasteye.net/columns/trumps-attempts-redefine-who -palestinian-refugee-racist-and-non-sensical-1702556026.

Esmeir, Samara. *Juridical Humanity: A Colonial History.* Palo Alto, CA: Stanford University Press, 2012.

Espinoza, Mary Kay, Nena MacDonald, and Howard Witt, "Sanctuary Activists Lose Conspiracy Trial." *Chicago Tribune,* May 2, 1986.

"Executive Order Protecting the Nation from Foreign Terrorist Entry into the United States," January 27, 2017. www.whitehouse.gov/presidential-actions/executive-order-protecting -nation-foreign-terrorist-entry-united-states/.

García, María Cristina. *The Refugee Challenge in Post-Cold War America.* New York: Oxford University Press, 2017.

Garfinkle, Adam M. "On the Origin, Meaning, Use and Abuse of a Phrase." *Middle East Studies* 27, no. 4 (1991): 539–55.

Giatarelli, Anna. "Border Police, Troops Brace for Caravan Surge in Arizona." *Washington Examiner*, December 5, 2018. www.washingtonexaminer.com/news/border-police-troops-brace-for-caravan-surge-in-arizona.

Gladstone, Rick, and Satoshi Sugiyama. "Trump's Travel Ban: How It Works and Who Is Affected." *New York Times*, July 1, 2018. www.nytimes.com/2018/07/01/world/americas/travel-ban-trump-how-it-works.html.

Golden, Renny, and Michael McConnell. *Sanctuary: The New Underground Railroad*. Maryknoll, NY: Orbis Books, 1986.

Goodwin Gill, Guy S. "Introductory Note" to "Declaration on Territorial Asylum." United Nations Audiovisual Library on International Law. legal.un.org/avl/ha/dta/dta.html (accessed May 25, 2018).

Greenstein, Ron. *Zionism and Its Discontents: A Century of Radical Dissent in Israel/Palestine*. London: Pluto Press, 2014.

Gulasekaram, Preethepan, and S. Karthick Ramakrishnan. "Immigration Federalism: A Reappraisal." *New York University Law Review* 88 (2013): 2074–145.

Harvard Law Clinic and Cosecha. "Sanctuary Campus: Frequently Asked Questions." today.law.harvard.edu/wp-content/uploads/2017/02/Sanctuary-Campus-Toolkit.pdf (accessed September 14, 2018).

Harwood, Edward. *In Liberty's Shadow: Illegal Aliens and Immigration Law Enforcement*. Palo Alto, CA: Stanford University Press, 1986.

"Havens of Refuge." New York: Center for Constitutional Rights, 1985.

Hawkins, Derek. "Federal Judge Blasts ICE for 'Cruel' Tactics, Frees Immigrant Rights Activist Ravi Ragbir." *Washington* Post, January 30, 2018. www.washingtonpost.com/news/morning-mix/wp/2018/01/29/federal-judge-blasts-ice-for-cruel-tactics-frees-immigrant-rights-activist-ravi-ragbir/?utm_term=.52ed773b0467.

Hennessey-Fiske, Molly. "Migrants, Young and Old, Are Not Always Related. Border Patrol Says Fear of Child Trafficking Forces Separations." *Los Angeles Times*, May 8, 2018. www.latimes.com/nation/la-na-border-patrol-dna-20180508-htmlstory.html.

Hernández, David. "Habitual Punishment: Family Detention and the Status Quo." *Europe Now*, November 8, 2018. www.europenowjournal.org/2018/11/07/habitual-punishment-family-detention-and-the-status-quo/.

Hernandez, Kelly Lytle. *Migra! A History of the U.S. Border Patrol*. Berkeley: University of California Press, 2010.

Hester, Torrie. *Deportation: The Origins of U.S. Policy*. Philadelphia: University of Pennsylvania Press, 2017.

Jordan, Miriam. "Breaking Up Families: A Look at the Latest Border Tactic." *New York Times*, May 12, 2018. www.nytimes.com/2018/05/12/us/immigrants-family-separation.html.

Karlip, Joshua M. *The Tragedy of a Generation: The Rise and Fall of Jewish Nationalism in Eastern Europe*. Cambridge, MA: Harvard University Press, 2013.

King, Wayne. "Trial Opening in Arizona." *New York Times*, October 21, 1985. www.nytimes.com/1985/10/21/us/trial-opening-in-arizona-in-alien-sanctuary-case.html.

Kinzer, Stephen. *All the Shah's Men: An American Coup and the Roots of Middle East Terror*. New York: Wiley Books, 2008.

Kinzer, Stephen. *Overthrow: America's Century of Regime Change from Hawaii to Iran*. New York: Times Books, 2007.

"Let My People Stay." Podcast 5 of series, "Indefensible." The Immigrant Defense Project. www.immigrantdefenseproject.org/indefensible-episode-5/ (accessed September 14, 2018).

Lindskoog, Carl. *Detain and Punish: Haitian Refugees and the Rise of the World's Largest Immigration Detention System*. Gainesville: University Press of Florida, 2018.

Madrigal, Alexis. "The Making of an Online Moral Crisis: How the Many-Chambered Heart of the Internet Turned the Trump Administration's Family-Separation Policy into a Different Kind of Scandal." *The Atlantic*, June 19, 2018. www.theatlantic.com/technology/archive/2018/06/the-making-of-a-moral-problem/563114/.

Maier, Martin. "Archbishop Romero and Liberation Theology." www.romerotrust.org.uk/sites/default/files/MartinMaier1500words.pdf (accessed September 13, 2018).

Martin, Bradford. *The Other Eighties: A Secret History of America in the Age of Reagan*. New York: Hill and Wang, 2011.

National Center for Youth Law. "Flores v. Reno." youthlaw.org/case/flores-v-reno/ (accessed November 6, 2018).

National Public Radio. "Border Patrol Union Official Discusses Family Separation Policy." National Public Radio, June 19, 2018. www.npr.org/2018/06/19/621578853/border-patrol-official-discusses-family-separation-policy.

"The National Security Entrance-Exit Registry." Arab-American Institute. www.aaiusa.org/nseers (accessed September 14, 2018).

New Sanctuary Coalition. "Sanctuary Caravan." www.sanctuarycaravan.org/ (accessed November 7, 2018).

Ngai, Mae. *Impossible Subjects: Illegal Aliens and the Making of Modern America*. Princeton, NJ: Princeton University Press, 2004.

Paik, Naomi. "Abolitionist Futures and the New Sanctuary Movement." *Race and Class* 54, no. 2 (2017): 3–25.

Paik, Naomi. *Rightlessness: Testimony and Redress in U.S. Prison Camps since World War II*. Chapel Hill: University of North Carolina Press, 2016.

Palestinian Stop the Wall Campaign. "Letter to the Via Crucis March of Migrants," April 2018. www.pueblosinfronteras.org/members.html (accessed May 14, 2018).

"Passing the Word: Our Alien Seamen." *The Pilot*, newspaper of the National Maritime Union, in NMU Reference File of the Sailors International Union, Record Group 267, Box 1, File 1, Robert F. Wagner Labor Archives, Tamiment Library, New York University.

Pianko, Noam. *Zionism and the Roads Not Taken: Rawidowicz, Kaplan, Kohn*. Bloomington: University of Indiana Press, 2010.

Plitman, Jacob. "On an Emerging Diasporism." *Jewish Currents*, Spring 2018. jewishcurrents.org/essay/on-an-emerging-diasporism.

Public Law 92-212, March 17, 1980, www.gpo.gov/fdsys/pkg/STATUTE-94/pdf/STATUTE-94-Pg102.pdf.

Pueblo Sin Fronteras. "Refugee Caravan 2018." www.pueblosinfronteras.org/index.html (accessed November 6, 2018).

Robles, Frances. "Marielitos Face Long Delayed Reckoning: Expulsion to Cuba." *New York Times*, January 14, 2017. www.nytimes.com/2017/01/14/us/cuba-us-migrants.html.

Romero, Dennis. "Migrants Met with Fear, Disdain, in Tijuana, Mexico." NBC News, November 18, 2018. www.nbcnews.com/news/world/migrants-met-fear-disdain-tijuana-mexico-n937506.

Romero, Oscar. "On Accompaniment." *Kalfou* 3, no. 2 (Fall 2016): 253.

Rubenberg, Cheryl. "Israel and Guatemala: Arms, Advise and Counterinsurgency." *Middle East Report* (May–June 1986).

Said, Edward. *The Question of Palestine*. New York: Vintage Books, 1992.

Schreiber, Rebecca M. *The Undocumented Everyday: Migrant Lives and the Politics of Visibility*. Minneapolis: University of Minnesota Press, 2018.

Schwartz, Daniel. "Searching for a New Sanctuary Movement." *Dissent*, June 25, 2010, www.dissentmagazine.org/online_articles/searching-for-a-new-sanctuary-movement.

Semple, Kirk, and Miriam Jordan. "Migrant Caravan of Asylum Seekers Reaches U.S. Border." *New York Times*, April 29, 2018.

Smith, M. L. R., and Sophie Roberts, "War in the Gray: Exploring the Concept of Dirty War." *Studies in Conflict and Terrorism* 31, no. 5 (May 2008): 377–98.

"Social Work in the Sanctuary Movement for Central American Refugees." *Social Work*, January 1, 1985.

"States Parties to the 1951 Convention on the Status of Refugees and the 1967 Protocol." www.unhcr.org/afr/3b73b0d63.pdf (accessed June 3, 2018).

Stein, Jason, and Patrick Marley. "State Senate Unlikely to Take Up Sanctuary Cities Bill." *Milwaukee Journal Sentinel*, February 19, 2016. archive.jsonline.com/news/statepolitics/state-senate-unlike-to-take-up-sanctuary-cities-bill-b99673340z1-369431031.html/.

Stop the Wall. "Call for Global Day of Action." November 8, 2018. www.stopthewall.org/call-global-day-interaction-worldwithoutwalls-november-9-2018.

Tomlinson, Barbara, and George Lipsitz. "American Studies as Accompaniment." *American Quarterly* 65, no. 1 (2013): 1–30.

United Nations High Commissioner for Refugees. *Convention and Protocol Relating to the Status of* Refugees. Geneva: UNHCR, 2010. www.unhcr.org/en-us/3b66c2aa10.

United Nations Relief and Works Agency for Palestine. "Who We Are." www.unrwa.org/who-we-are (accessed May 30, 2018).

"The UN Resolution on Zionism." *Journal of Palestine Studies* 5, no. 1/2 (1975): 252–54.

U.S. Citizenship and Immigration Services. "Obtaining Asylum." www.uscis.gov/humanitarian/refugees-asylum/asylum/obtaining-asylum-united-states (accessed November 7, 2018).

Valverde, Miriam. "What You Need to Know about the Trump Administration's Zero Tolerance Policy." Politifact, June 6, 2018. www.politifact.com/truth-o-meter/article/2018/jun/06/what-you-need-know-about-trump-administrations-zer/.

Whitfield, Joshua J. "The Immigration Caravan Lays Bare the Conflict between Jesus and Power." *Dallas News*, May 12, 2018. www.dallasnews.com/opinion/commentary/2018/05/12/immigration-caravan-lays-bare-conflict-jesus-power.

Sanctuaryscapes in the North American Southwest

Aimee Villarreal

The old San Gerónimo Mission at Taos Pueblo, located seventy miles north of Santa Fe, New Mexico, is material evidence of a violent end. There are no public memorials that recall the massacre at Taos Pueblo, but the community remembers. The charred, crumbling adobe remains of the mission, the crosses that crowd the graveyard and wander out into the llano, the disfigured santos tossed from the flames. These materialities live on to remind us. On January 18, 1847, two thousand Mexican and Pueblo Indian dissidents joined Mexican nationalists Pablo Montoya and Manuel Cortés and Tiwa leader Tomás Romero in rebellion against the US occupation of New Mexico. They assassinated the territorial governor, Charles Bent, and brutalized anyone deemed a traitor to Mexico.[1] US troops were deployed from Santa Fe to Taos to put down the rebellion, which had quickly spread to the neighboring villages of Mora, La Cañada, and Arroyo Hondo.

Outnumbered and out of ammunition, a large faction of the Mora insurgents took refuge in the mountains among the Jicarilla Apache, where they continued to resist the US occupation until the signing of the Treaty of Guadalupe Hidalgo in February 1848.[2] The Jicarilla Apache, however, refused to submit. Meanwhile, US forces brought down a campaign of fire and blood upon the people of Taos Pueblo. Those who could not escape to Apache-controlled regions of refuge, as the Mora rebels had done, turned to another custom in times of crisis. They took sanctuary within San Gerónimo Mission.[3] But the invaders did not recognize the privilege of

Radical History Review
Issue 135 (October 2019) DOI 10.1215/01636545-7607821
© 2019 by MARHO: The Radical Historians' Organization, Inc.

ecclesiastic immunity or the sanctity of church asylum, which remained inscribed in Mexican law until 1860.[4] The soldiers fired relentlessly on the mission and set the roof on fire.[5] Billows of black smoke choked down screams of unimaginable pain and terror as the 150 men, women, and children trapped inside its earthen walls were reduced to ashes.

The imprints of lives lost and stories untold smudge contemporary sanctuary practices and movements in the North American Southwest and haunt the religious narratives that frame them. Sanctuary is fundamentally about the search for home and the remaking of homelands through space-making projects that mobilize individual and collective acts of spiritual and material regeneration. It involves productions of place and space—the differentiation of space and the spatialization of difference—and draws upon culturally defined notions of solidarity, mutuality, and exchange. Further, spaces of protection are configured in relation to external conditions of violence that force people to flee from their homes and to depend on the generosity of strangers for survival. Sanctuary, in concept and practice, is inherently contradictory and contingent. It depends on multiple kinds of negotiations (moral, spiritual, political, economic) about who belongs within the circle of community and who is worthy of protection and care.

Sanctuary is said to have ancient roots and universal dimensions but also particular historical and cultural expressions.[6] However, it is often assumed that the origins of sanctuary, or more specifically, the practice of creating safe spaces for the persecuted or accused and offering hospitality to people in need of protection, derives its sacred character and institutional authority from Christian providence and its corresponding medieval European legal codes and theologies.[7] This article challenges these conventional perspectives and calls for a situated historiography of sanctuary in the Americas, one that acknowledges its coloniality as an instrument of pastoral power and centers Indigenous regions of refuge and negotiations with settler colonialism.

Opening this dialogue requires a radical reorientation of sanctuary's given terms and historical trajectories. I begin by redefining sanctuary as a dynamic autochthonous tradition and Indigenous survival strategy cultivated (and continuously remade) in regions of refuge and rebellion.[8] As Indigenous people were displaced from their homelands or forced to congregate in missionary compounds they became refugees in their own homelands. They capitalized on their intertribal relations and knowledge of the landscape and sometimes banded together with other persecuted or displaced groups to create new multiethnic communities. Indigenous "sanctuaryscapes" can be understood as "transformative space-making projects" that allowed Indigenous peoples and knowledges to survive colonialism and continue into the present.[9] Sanctuaryscapes were mobile, collective, and often precarious but they were also spiritually grounded and politically strategic. Restoring Indigenous and African sanctuaryscapes to the origin stories of sanctuary movements in the Americas revitalizes and also complicates contemporary imaginings of sanctuary's potential as a radical or transformative practice.[10]

The most common understanding of sanctuary is rooted in Christian notions of sacred space as set apart from the mundane world. The inner sanctum of the church is where the altar and the tabernacle reside. In contrast to the mobility and diversity of sanctuaryscapes, church asylum is confined to consecrated grounds—the mission, *convento*, or church and their environs including courtyards and cemeteries. Church asylum is a specific practice of sanctuary that evolved in tandem with Christendom and Western European legal systems. The notion that fugitives who fled to churches received impunity (at least temporarily) occupied a central place in medieval legal traditions and debates.[11] The laws and rationales that governed the right of asylum had both secular and spiritual provenance and balanced powers between church and state.[12]

The privilege of church asylum was exclusive to Christians and conferred to individuals.[13] Ecclesiastical judges, in negotiation with civil authorities, adjudicated cases in consideration of the circumstance and the gravity of the crime committed with reference to both civil law and theological sources. Spanish legal and theological treatises, which extended to Spain's American colonies, regulated church asylum and clearly outlined the rules regarding the treatment of the accused, but distance from the metropole and the specificity of local conditions allowed for a wide array of interpretations. Sanctuary and clemency were inscribed in law and subject to intense juridical debate, but they were also embedded in religious vocation or the clergy's obligation to care for the material and spiritual well-being of the flock.[14] The institution of ecclesiastic immunity, which gave the clergy jurisdiction over church asylum, was rooted in Christian notions of sin and redemption and matters of divine authority, but it was also premised upon pastoral power—the clergy's special charge to procure converts, hear confessions, bestow sacraments, and ultimately to manage the social, spiritual, and moral life of the community.

Situated within the matrix of colonial governmentality, sanctuary was integrated in the techniques and ideologies of imposing rule over Indigenous populations, including forced congregation in missions and settlements. As an instrument of colonial governance, sanctuary was embedded in the logics and infrastructures of colonization and Christian conversion, which defined Indigenous sovereignties, spiritualities, and ways of knowing and relating to the land as aberrant and in need of reform or eradication. I argue that church asylum, which was the primary way that sanctuary was practiced in Spanish America, was another enclosure within an already colonized space and therefore, implicated if not fully entrenched in the very forms of violence and domination that made Indigenous people refugees in their own homeland. At the same time, Indigenous people maintained their own spatial autonomies inside and outside colonized spaces.

Mission compounds were inside Indigenous territories and became embedded within them over time because they were places where goods were produced and traded. Pueblo people who lived within or adjacent to missions and colonial settlements made astute use of pastoral care as Christian converts and in some cases took sanctuary in churches to evade punishment by secular authorities. Spanish missions were not isolated colonial outposts. They were economic and spiritual centers positioned within preexisting Puebloan ceremonial geographies that nested the village within concentric sources of power such as sacred mountains, reservoirs, cultivation grounds, shrines, and other features of the landscape.[15] The mission enterprise also extended beyond its physical boundaries as priests traveled between settlements or ventured out to seek potential converts and track down apostates who had fled to Indigenous sanctuaryscapes.[16]

Therefore, it is necessary to locate sanctuary practices more broadly within the racial geographies and rationalities of colonial rule that differentiated Indigenous from European humanity and ways of life while also compelling them together and drawing them violently apart. The Indian that filled the landscape and so occupied and preoccupied the Spanish imagination was docile and hospitable or barbarous and hostile, ripe for conversion or violently recalcitrant.[17] Following Saldaña-Portillo's observation that the drive to know, reform, and, ultimately, control Indian souls and sovereignties was the precondition of Spanish colonialism and in turn, for the production of "settled" and secure spaces, sanctuary was part of the terrain of possibilities that shaped and also constrained Indigenous agencies and struggles for autonomy. Therefore, Indigenous regions of refuge and colonial sanctuary can be understood as adversarial but also co-constituted spatial practices.

I bring an eclectic collection of sources and a time-traveling methodology to this investigation of sanctuary practices and relations in the North American Southwest, which is understood today as a politically bifurcated yet restless cultural and geographic space whose unevenly integrated transborder region encompasses northern Mexico and the southwestern United States.[18] My analysis juxtaposes fragmented church asylum cases that date from the seventeenth and eighteenth centuries in New Mexico and El Paso de Norte (1681–1796)[19] with historical and archeological studies of Pueblo cities of refuge and Apache defensive enclaves from the same period. Through the methodology of juxtaposition, Indigenous regions of refuge are placed alongside church asylum to reveal the generative diversity of sanctuary relations and practices that emerged during the colonial period in unsettled regions of the Spanish Empire.

Drawing on Anthony Tyeeme Clark and Malea Powell's concept of Indigenous groundwork and "homescapes,"[20] which advance a Native American politics of place and space "at the intersection of colonizing ideologies and Native epistemologies,"[21] I introduce "sanctuaryscapes" as a framework for understanding the mobile, diverse, and generative regions of refuge that Pueblo and Athapaskan peoples forged to confront colonialism. These networks, escape routes, and defensive enclaves were often unstable and temporary, but they allowed Indigenous people to selectively accommodate to Spanish/Mexican rule and evade the coercive protection and care of the mission. Sanctuaryscapes could be defined as "radically conservative" in that traditional ways of gaining status and creating alliances through trade and raiding, kinship relations, and exchange of captives (women and children) were creatively adapted to fit new circumstances and accommodate diverse tribal practices.[22] These altered relations were solidified and sanctified through origin myths, marriages, and markings on the landscape.[23] Therefore, Indigenous practices of hospitality and mutuality were not merely improvised but part of a broader moral and spiritual economy comprised of material and symbolic forms of solidarity that mobilized sanctuaryscapes and held them together.

According to historian Juliana Barr, areas that the Spanish considered barbarous or unpacified were identified as the Indigenous nation's borders and marked the limits of the Spanish Empire.[24] Barr notes that when Spanish maps identified Indigenous territories their borders were amorphous, disorderly, and unknown, whereas the boundaries of Spanish towns were clearly defined. Euro-American mappings intentionally erased or obscured Indigenous territories. The Comanches and other seminomadic tribes controlled vast territories of northern New Spain, a region the Spanish entered with great trepidation and disparaged as La Gran Chichimeca. Despite their physical presence and continual occupation of the landscape, Indigenous peoples were considered landless and itinerant from the Euro-American perspective. When we ignore Indigenous homelands and relationships to the land in our renderings of national borders and territories, we reproduce the colonial logic that holds this racial geography in place—an inert landscape emptied of its Native inhabitants and ripe for the taking.[25] With regard to the historiography of sanctuary as a mode of representation, we participate in a similar process of erasure when we ignore how colonialism and slavery disrupted Indigenous societies and reconfigured territories, economies, land-based spiritualities, and intertribal relations. These social and political upheavals and displacements gave rise to sanctuaryscapes.

Therefore, "sanctuaryscape" acknowledges how geopolitical and cultural borders were shaped by colonialism and also how sanctuary was and continues to be a form of containment or enclave in which internal spaces of protection are configured by external spaces of violence. While the Spanish may have imagined territories controlled by barbarous Indians as the space of violence that required taming, and Spanish towns as "green zones" with military installations and armies to protect their integrity and resources from dangerous and hostile outsiders, Indigenous peoples viewed space and place differently. The territories that they controlled were bulwarks against colonial rule, and peaceable spaces where Indigenous life could flourish independently. "Sanctuaryscape" recognizes the spatial dimensions of

Indigenous assertions of power. As Barr asserts, "Indians knew the regions within which they were safe or vulnerable. Far more than that, confederacies, chiefdoms, and nomadic hunter-gatherers circumscribed the geographic areas within which they asserted control over resources, people, relationships, culture, ritual, and historical memory."[26]

The Revivals of Sanctuary

The ancient roots of Western European asylum practices within the Christian sanctuary tradition have served as a source of inspiration and legitimacy for contemporary sanctuary movements. Scholars who have written about the revival of sanctuary in relation to the Central American refugee crisis during the eighties have done considerable work documenting ancient sanctuary practices and offer a compelling historical context for these faith-based movements.[27]

The majority of these case studies acknowledge sanctuary's Christian origins in references to cities of refuge in the Old Testament or the ethic of offering hospitality to the stranger. Movement participants clung to biblical sources of justification for enacting sanctuary against the law, which motivated scholars to recover the ancient roots of the concept. The focus of these studies is contemporary sanctuary movements and politics in the United States, Canada, and Europe. However, few provide detailed or comprehensive cross-cultural or transhistorical analysis of sanctuary traditions. To clarify this point, while scholarship on the sanctuary movements of the 1980s illuminates how white, middle-class Christians and Jews formed durable transnational alliances and authentic cross-cultural connections with Central American refugees,[28] the literature on sanctuary and asylum in non-Christian and non-Western societies is rather thin. Further, there is a wide scholarly gap on Native American, Polynesian, Aboriginal Australian, and African sanctuary and asylum practices especially in relation to colonialism.[29]

From an anthropological perspective, sanctuary is built into the fabric of human evolution and the development of sociality and mutuality. Linda Rabben explains that "giving asylum or sanctuary may be seen as one of the basic manifestations of altruistic behavior and human morality."[30] "Survival of our species," she posits, "depended on extending bonds beyond immediate kin by making alliances through marriage partners or other kinds of reciprocity."[31] Rabben shores up sanctuary's universality with a robust assortment of cross-cultural comparisons, but the bulk of her historical research is on Christian and Western European practices. This bias is partly the result of the content of the archive and the availability of sources, yet as Anna Tsing contends, "universalisms are not politically neutral."[32] Universal reasoning is part of the coloniality of power in which European knowledge is viewed as representative of all of humanity whereas the cultures and knowledges of the colonized are considered particular and therefore trivial.[33]

Ignatius Bau traces the ancient origins of sanctuary from Greek and Roman temple asylum to Old Testament cities of refuge, and to medieval privilege of church asylum in England, which he notes became riddled with corruption and eventually outlawed by Parliament in 1624. His chapter on sanctuary in US history begins with the familiar story of Puritan and Pilgrim exiles in a promised land emptied of Indigenous inhabitants. Church asylum disappears in colonial America but reemerges in the text as radical hospitality in opposition to unjust laws, specifically the Fugitive Slave Act of 1850, which mobilized the Underground Railroad to help African Americans escape to free states in the north. Sanctuary activism makes a brief appearance in the United States and Europe during World War II in response to the Holocaust,[34] but Bau and others pin the revival of contemporary sanctuary movements to the Vietnam War era when conscientious objectors began taking refuge in churches and universities.[35] Admittedly, the origin story that he narrates and others recite maps onto sanctuary activists' own spiritual and cultural justifications for harboring or assisting refugees and participating in the movement to end US military intervention in Central America. However, this origin story, which has become essentialized within sanctuary movements and scholarship about them, has a notable Protestant overtone that curiously overlooks Native American practices of hospitality as well as the robust Catholic tradition of church asylum that flourished in Spanish colonial America.

Native American and other non-Western traditions of sanctuary and hospitality are not well documented, but they must also have ancient roots. Political exchanges and alliances beyond immediate kin were essential to the survival of tribal groups. These alliances and relations were radically transformed with the advent of European colonialism (and the imposition of Christianity and the slave economy) producing mass displacements of people, tensions between former allies and trading partners, and causing widespread social and political unrest. Indigenous sanctuaryscapes existed long before the arrival of Europeans, but these practices of protection and hospitality became more pronounced and essential to survival in response to colonialization.

Another area of great scholarly interest is the relationship between secular and religious authority in movements that mobilized Christian notions of hospitality and sanctuary to contest what activists saw as unjust immigration laws.[36] Foucault's theories of governmentality and pastoral power and Agamben's notion of the exception have been useful for positioning sanctuary squarely within modern forms of domination and the rule of law.[37] Pastoral power is of particular interest because, as Randy Lippert suggests, it "entails certain spatial imagining" that allows for the protection and care of migrants but also the constant monitoring, counseling, and surveillance of them as pastoral objects entrapped within sanctuary's enclosures.[38] Put another way, pastoral care involves total knowledge of the other, which has a panoptic effect of creating individuals who are willing to make themselves docile and controllable. The politics of discernment—the power to decide who is deserving of or eligible for protection and care—is of particular value for understanding how seemingly benevolent actions can also involve coercion, confinement, and other forms of discipline.

The contradictions of pastoral power and care underlie the secular and sacred tensions at the heart of sanctuary. Spanish colonial documents and Native oral histories tell of Catholic missionaries loving their neophytes to death through infrastructures of congregation that dispersed and contained Indigenous people within colonized spaces.[39] Congregation was an infrastructure of racial differentiation that traversed public and private domains. Historian Daniel Nemser's research on early colonial Mexico illuminates how architecture and spatialization of difference configured secular and religious notions of Indian humanity as aberrant yet potentially redeemable. The connections he makes between colonial logic and actual structures—roads, plazas, missionary compounds, military installations, and houses—furthers my argument that sanctuary's enclosures tightened the coercive embrace of pastoral care while simultaneously creating secular notions of protection that demarcated European spaces, bodies, and ways of living from Indigenous ones.

Recent studies of sanctuary cities tend to brush over historical accounts of sanctuary. They are secular in orientation and bypass the religious side of the concept altogether. Instead, these studies investigate forms of governance such as local immigration politics and policymaking, citizenship and immigrant rights, and the relationship between municipal governments and policing.[40] The relations of power that organize sanctuary's conditions of possibility are unmoored from religion as it enters policy worlds. Some scholars argue that churches and states, refugees and advocates, are systematically entangled in a secular politics of discernment that sorts criminal from law-abiding immigrants and deepens law enforcement and municipal governments' participation in securing the sanctuary city.[41] Nevertheless, immigrant rights advocates use public safety arguments strategically to get sanctuary city resolutions passed. Reforming policing practices can reduce racial profiling and in turn protect immigrants from being targeted by police and then questioned about their citizenship status. Sanctuary cities aim to protect all residents by decreasing deportations and promoting an ethic of inclusion.[42]

Modern international asylum laws are tied to nation-states and their particular political interests, but sanctuary has operated inside and outside the rule of law, tradition, or custom.[43] Today, as in the past, sanctuary is subject to defilement and moral corruption as witnessed with the rise in conservative backlash against sanctuary cities and the 2017 immigration roundups branded "Operation Safe City," which targeted them. Securing a place to belong and build a livable life is fundamental to human survival. Deciding who is eligible for protection with regard to the politics of care belies the secular and religious tensions at the heart of sanctuary. The search for belonging and safety impresses upon sanctuary in a variety of ways.

In sum, sanctuary carries diverse forms of power that flow between church and state, public and private spaces, the temporal and the eternal. Sanctuary is a political act hedged with restrictions, ideological conflicts, and power struggles. Municipal policies also promise protection and care to undocumented residents. Echoing the contractions of pastoral care discussed earlier, providing limited protections and services to these vulnerable denizens can also, as Jennifer Bagelman contends, create "docile subjects who are willing to defer the rights of citizenship" and wait indefinitely in legal limbo without permanent status.[44] As sanctuary has entered the secular arenas of law and policy, it has become part of the machinery of governance and bureaucratic systems. However, sanctuary is also a grassroots movement—a stand against injustice that empowers local communities to work together to create spaces of protection and belonging and in solidarity with the marginalized, the undocumented, the refugee.

Regions of Refuge and Rebellion

The concept of *regiones de refugio* (regions of refuge) derives from anthropological studies in the 1970s of Indigenous communities in Mexico that had long been neglected by the state and lived under conditions of extreme poverty.[45] It was used to describe the subsistence strategies and selective processes of acculturation that Indigenous peoples adopted to survive colonialism. Fleeing to inhospitable regions of refuge relatively isolated from urban settlements was a forced choice. These defensive spaces provided Indigenous people a measure of autonomy that allowed them to maintain their customs and lifeways while bearing the brunt of failed economic policies and land reforms that further impeded their development and sustainability. This strategy of resiliency to colonial oppression (past and present) and racialized subordination in regions of refuge was described as a process of ethnic enclavement, a concept that gained considerable traction in anthropological studies of urban immigrant communities in the United States.

Sanctuary practices in the Americas cannot be fully appreciated without attention to coloniality. Regions of refuge emerged within the context of colonial violence, the genocide and forced removal of Indigenous peoples, the transatlantic slave trade, and other forms of persecution and unfreedom that marginalized groups suffered under European colonialism. During the Spanish colonial period and up until the nineteenth century, Indigenous people, mestizos and African runaways (*cimarrones* or maroons) intermarried and frequently rebelled against colonial rule, escaping to regions of refuge high in the mountains or deep into forestlands or swamps where they created sanctuaryscapes for themselves.[46]

While life in regions of refuge was (and continues to be) precarious, these defensive spaces were also sites of resistance where Indigenous peoples and escaped

African slaves gathered their resources, planned rebellions, and established communities that withstood settler colonialism for generations. African sanctuaryscapes are also part of this story. In Spanish Florida, African slaves routinely fled from British plantations to missions where they were given sanctuary, converted to Catholicism, and granted land to establish a free black town, Gracia Real De Santa Teresa de Mose, near St. Augustin (1738–63).[47] Slave revolts involving Indians, Africans, and mixed-raced people erupted throughout Mexico, Latin America, and the Caribbean throughout the colonial period. Runaways known as *cimarrones* in Mexico rebelled against Spanish rule in 1607 in the Port of Veracruz, under the leadership of an African man called Yanga. His band of insurgents was so tenacious that the Spanish granted them a settlement.[48]

During the Spanish colonial period and through the nineteenth century, Mexico's northern hinterlands were considered hostile and dangerous. Nevertheless, Spanish/Mexican elites believed that the unruly northern territories held strategic and economic promise with mineral wealth and a new harvest of souls for the expansion of Christendom and the Spanish Empire. The arid and mountainous terrain, which includes the Mexican states of Chihuahua, Coahuila, Sonora, and parts of what is now New Mexico, Texas, and Arizona, acquired the moniker La Gran Chichimeca.[49] The Spanish defined the region as savage and inhospitable, populated with cruel and murderous bands of nomads or *indos bárbaros* who refused to become civilized. The imaginary of La Gran Chichimeca was created in opposition to the pacified and cultured agriculturalists of the south. This cultural and regional divide persisted well into the nineteenth century and has continued to shape national histories and research agendas.[50]

Endemic warfare between colonists and Indigenous peoples defined the Chihuahuan frontier. A culture of perpetual warfare, retribution, and violence came to define *norteño* society.[51] The constant state of rebellion to the forms of subjugation that the colonists, the church, and the colonial state imposed on Indigenous populations ensured that their transformation into docile colonial subjects was never fully realized. Historian Ana Maria Alonso observes that "throughout the seventeenth century indigenous peoples of Chihuahua, such as the Toboso, the Manso, the Conchos, and the Tarahumara, were in a nearly continuous state of 'rebellion' engendered by the advance of the colonial frontier and by the processes of subjection that the colonists, the church, and the state tried to impose on them."[52] While some of these groups were exterminated or deported, the Tarahumara fled to the most inaccessible regions of the Sierra Madre Occidental, where they continue to live today.[53]

In other cases, Indians and lower-class mestizos were given incentives and land grants to establish free colonies in exchange for their military service to Spain and later, the Mexican state, in wars against the Apache and other rebellious tribes that raided and ravished colonial settlements and rural towns. Service in Indian auxiliaries was a way to show personal valor, gain prestige, and move up the social ladder, or to essentially "whiten" as citizens of frontier society. Alonso argues that the frontier was a zone of "intercultural exchange and transformation" where the boundaries of race and ethnicity, civilization and barbarism, were fluid and unstable.[54]

While a full analysis of the social, political, and cultural complexities of the Spanish borderlands is beyond the scope of this study, Indigenous people, mestizos, African slaves, and plebeian fugitives from colonial society sometimes banded together and rebelled against Spanish colonial rule. In other instances, they became further integrated into the colonial state as guides and scouts, military auxiliaries, and settlers in their own right. Indigenous and mixed-raced people also escaped from missions or avoided them by fleeing to regions of refuge high in the mountains or deep in forestlands and swamps, where they created sanctuaryscapes. They also took refuge with allied tribes across medicine lines (Native American territorial boundaries), capitalized on European territorial disputes, and built new communities where new alliances, intercultural subjectivities, and blended spiritual and material cultures emerged. In this context, sanctuary emerges as a site of collective action, transculturation, and social transformation.

In light of this evidence, our definition of sanctuary can be expanded to include regions of refuge. Indigenous sanctuaryscapes facilitated large and small resistance movements whose goals were political and decolonial. While the outcomes of these movements were diverse, they were not simple cultural revitalization movements that demanded a return to an Indigenous past that was no longer viable. They were future-oriented, not necessarily directed at eradicating all vestiges of European culture (although this may have served as a call to unity) or dismantling colonial society and establishing control over its resources but at finding a safe place to call home. In the next section, I will discuss two different but interconnected examples of sanctuaryscapes that emerged in the North American Southwest, Pueblo cities of refuge and Apache autonomous enclaves. I have chosen to concentrate on these specific cases because they exemplify intertribal relations, practices of hospitality, and cultural creativity in the making of sanctuaryscapes.

Pueblo Cities of Refuge

On August 10, 1680, the Pueblos of New Mexico and their mestizo allies rose up against the Spanish Empire. The rebellion had many causes—religious oppression, labor coercion, sexual abuse, conflicts between soldiers and priests, drought, disease, and famine—all of which came to a head in the mid-1600s. Jemez Pueblo scholar Joe Sando called the Pueblo Revolt "the First American Revolution."[55] Today, many Pueblo communities continue to commemorate the revolt as an important declaration of their sovereignty that inaugurated the modern era. It is said that the revolt had to happen in order to restore balance to the Pueblo world and to ensure the continuance of the people.[56] Scholars who have evaluated the fragmented historical and archaeological evidence suggest that the primary reason for the uprising was slavery and the cultural breakdown that resulted as social systems, economies, households, and tribal relations were disrupted with the arrival of the Spanish and their Native allies.[57]

The Pueblo Revolt has been termed the "Pueblo-Athapaskan Revolt" because of the participation of Apache and Navajo allies and other non-Pueblo tribes.[58] The uprising was preceded by numerous premeditated rebellions that began near the silver mines of Parral, Chihuahua, where Indigenous people captured from as far away as the Dakotas had been enslaved to work in the mines. One of the most significant of these rebellions was the Tepehuan Revolt of 1616, which embroiled Durango in warfare for over two years, and the Tarahumara rebellions in Chihuahua that erupted in the mid and late seventeenth century. In both cases, the survivors fled to the sierras, where they regrouped in multicultural sanctuaryscapes that sustained numerous households, and subsisted on a combination of agriculture and resources acquired from raiding Spanish settlements.[59] These autonomous communities remained hostile to the Jesuit and Franciscan missionaries, and constant raiding drained military resources and slowed economic development throughout Nueva Vizcaya.[60]

The Pueblos likely knew about these rebellions and the deleterious impact they had on Spanish colonial rule in the south. They also learned from them. Pueblo and Athapaskan people had resisted Spanish colonization since the arrival of the outsiders, but the 1680 revolt was stunning. Po'pay, a spiritual leader from Ohkay Owingeh Pueblo strived for a spiritual return to Native ways and set out to realize his vision. Po'pay and his war captains (some of whom were mestizos and mulatos) from various mission communities planned the rebellion in secret over a ten-year period and formed an unprecedented pan-Indigenous alliance in the process. It is important to note that not all of the Pueblos were unified in this cause and not all of them respected Po'pay's messianic vision or his leadership; nevertheless, his envoys were able to galvanize a powerful anticolonial coalition. Because of its efficacy in banishing the Spanish from New Mexico and the ripple effect it had on settlements in Nueva Vizcaya, it was also a Great Northern Rebellion.

The complete eradication of symbols of Spanish culture and Catholicism may have been Po'pay's imperative, but not all Pueblo communities joined in the rebellion, killed their priests, or destroyed sacred icons. In the twelve years between the uprising and the return of Spanish authority in 1692, along with a motley group of settlers and soldiers recruited from Chihuahua and Zacatecas, the Pueblo people, reorganized as the pan-Pueblo alliance, began to fracture, and conflicts ensued.[61] The Keres of Zia and Santa Ana Pueblos, whose participation in the revolt had been tenuous, consolidated at Cerro Colorado and broke ties with the northern Tewa. This rift strengthened revolutionary solidarity between the Tewa, the Jemez, and the Keres of Kotyiti.

The postrevolt landscape was flooded with migrants and refugees. Some remained in mission villages founded before the uprising, while others occupied Spanish colonial settlements such as the Governor's Palace in Santa Fe. Pueblos from diverse tribes abandoned their mission villages and, following the sacred migration stories passed down to them from their ancestors, they built new communities atop high mesas empowered with Pueblo cosmovision (stories, sacred places and directions, celestial coordinates, and other significant markers).[62] However, many Tiwa and some Tewa families took refuge with their Apache and Navajo allies and kin.

Archeologists have identified six Pueblo cities of refuge: Dowa Yalanne (Corn Mountain) near Zuni; Tunyo (Black Mesa) at San Ildefonso; Kotyiti, southwest of Cochiti; and three villages in the vicinity of Jemez: Astialakwa, Potokwa, and Bolestsakwa.[63] These urban sanctuaryscapes displayed social experimentation and innovations in art and architecture. The entire Zuni population, which was previously settled in seven different villages, consolidated at Dowa Yalanne. Different kinds of social units were formed with the unification of households, clans, kiva groups, medicine societies, and priesthoods.[64] Corn Mountain was inhabited various times after the Pueblo independence period and continues to be a sacred place where ceremonies are performed at certain times of the year. According to Pueblo archeologist Joseph Aguilar, who is currently surveying Tunyo (the site of the final battle of the reconquest in 1692), this mesa-top city functioned as a garrison where men of the warrior classes resided. Their families remained camped in the river valley below the mesa. He also confirms that Tunyo features prominently in the migration stories of the Tewa people and is considered a sacred place.[65]

Another unique feature of Pueblo cities of refuge is that they incorporated diverse Puebloan refugees who spoke different languages, and welcomed some Nadé (Apache) and Diné (Navajo) allies. For instance, at Potokwa, Towa-speaking people from the Jemez area lived together with Keres speakers from farther south and a few Diné. It was also well fortified with all of the rooms facing inward, encircling the central plaza. Houses could only be entered from rooftop openings using ladders that could be removed if the village came under attack. They created a dual-moiety social organization with twin kivas and plazas, which symbolized duality and solidified seasonal rotation of leadership to unite previously segmented groups.[66]

Women were also active agents in reorganizing households and reshaping social and political identities in the postrevolt period as cultural producers. At Kotyiti, pottery makers created ceramic designs that revitalized older styles. The reemergence of the double-headed key motif, which dates to the 1400s, provides a cogent example.[67] This style was not in circulation before the revolt but reemerged as a rebellious symbol during the revitalization period. Barbara J. Mills observes that Zuni potters stopped using Spanish-era glazeware and kachina imagery, opting instead for solid red and black paint on white slips with a matte finish and feather motifs.[68] These styles may have been more easily standardized across the different symbolic vocabularies and styles that were commonly used by culturally distinct Puebloan groups.

In light of the material evidence, Pueblo women and men created art forms that bridged cultural and linguistic differences through reinvention of older designs that moved across tribal communities. This strategy may have been used to achieve solidarity and project a revolutionary and pan-Indigenous identity among allied tribes.[69] Archeologists and historians of the postrevolt period interpret semiotic reinventions of tradition as nation-building projects that promoted a communitarian vision and Pan-Indigenous subjectivity for the first time in recorded history among Pueblos and their Athapaskan partners.[70] They also suggest that Po'pay and his war captains revalued and mobilized the social and cultural flattening that the Spanish had imposed to reduce tribal distinctiveness to one racialized designation—Pueblo—to create a form of solidarity.[71]

Another significant sanctuaryscape was El Cuartelejo, an Apache-controlled region located along the present-day Colorado and Kansas border, where at least five different bands resided. Pueblo people routinely escaped from Spanish missions and took refuge with their Plains allies. The existence of these autonomous regions was a constant threat to the clergy's reeducation project. Converts frequently fled to El Cuartelejo, becoming apostates and reverting to their old way of life. In fact, after the Pueblo Revolt, the Picuris survivors (including two war captains who had helped orchestrate the rebellion) took refuge at El Cuartelejo. Archaeologist Sunday Eiselt suggests that the communities most resistant to conversion and colonization were the frontier Pueblos, who had closer ties with Apache and Navajo bands. She explains that "the Apaches played a major role in the resulting conflicts by harboring Puebloan fugitives, assisting Puebloan rebels, and attacking the missionized Pueblos who were allied with the Spanish."[72]

Some Apache bands, the Jicarilla in particular, spent part of the winter near fortified Pueblo villages such as Taos and Picuris. The Pueblos provided their Plains trade partners and kin with hospitality in hard times. This kindness was returned when Tiwa allies sought refuge from Spanish domination. These relationships of reciprocity were also important in warfare. Eiselt also posits that sanctuaryscapes allowed Indigenous people to share and maintain cultural knowledge and interrupt Spanish attempts to assimilate or convert them.[73] On the other hand, the interior Tewa villages were more vulnerable to Spanish domination because they did not have a sanctuary relationship with Athapaskan groups. They were entrapped, to some extent, within their own fortified communities alongside missions and Spanish/Mexican villages. As Pueblo people become more integrated into colonial economies, contact between Tewas and Athapaskans, which had become increasingly conflictual, resulted in outbreaks of violence.

However, many of these partnerships of exchange and kinship broke down due to intensification of the slave trade, which, according to Eiselt, made "relations between Apaches and the lowland frontier Pueblos tenuous and unpredictable" in the late 1600s.[74] The same occurred in Towa communities in Jemez. Eiselt explains that following the rebellions of 1649 and 1653, the Jemez fled and took sanctuary with the Navajo, which gave rise to the Navajo Coyote Pass Clan, composed of Jemez women and their descendants.[75] Family ties tend to be durable, but hospitable relations and intermarriage between the Jemez and Navajo deteriorated as Pueblo and Athabaskan communities in the region became ensnared in the slave trade. As anguished Pueblo and Navajo families made separate deals with the Spanish for the return of their relatives, allies soon became enemies and former sanctuaryscapes turned inhospitable.

By 1693, when the Spanish returned to New Mexico, Jemez Pueblo was fighting with their former Navajo neighbors who had allied with Cochiti Pueblo against the Gila Apaches. A few years later in 1706, sixty-two men and women and seventeen children from Picuris who had taken refuge and, in the words of Spanish authorities, had been "living as apostates in the remote providence of Santo Domingo del Cuartelejo" were returned by military escort to the "holy custody of the village and mission of San Gerónimo de Taos."[76] According to Spanish testimonies, the Picuris had been held there as captives of the Apache and were more than happy to return to their homeland.[77] While it is possible that the Picuris had overstayed their welcome at El Cuartelejo or that the Apache had exchanged the refugees for Spanish provisions, based on their deep historical ties, it is unlikely that they were overjoyed to return to the mission. Shortly before their departure, Spanish authorities held a solemn ceremony declaring El Cuartelejo "pacified" and under the control of church and crown.[78]

In sum, the diverse sanctuaryscapes that Pueblo and Athapaskan peoples had forged before and after the revolt were important sites of transculturation. Because they depended on kinship ties and captive exchanges, women were important actors in maintaining peaceful relations and producing material and symbolic offerings of hospitality.[79] These dense relations were codified in myth, language, and religious practices, as well as a shared sense of identity, and for this reason, they remained steadfast for generations while thin alliances fractured under the pressures of colonialism.[80] Therefore, Indigenous sanctuaryscapes ebbed and flowed with some being more durable and dependable than others. The influence of Christianity was ever present. Many Indigenous people, Pueblos in particular, accepted elements of the faith, creating balance with their Native traditions. Additionally, the protection and provisions that Pueblos and Apaches were promised in missions, presidios, and on reservations known as "peace establishments" competed with sanctuaryscapes, which were difficult to sustain in a land embroiled in warfare.[81]

In the final section of this article, I focus on the Spanish institution of church asylum. Indigenous people and mestizos and mulatos created sanctuaryscapes, but they also took refuge in churches, missions, and *conventos*. But colonial authorities, both secular and religious, presided over church asylum. The privilege was only available to Christians or to those willing to submit to baptism, and was confined to sacred enclosures within colonized space. Submitting to baptism could be a strategic decision, but it came with consequences. Fleeing a mission was apostasy, a grave crime against God and the colonial state. The majority of New Mexican church asylum cases that I examined were originally compiled by Elizabeth Howard West in 1928.[82] The bulk of these cases derive from a period in which church asylum had come under intense scrutiny in both Spain and its American colonies in response to widespread abuses and protracted conflicts between church and state (1680–1796).

The right to ecclesiastical immunity formed the basis of sanctuary in Spain and in the Americas. The practice was codified in civil laws, religious canons, and municipal charters or *fueros*. The *Siete Partidas* (1251–65) was a robust book of legal codes based on Roman and canon law. The volumes outlined the jurisdictions between church and crown (and other civil matters), and the *Recopilación de Leyes de los Reinos de las Indias* were civil laws that set forth the legalities of sanctuary. In addition, theological manuals such as *Sumas de Teología Moral*, which set down guidelines for correct and incorrect behavior expected of all Christians, were equally important statutes that dictated the right to asylum and the treatment of the accused.[83] Individuals accused of crimes such as rape, forgery, desertion, and tax evasion were excluded from taking sanctuary in some cases, but debtors and people indicted of murder, assault, and other wrongdoing were not prohibited.[84] In Spain as in America, sanctuary was a privilege afforded exclusively to Christians. Jews, Muslims, and heathens were considered ineligible.[85]

There were special rules guiding the extradition of the accused. In order to extract a person from sanctuary, a special bond, or *caución juratoria*, had to be issued, which served as an oath that the accused would not be harmed once removed from refuge.[86] The bond had to be approved and signed by an ecclesiastical judge. The penalty for forcibly removing a person from sanctuary or for not following the proper procedure was excommunication. Sometimes disputes erupted between secular and ecclesiastical authorities involving sanctuary cases that became so intense and drawn out that priests exerted their wrath over entire communities, refusing to give mass, communion, or to perform sacraments until the conflict was resolved.[87] The clergy's pastoral power over the right of asylum balanced the authority to judge on matters both worldly and spiritual between religious and secular spheres. Ultimately, an individual's moral failings and crimes against the church or state incurred eternal and temporal consequences.

In Spanish America, church asylum was widespread and unregulated. It was almost entirely governed by local authorities and situations. As a colonial institution, church asylum figured into prolonged disputes between church and crown. Unlike other European countries that outlawed the once robust practice by the late 1700s, its relatively long duration in Spain and its colonies attests to the power of the Catholic Church in all aspects of life and the centrality of the church in deciding on the exception.[88] Criminal inclinations and actions were interpreted as moral failings, lack of faith, or even being under the influence of evil or demonic forces rather than as a social or psychological problem. Therefore, the church's authority to deliberate and adjudicate was considered righteous and extended well beyond the purview of faith.[89]

Church sanctuary was often misused and abused, and clergy often profited, as did people of all races and classes who took advantage of the system for their own benefit. As a result, sanctuary came under scrutiny in the 1700s in both Spain and the Americas. The Bourbon Reforms were particularly harsh on sanctuary. Many of the reforms of the period targeted ecclesiastic immunity to limit the role of the Catholic Church in matters related to criminal justice and clemency. The crown issued various royal *cédulas* focused on limiting the practice of church asylum and regulating procedures related to the treatment of prisoners and the accused. Interestingly, the majority of recorded New Mexico sanctuary cases that have survived date from this period of heightened surveillance and reform. Although the archive is fragmented, it seems significant that there was an uptick in recorded cases from this period of conflict and transition, which reflects a broader transatlantic cultural and political shift toward secularization.

Church Asylum in New Mexico, 1685–1796

The first recorded incident involving sanctuary in New Mexico occurred in 1663. Governor Diego de Peñalosa arrived in Santa Fe to replace Bernardo López Mendizábal, who had been charged by the Holy Office of the Inquisition as being a crypto-Jew and also for allowing the Pueblos to perform their traditional dances, which were believed to be diabolical. Mendizábal and his wife had been taken to Mexico City in chains to stand trial for religious crimes. Mendizábal died during his trial in prison. Peñalosa's transition to the governorship was rocky, to say the least. He found himself in the middle of warring factions of Franciscans and unfortunately seems to have sided with the weaker faction, which placed him in the line of fire.

Governor Peñalosa was indicted on a variety of grave offenses to church and crown from all sides. He was accused of committing adultery, having consorted with a concubine, Maria de Barrios, whom he had brought from Casas Grandes and who was living with him in the Governor's Palace. Peñalosa was also accused of illegally confiscating all of Mendizábal's property. But his most notorious crime, according to the witnesses who testified against Peñalosa, was removing Pedro Duran de Chávez from the sanctuary by force. Duran de Chávez had taken sanctuary at the convent of Santo Domingo after being accused of assault. The manner in which he escaped from bondage is quite dramatic. As the soldiers were taking him through Santo Domingo Pueblo on their way to Santa Fe, they stopped for a break. While the soldiers were occupied, the prisoner, who was bound, convinced an Indian to carry him into the convent. This situation was quite an embarrassment for the soldiers who were unable to secure the prisoner, and for Peñalosa, who saw the aiding and abetting of Duran de Chávez's escape as an affront to his authority. He decided to take matters into his own hands and take the prisoner out of sanctuary by force. Witnesses reported that the governor had not only removed Duran de Chávez from sanctuary without proper documentation or permission from an ecclesiastical judge, but he had done so on a Sunday after mass. For this incorrigible offense against the church, Peñalosa was excommunicated and sent back to Mexico City, where he languished in the "secret prisons" of the Holy Inquisition.[90] This case exemplifies the importance of the privilege of sanctuary not only in terms of the church's authority but also in terms of community relations. The average resident respected the right to asylum, and Peñalosa's disrespect of sanctuary was the last straw.

The majority of cases of documented church asylum in the archive occurred after the Pueblo Revolt of 1680 and involve individuals of all races and classes. However, the vast majority of asylees were men. There is one recorded case of a woman taking sanctuary in a church in Santa Fe, but she is only mentioned briefly in a case involving her sons, who had apparently, with the help of their mother, robbed a public warehouse.[91] However, there are many documented cases of women taking sanctuary in Mexico City and Guadalajara. Some of these women were notorious rebels, but the majority were of the mixed-race lower classes and living in precarious conditions. It is possible that they committed petty theft or even feigned being accused of a crime in order to be fed and given shelter temporarily while in sanctuary.[92]

Presumably cases of women taking sanctuary in the New Mexico are lost to history. But it is also possible that taking sanctuary in churches, missions, or convents alone with priests notorious for having concubines and sexually violating women was not seen as safe or proper. Maybe there was no sanctuary for women, especially those of Indian or mixed-racial heritage who were vulnerable within the domestic space and within colonial institutions that did not recognize them as persons with the same rights or social status as men. Exercising the right to asylum usually worked out well for members of the elite classes and for commoners who had much-needed skills such as carpentry, masonry, or ironworking. These individuals were usually released on bond and resumed their lives after paying fines, serving in the military, or doing public works. Pueblo converts, women, and mixed-race plebeians were not so fortunate.

Church asylum was also used to subvert authority. Juan Tafoya of Isleta Pueblo was an unruly mestizo and a thorn in the side of Governor Pañuela. In 1712, he was accused of sedition and stirring up rebellion among the Christian Indians. He evaded capture by going from "pueblo to pueblo taking refuge in their convents and tampering with the Indians causing inquietude and apostasy."[93] The governor issued a warrant for his arrest and summoned him to appear in Santa Fe for questioning. His failure to appear after being summoned three times was considered an act of rebellion against the empire. Pañuela declared Tafoya a traitor, authorized anyone who found him outside the sanctuary to execute him on sight, and warned that anyone found assisting him would be charged with sedition. The rebel and apostate Juan Tafoya apparently was never captured. He disappeared from the record, so his fate remains unknown.

This case exemplifies how sanctuary could be used to evade authorities and even to further rebellious acts against Spanish rule. One may wonder why clergy would condone these abuses or take a man accused of inciting rebellion among the Pueblo converts into sanctuary. Although it seems incongruous, as an institution that kept religion and politics in balance and in tension, the clergy's power to judge could supersede the content or magnitude of the crimes a person in sanctuary was accused of committing. However, because apostasy was a particular threat to the mission enterprise and the success of the colonial project more generally, this crime was treated with special pastoral care and vigilance. Apostasy was not only a crime against Spanish authority, it was a crime that placed one's eternal soul in jeopardy. Therefore, it is not that surprising that clergy were willing to accept Tafoya into sanctuary. Perhaps they saw it as an opportunity to counsel him and bring him back into the fold of the Christian faith. After all, he had voluntarily placed himself at their mercy by taking sanctuary in the church, and it was the priest's obligation to respond appropriately in accordance with his Christian vocation.

Spanish officials saw abuses of church asylum and Indigenous sanctuaryscapes as threats to the colonial state. In a case that occurred in 1757, two prisoners, Diego Antonio Marqués and Juan de Venavides, escaped from jail and took refuge in La Parroquia de Santa Fe. Guards were placed outside the church entrance to ensure the criminals did not escape. The *alcalde mayor* of Santa Fe, Francisco Guerrero, wrote a letter to the vicar and ecclesiastical judge, Don Santiago de Roibal. In his letter Guerrero expresses his concern that the men would flee and "become apostate, passing to the *rancherías* of infidel Indians of the barbarous nations who inhabit these environs."[94] Father Roibal was willing to comply with the alcalde's request, but the refugees had testified that they would only return to jail if they were promptly executed. Therefore, he was burdened with a moral dilemma. The vicar did not want to be complicit in the refugees' suicides, which weighed heavily on his conscience.[95] Suicide, in his view, was a greater crime against God and a more serious act of apostasy than escaping to the autonomous *rancherías*.

The clergy's investment in the institution of sanctuary as a matter of pastoral power and care was equally important (if not more important) as maintaining law and order. Furthermore, the Christian Pueblos, in this case, are represented as being vulnerable to disobedience and evil influences. This paternalistic perspective covers the reality that the Pueblos were never fully under the control of the padres or the alcaldes. There was always the looming potential of rebellion and apostasy even among the seemingly "docile" Pueblo converts. Just beyond the mission walls the province of "barbarous infidels" beckoned.

However, Pueblo converts also used church asylum strategically. In 1731, two Indians from Santa Clara Pueblo had a violent altercation, and one of the men involved was gravely injured. The survivor, Joseph Naranjo, took sanctuary in the mission at Santa Clara. The deputy alcalde attempted to interrogate Naranjo after taking the testimony of his dying victim. Naranjo responded, "Iglesia me llamo" (my name is church) to every question the inquisitor asked him. He even refused to give his name.[96] He continued to evade questioning for three days using the prescribed response, which indicates that Naranjo was confident that he would not be removed from the church if he refused to admit to any wrongdoing. After two months, the governor ordered both men to appear in Santa Fe or be charged with rebellion and disobedience. The injured man had died by that time, and Joseph Naranjo failed to appear for questioning. After two years in sanctuary, his small plot of farmland had been seized and his family was on the brink of starvation. Finally, the victim's widow dropped the charges against Naranjo and petitioned the governor for his release so that he could return to his wife and children.

This case illustrates that even a personal altercation could be considered an act of sedition when Pueblo converts were implicated. In the end, the community had to find its own form of restorative justice. The wives of the two men involved in the altercation came to a resolution that would serve the best interests of both families. Naranjo remained in sanctuary for two years and he cleverly used his right to remain silent in order to stay out of jail, although in so doing he basically imprisoned himself in another enclosure confined within the space of the mission.

The Catholic Church remained central to the administration of justice beyond crimes against the faith or the clergy in colonial New Mexico (and elsewhere in Mexico and Latin America). Clergy had a say in punishment and mercy as managers of morality and envoys of divine justice. On the other hand, sanctuary also benefited the commoner and the rebel who could use it to avoid or delay punishment, evade the law, or even receive shelter and a free meal while in sanctuary. The church asylum was a Spanish institution dictated by the metropole, but it was enacted in the colonies in accordance to local customs, political systems, and social hierarchies. Sanctuary privileges were diverse and open to interpretation but also to widespread abuse and corruption. But sanctuary was an exclusive right only available to Christians (or those willing to submit to baptism), individuals already within the folds of Spanish colonial society.

In reclaiming the sanctity and historicity of sanctuary, its multifaceted nature is revealed. Sanctuary can simultaneously work against and in collaboration with power. It could be confined within the sanctified enclosures of the church regulated by colonial authority or, alternatively, dispersed in the form of autonomous and mobile Indigenous sanctuaryscapes. When Indigenous people fled to regions of refuge or created defensive spaces for themselves to resist or evade colonial domination, it was often temporary and precarious. However, the solidarities and cultural innovations that emerged from both rural and urban Indigenous sanctuaryscapes had enduring social and political implications not solely for those who created these protective enclaves, but for Spanish authorities and settlers who lived in fear of rebellion from within and from afar.

Church asylum, on the other hand, offers an example of institutionalized forms of sanctuary that are hedged on state and pastoral power as an aspect of colonial governance. While this structure could be manipulated from below, sanctuary was implicated in the clergy's power to decide on religious and secular matters. However, clergy sometimes allowed crimes that undermined colonial rule to go unpunished or deferred to uphold their Christian priorities and obligations to care for the spiritual and material well-being of those under their charge. Sanctuary power writ large was a stage upon which the perpetual struggle between the secular and the religious played out, one of the many threads in the making of the secular borderlands.

Legacies of radical hospitality hold profound historical, political, and spiritual relevance for immigrant rights advocates in New Mexico today. They recall the mesa-top Pueblo cities of refuge that flourished in the wake of the Great Northern Rebellion of 1680 and continue to inspire contemporary social movements. In December 2016, residents packed city hall in Santa Fe to register support for the Welcoming City Resolution, one of the most progressive sanctuary city proposals in the nation. The resolution passed unanimously in open defiance of the Trump administration's legally dubious sanctions on sanctuary cities. Santa Fe was one of the first cities in the country to become a sanctuary for Central American refugees in 1985 at the height of the faith-based sanctuary movement. The following year, Governor Toney Anaya declared New Mexico a "state for sanctuary" in solidarity with the Central American cause.[97]

A prominent theme that runs through New Mexico's prior sanctuary proclamations and resurfaced in the array of testimony given in support of Santa Fe's Welcoming City Resolution is that providing safe harbor to those in need is a longstanding local tradition. City councilor Renee Villarreal, one of the representatives who introduced the resolution, asserted: "New Mexico has a long tradition of providing sanctuary to those fleeing harm, from the Pueblo Revolt to those fleeing persecution in Central America during the 1980s. We won't turn our back on our sacred traditions now. Instead, we must strengthen those policies."[98] When advocates evoke the language of tradition, they awaken a particular politics of locality and belonging, one that enfolds sanctuary within a homeland that predates the nation-state.[99] At once aspirational and haunting, this imagined and contested homeland lives among the ruins and revivals of sanctuary.

In New Mexico, legacies of resistance to colonialism coalesce in movements against unjust immigration laws in our current moment of social and political crisis. If sanctuary can be understood as a form of collective action against injustice, its deep historical memory is what sets it apart from other movements in the North American Southwest. As a cultural tradition that is prior to US nationalism and its exclusionary forms of citizenship, sanctuary offers a counternarrative that anchors an alternative vision of solidarity and belonging—a local citizenship or ethic of solidarity and belonging that must continuously be remade and reclaimed in relation to changing circumstances of struggle.

Aimee Villarreal is assistant professor and program director of Comparative Mexican American Studies at Our Lady of the Lake University. Villarreal coproduced an award-winning documentary animation about the 1680 Pueblo Revolt, *Frontera! Revolt and Rebellion on the Río Grande* (2014): https://vimeo.com/75840615. Her forthcoming book *Places of Sanctuary in the Secular Borderlands* is a multidisciplinary study of sanctuary practices and movements at the intersections of the sacred and the secular.

Notes

1. Mora, *Border Dilemmas*, 49–53.
2. Eiselt, *Becoming White Clay*, 130.
3. In the documentary *Surviving Columbus* (1993; dir. Diane Reyna), Roxanne Swentzell, a native of Taos Pueblo, is interviewed about what happened at the old San Gerónimo Mission. She talks about the burnt statue of a saint that her grandmother cherished and cared for and also asserts that the people took sanctuary in the mission expecting to be protected.
4. West, "The Right of Asylum in New Mexico in the Seventeenth and Eighteenth Centuries," 362. According to archaeologist Michael Adler (personal communication, October 25, 2018), residents of Taos Pueblo are resolute that their ancestors indeed took sanctuary in the mission with the expectation of immunity.
5. Vargas, *Crucible of Struggle*, 88–90.
6. Rabben, *Sanctuary and Asylum*.
7. Bau, *This Ground Is Holy*; Rabben, *Sanctuary and Asylum*.
8. Aguirre-Beltrán, *Regions of Refuge*; Vélez-Ibáñez, "Regions of Refuge."
9. Saldaña-Portillo, *Indian Given*, 15.
10. Yukich, *One Family Under God*, 1–38.
11. Shoemaker, "Sanctuary for Crime in the Early Common Law," 16–17.
12. Rojas, "Bajo el amparo del Altísimo."
13. Sánchez Aguirreolea, "El derecho de asilo en España durante la Edad Moderna," 586.
14. Nemser, *Infrastructures of Race*.
15. Leckman, "Meeting Places," 76–77.
16. Schneider and Panich, "Native Agency at the Margins of Empire."

17. Saldaña-Portillo, *Indian Given*, 26–27.

18. Vélez-Ibáñez defines the Southwest North American region in terms of political ecology, economic integration, and shared cultural geography. He excludes Mesoamerica from his analysis and instead focuses on the Mexican states of Chihuahua, Sonora, Coahuila, Nuevo León, and Tamaulipas, which form the transborder region. See Vélez-Ibáñez, "Continuity and Contiguity of the Southwest North American Region."

19. Most of these cases were originally collected by Elizabeth Howard West when she was cataloging materials for Ralph Emerson Twitchell's *Spanish Archives of New Mexico* in 1914. She published the cases and her interpretation of them in "The Right of Asylum in New Mexico in the Seventeenth and Eighteenth Centuries," which was published in 1928 in the *Hispanic American Historical Review*.

20. The term "homescapes" was composed by Muskogee literary critic and novelist Craig Womack. See Womack, *Red on Red*.

21. Squint, "Choctaw Homescapes," 115.

22. Pearsall, "'Having Many Wives' in Two American Rebellions," 1023.

23. Leckman, "Meeting Places," 86–87.

24. Barr, "Geographies of Power," 5–6.

25. Saldaña-Portillo, *Indian Given*, 24–25.

26. Barr, "Geographies of Power," 9.

27. Bau, *This Ground Is Holy*.

28. Coutin, *The Culture of Protest*; Cunningham, *God and Caesar at the Rio Grande*; Lorentzen, *Women in the Sanctuary Movement*; Smith, *Resisting Reagan*; Yukich, *One Family Under God*.

29. It is interesting to note that people from the global South are more often represented as migrant/asylum seekers than as producers of alternative sanctuary spaces. In addition, although Indigenous people have suffered forced removals, religious persecution, state-sponsored genocide, slavery, and other horrors, they are rarely defined as refugees or people in need of sanctuary within settler colonial nations. As far as I can tell, there are no sanctuary movements before the 1980s that centered on protecting Indigenous people from unjust laws or genocidal polices. While revivals of sanctuary in the United States are traced to the Underground Railroad, which mobilized following the passage of the Fugitive Slave Act of 1850 to assist escaped African American slaves, no faith-based movement arose to protect the Cherokee and Choctaw after the passage of the Indian Removal Act in 1830.

30. Rabben, *Sanctuary and Asylum*, 27–28.

31. Rabben, *Sanctuary and Asylum*, 28.

32. Tsing, *Friction*, 9.

33. Quijano, "Coloniality of Power, Eurocentrism, and Social Classification," 181–224.

34. Golden and McConnell, *Sanctuary*.

35. Bau, *This Ground Is Holy*, 161–71.

36. Coutin, *The Culture of Protest*; Cunningham, *God and Caesar at the Rio Grande*; Lorentzen, *Women in the Sanctuary Movement*.

37. Lippert, *Sanctuary, Sovereignty, Sacrifice*, 89–139.

38. Lippert, *Sanctuary, Sovereignty, Sacrifice*, 126.

39. Nemser, *Infrastructures of Race*.

40. Provine, Varsanyi, Lewis, and Decker, *Policing Immigrants*; Ridgeley, "Cities of Refuge."

41. Mancina, "The Birth of a Sanctuary City," 206–8.
42. Villarreal, "Places of Sanctuary," 244–45.
43. Rabben, *Sanctuary and Asylum*, 28–38.
44. Bagelman, *Sanctuary City*.
45. Aguirre Beltrán, *Regions of Refuge*, 5–8.
46. Proctor, "Slave Rebellion and Liberty in Colonial Mexico," 5–7.
47. Landers, "Gracia Real de Santa Teresa de Mose," 9–10.
48. Richmond, "The Legacy of African Slavery in Colonial Mexico," 10.
49. According to Pedro Tomé, this term derives from the Mexica word *Chichimecatlalli*, which referred to the north. See "Redescubriendo la Gran Chichimeca."
50. Tomé, "Redescubriendo la Gran Chichimeca."
51. Alonso, *Thread of Blood*.
52. Alonso, *Thread of Blood*, 25.
53. Alonso, *Thread of Blood*, 25.
54. Alonso, *Thread of Blood*, 70–71.
55. Sando and Agoyo, *Po'pay*.
56. Villarreal and Leaños, "Animating Resistance."
57. Liebmann, *Revolt*; Reséndez, *The Other Slavery*, 149–71.
58. Eiselt, *Becoming White Clay*, 100.
59. Gradie, *The Tepehuan Revolt of 1616*.
60. Merrill, "Cultural Creativity and Raiding Bands in Eighteenth-Century Northern New Spain."
61. Liebmann, Preucel, and Aguilar, "The Pueblo World Transformed," 151–52.
62. Liebmann, Preucel, and Aguilar, "The Pueblo World Transformed," 145.
63. Liebmann, *Revolt*.
64. Liebmann and Preucel, "Pueblo Settlement, Architecture, and Social Change."
65. Joseph Aguilar, personal communication, June 29, 2017.
66. Liebmann, *Revolt*, 83–95.
67. Capone and Preucel, "Ceramic Semiotics."
68. Mills, "Acts of Resistance."
69. Mobley-Tanaka, "Crossed Cultures, Crossed Meanings."
70. Preucel, "Writing the Pueblo Revolt," 4–5.
71. Liebmann, *Revolt*, 141.
72. Eiselt, *Becoming White Clay*, 78.
73. Eiselt, *Becoming White Clay*, 78.
74. Eiselt, *Becoming White Clay*, 79.
75. Eiselt, *Becoming White Clay*, 79–81.
76. "Fray Francisco Jiménez, of Taos, certifies that he has received the apostate Picuris, 31 August 1706." Archivo General de la Nación de México (AGN), PI 36, page 95, fol. 37r.
77. Thomas, *After Coronado*, 64–67.
78. "Ensign Francisco de Valdés Sorribas certifies to Ulibarri's taking possession and pacification of the new province, 4 August 1706," AGN PI 36, p. 94, 36r.
79. Pearsall, "'Having Many Wives' in Two American Rebellions." See also Barr, *Peace Came in the Form of a Woman*.
80. Eiselt, *Becoming White Clay*, 93.
81. Babcock, *Apache Adaptation to Hispanic Rule*, 219.

82. West, "The Right of Asylum in New Mexico in the Seventeenth and Eighteenth Centuries."
83. Rojas, "Bajo el amparo del Altísimo," 5.
84. Uribe-Uran, "'Iglesia me llamo.'"
85. Sánchez Aguirreolea, "El derecho de asilo en España durante la Edad Moderna," 583.
86. Uribe-Uran, "'Iglesia me llamo,'" 450.
87. Uribe-Uran, "'Iglesia me llamo,'" 451.
88. Uribe-Uran, "'Iglesia me llamo,'" 471–72.
89. Rojas, "Bajo el amparo del Altísimo."
90. "Church-State Relations in New Mexico 1609–1659," 5–7.
91. West, "The Right of Asylum in New Mexico in the Seventeenth and Eighteenth Centuries," 384.
92. Uribe-Uran, "'Iglesia me llamo,'" 465–66.
93. "Church-State Relations in New Mexico 1609–1659."
94. West, "The Right of Asylum in New Mexico in the Seventeenth and Eighteenth Centuries," 380.
95. West, "The Right of Asylum in New Mexico in the Seventeenth and Eighteenth Centuries," 381.
96. West, "The Right of Asylum in New Mexico in the Seventeenth and Eighteenth Centuries," 375–76.
97. "Sanctuary Proclamation," March 28, 1986, Toney Anaya Papers, Center for Southwest Research, University of New Mexico.
98. Dax, "The Defiant, Refugee-Loving History of New Mexico."
99. In "The Hispano Homeland Debate Revisited," Sylvia Rodríguez traces the emergence of the homeland concept in northern New Mexico as a product of different ethnopolitical mobilizations since the 1960s. It encompasses competing ethnic nomenclatures (Hispana/o, Mexicana/o, Chicana/o) class interests, and religious perspectives.

References

Aguirre Beltrán, Gonzalo. *Regions of Refuge.* Monograph Series 12. Washington, DC: Society for Applied Anthropology, 1979.

Alonso, Ana María. *Thread of Blood: Colonialism, Revolution, and Gender on Mexico's Northern Frontier.* Tucson: University of Arizona Press, 1995.

Babcock, Matthew. *Apache Adaptation to Hispanic Rule.* New York: Cambridge University Press, 2016.

Bagelman, Jennifer. *Sanctuary City: A Suspended State.* New York: Palgrave Macmillan, 2016.

Bandelier, Adolph F. A., and Fanny R. Bandelier. "Church State Relations in New Mexico." In *Historical Documents Relating to New Mexico, Nueva Vizcaya, and Approaches thereto, to 1773, Volume III,* edited by Charles Wilson Hackett, 5–16. Washington, DC: Carnegie Institution of Washington, 1937.

Barr, Juliana. *Peace Came in the Form of a Woman: Indians and Spaniards in the Texas Borderlands.* Chapel Hill: University of North Carolina Press, 2007.

Barr, Juliana. "Geographies of Power: Mapping Indian Borders in the "Borderlands" of the Early Southwest." *William and Mary Quarterly* 68, no. 1 (2011): 5–46.

Bau, Ignatius. *This Ground Is Holy: Church Sanctuary and Central American Refugees.* New York: Paulist Press, 1985.

Capone, Patricia W., and Robert W. Preucel. "Ceramic Semiotics: Women, Pottery, and Social Meanings at Kotyiti Pueblo." In *Archaeologies of the Pueblo Revolt: Identity, Meanings and Renewal in the Pueblo World*, edited by Robert W. Preucel, 99–113. Albuquerque: University of New Mexico Press, 2007.

Clark, Anthony Tyeeme, and Malea Powell. "Resisting Exile in the 'Land of the Free': Indigenous Groundwork at Colonial Intersections." *American Indian Quarterly* 32, no. 1 (2008): 1–15.

Coutin, Susan Bibler. *The Culture of Protest: Religious Activism and the U.S. Sanctuary Movement*. Boulder, CO: Westview Press, 1993.

Cunningham, Hilary. *God and Caesar at the Rio Grande: Sanctuary and the Politics of Religion*. Minneapolis: University of Minnesota Press, 1995.

Dax, Michael. "The Defiant, Refugee-Loving History of New Mexico: How the State's Unique and Open Relationship with Mexico Is Overshadowing Trump's Immigration Policies." *Yes!*, July 11, 2017. www.yesmagazine.org/issues/sanctuary/the-defiant-refugee-loving-history-of -new-mexico-20170711.

Eiselt, B. Sunday. *Becoming White Clay: A History and Archaeology of Jicarilla Apache Enclavement*. Salt Lake City: University of Utah Press, 2012.

Golden, Renny, and Michael McConnell. *Sanctuary: The New Underground Railroad*. Maryknoll, NY: Orbis Books, 1986.

Gradie, Charlotte M. *The Tepehuan Revolt of 1616: Militarism, Evangelism, and Colonialism in Seventeenth-Century Nueva Vizcaya*. Salt Lake City: University of Utah Press, 2000.

Landers, Jane. "Gracia Real de Santa Teresa de Mose." *American Historical Review* 95, no. 1 (1990): 9–30.

Leckman, Phillip O. "Meeting Places: Seventeenth-Century Puebloan and Spanish Landscapes." In *New Mexico and the Primería Alta: The Colonial Period in the American Southwest*, edited by John G. Douglass and William M. Graves, 75–114. Boulder: University Press of Colorado, 2017.

Liebmann, Matthew. *Revolt: An Archaeological History of Pueblo Resistance and Revitalization in Seventeenth-Century New Mexico*. Archaeology of Colonialism in Native North America. Tucson: University of Arizona Press, 2012.

Liebmann, Matthew, and Robert W. Preucel. "Pueblo Settlement, Architecture, and Social Change in the Pueblo Revolt Era, A.D. 1680 to 1696." *Journal of Field Archaeology* 30, no. 1 (2005): 45–60.

Liebmann, Matthew, Robert Preucel, and Joseph Aguilar. "The Pueblo World Transformed: Alliances, Factionalism, and Animosities in the Northern Rio Grande." In *New Mexico and the Primería Alta: The Colonial Period in the American Southwest*, edited by John G. Douglass and William M. Graves, 143–56. Boulder: University Press of Colorado, 2017.

Lippert, Randy K. *Sanctuary, Sovereignty, Sacrifice: Canadian Sanctuary Incidents, Power, and Law*. Vancouver: UBC Press, 2005.

Lorentzen, Robin. *Women in the Sanctuary Movement*. Philadelphia: Temple University Press, 1991.

Mancina, Peter. "The Birth of a Sanctuary City: Municipal Migrant Rights and the City of Toronto." In *Sanctuary Practice in International Perspectives: Migration, Citizenship, and Social Movements*, edited by Randy K. Lippert and Sean Rehaag, 205–18. Abingdon, UK: Routledge, 2012.

Merrill, William L. "Cultural Creativity and Raiding Bands in Eighteenth-Century Northern New Spain." In *Violence, Resistance, and Survival in the Americas: Native Americans and the Legacy of Conquest*, edited by William B. Taylor and Franklin Pease G. Y., 124–52. Washington, DC: Smithsonian Institution Press, 1994.

Mills, Barbara. "Acts of Resistance: Zuni Ceramics, Social Identity, and the Pueblo Revolt." In *Archaeologies of the Pueblo Revolt: Identity, Meaning, and Renewal in the Pueblo World*, edited by Robert Preucel, 85–98. Albuquerque: University of New Mexico Press, 2002.

Mobley-Tanaka, Jeannette L. "Crossed Cultures, Crossed Meanings: The Manipulation of Ritual Imagery in Early Historic Pueblo Resistance." In *Archaeologies of the Pueblo Revolt: Identity, Meaning, and Renewal in the Pueblo World*, edited by Robert Preucel, 77–84. Albuquerque: University of New Mexico Press, 2002.

Mora, Anthony. *Border Dilemmas: Racial and National Uncertainties in New Mexico, 1848–1912*. Durham, NC: Duke University Press, 2011.

Nemser, Daniel. *Infrastructures of Race: Concentration and Biopolitics in Colonial Mexico*. Austin: University of Texas Press, 2017.

Pearsall, Sarah. "'Having Many Wives' in Two American Rebellions: The Politics of Households and the Radically Conservative." *American Historical Review* 188, no. 4 (2013): 1001–28.

Preucel, Robert W. "Writing the Pueblo Revolt." In *Archaeologies of the Pueblo Revolt: Identity, Meaning, and Renewal in the Pueblo World*, edited by Robert Preucel, 3–29. Albuquerque: University of New Mexico Press, 2002.

Proctor, Frank, III, "Slave Rebellion and Liberty in Colonial Mexico." In *Black Mexico: Race and Society from Colonial to Modern Times*, edited by Ben Vinson III and Mathew Restall, 5–23. Albuquerque: University of New Mexico Press, 2009.

Provine, Doris Marie, Monica Varsanyi, Paul G. Lewis, and Scott H. Decker. *Policing Immigrants: Local Law Enforcement on the Front Lines*. Chicago: University of Chicago Press, 2016.

Quijano, Anibal. "Coloniality of Power, Eurocentrism, and Social Classification," In *Coloniality at Large: Latin America and the Postcolonial Debate*, edited by Mabel Moraña, Enrique Dussel, and Carlos A. Jáuregui, 181–224. Durham, NC: Duke University Press, 2008.

Rabben, Linda. *Sanctuary and Asylum: A Social and Political History*. Seattle: University of Washington Press, 2016.

Reséndez, Andrés. *The Other Slavery: The Uncovered Story of Indian Enslavement in America*. New York: Houghton Mifflin Harcourt, 2016.

Richmond, Douglas. "The Legacy of African Slavery in Colonial Mexico." *Journal of Popular Culture* 35, no. 2 (2001): 1–16.

Ridgeley, Jennifer. "Cities of Refuge: Immigration Enforcement, Police and the Insurgent Genealogies of Citizenship in US Sanctuary Cities." *Urban Geography* 29, no. 1 (2008): 53–77.

Rodríguez, Sylvia. "The Hispano Homeland Debate Revisited." *Perspectives in Mexican American Studies* 3 (1992): 95–116.

Rojas, María Odette. "Bajo el amparo del Altísimo: El asilo eclesiástico a finales del siglo XVII." *Historias: Revista de la Dirección de Estudios Históricos* 73 (2009): 19–21.

Saldaña-Portillo, María Josefina. *Indian Given: Racial Geographies across Mexico and the United States*. Durham, NC: Duke University Press, 2016.

Sánchez Aguirreolea, Daniel. "El derecho de asilo en España durante la Edad Moderna." *Mundo Moderno: Hispania Sacra* 55 (2003): 571–98.

Sando, Joe S., Herman Agoyo. *Po'pay: Leader of the First American Revolution*. Santa Fe, NM: Clear Light Publishers, 2005.

Schneider, Tsim D. and Lee M. Panich. "Native Agency at the Margins of Empire: Indigenous Landscapes, Spanish Missions, and Contested Histories," In *Indigenous Landscapes and Spanish Missions: New Perspectives from Archaeology and Ethnohistory*, edited by Lee M. Panich and Tsim D. Schneider, 5–22. Tucson: University of Arizona Press, 2014.

Scott, David. "Colonial Governmentality." *Social Text* 43 (1995): 191–220.

Shoemaker, Karl. "Sanctuary for Crime in the Early Common Law." In *Sanctuary Practices in International Perspectives: Migration, Citizenship, and Social Movements*, edited by Randy K. Lippert and Sean Rehaag, 15–27. New York: Routledge, 2013.

Squint, Kirstin L. "Choctaw Homescapes: LeAnne Howe's Gulf Coast." *Mississippi Quarterly: Journal of Southern Cultures* 66, no. 1 (2013): 115–37.

Tomé, Pedro. "Redescubriendo la Gran Chichimeca: Revalorización Regional y Antropología Social en la Recuperación de una Pluralidad Étnica Mexicana." *Revista de Dialectología y Tradiciones Populares* vol. LXV, no. 1 (2010): 155–84.

Thomas, Barnaby Alfred. *After Coronado: Spanish Exploration Northeast of New Mexico, 1696–1727. Documents from the Archives of Spain Mexico and New Mexico.* Norman: University of Oklahoma Press, 1935.

Tsing, Anna Lowenhaupt. *Friction: An Ethnography of Global Connection.* Princeton, NJ: Princeton University Press, 2005.

Uribe-Uran, Victor M. "The Great Transformation of Law and Legal Culture: 'The Public' and 'the Private' in the Transition from Empire to Nation in Mexico, Colombia, and Brazil, 1750–1850." In *Empire to Nation: Historical Perspectives on the Making of the Modern World*, edited by Joseph W. Esherick, Hasan Kayali, and Eric Van Young, 68–133. Oxford: Rowman and Littlefield Publishers, 2006.

Uribe-Uran, Victor M. "'Iglesia me llamo': Church Asylum and the Law in Spain and Colonial Spanish America." *Comparative Studies in Society and History* 49, no. 2 (2007): 446–72.

Vargas, Zaragosa. *Crucible of Struggle: A History of Mexican Americans from Colonial Times to the Present.* New York: Oxford University Press, 2010.

Vélez-Ibáñez, Carlos G. "Continuity and Contiguity of the Southwest North American Region: The Dynamics of a Common Political Ecology." In *The U.S.-Mexico Transborder Region: Cultural Dynamics and Historical Interactions*, edited by Carlos Vélez-Ibáñez and Josiah Heyman, 5–10. Tucson: University of Arizona Press, 2017.

Vélez-Ibáñez, Carlos G. "Malinowski Award Lecture, 2003: Regions of Refuge in the United States: Issues, Problems, and Concerns for the Future of Mexican-Origin Populations in the United States." *Human Organization* 63, no. 1 (2004): 1–20.

Villarreal, Aimee, and John Leaños. "Animating Resistance: Anthropology as Public Pedagogy." *Anthropology News*, May 2017. doi.org/10.1111/AN.468.

Villarreal Garza, A. "Places of Sanctuary: Religious Revivalism and the Politics of Immigration in New Mexico." PhD diss., University of California, Santa Cruz, 2014.

West, Elizabeth Howard. "The Right of Asylum in New Mexico in the Seventeenth and Eighteenth Centuries." *Hispanic American Historical Review* 8, no. 3 (1928): 357–91.

Womack, Craig. *Red on Red: Native American Literary Separatism.* Minneapolis: University of Minnesota Press, 1999.

Yukich, Grace. *One Family Under God: Immigration Politics and Progressive Religion in America.* New York: Oxford University Press, 2013.

"Returning Forest Darlings"

Gay Liberationist Sanctuary in the Southeastern Network, 1973–80

Jason Ezell

Carl Wittman opened his 1970 gay liberationist manifesto "Refugees from Amerika" with a stark statement on what it meant for a US city to serve as a gay sanctuary in the months following the Stonewall riots: "San Francisco is a refugee camp for homosexuals. We have fled here from every part of the nation, and like refugees elsewhere, we came here, not because it is so great here, but because it was so bad there. By the tens of thousands, we fled small towns."[1] By framing homosexuals as refugees, Wittman implied that the city line was equivalent to a national border and that San Francisco's gay residents were hardly full citizens in their new city. He stressed that the city was no "free territory" but rather a gay "ghetto," fully controlled by the police, lawmakers, and business owners who constrained the lives of the homosexuals who sheltered there. As a former East Coast activist involved with the Students for a Democratic Society (SDS) and with southern civil rights work, the newly out Wittman was acutely aware of the tenuous relationship between living within US borders and accessing safety within its system.

By 1973, many considered gay liberation dead. Most cities' Gay Liberation Front (GLF) chapters had folded, and the culture's audacious style—men, often bearded, in dresses—was being replaced by the hypermasculine "clone" look.[2] By 1974, Wittman had left the city behind. Traveling from North Carolina to rural Oregon with his partner Allan Troxler, the two stopped in Iowa. There they joined other

Radical History Review

Issue 135 (October 2019)   DOI 10.1215/01636545-7607833

© 2019 by MARHO: The Radical Historians' Organization, Inc.

gay liberationists to found *RFD*, a journal "for country faggots everywhere."[3] Proposed by Stewart Scofield at the 1974 Iowa Midwest Gay Pride following *Mother Earth News*'s refusal to publish an announcement for a gay rural collective, *RFD* professed a back-to-the-land variant of gay liberation.[4] It answered many readers' frustrations with feelings of containment in urban gay ghettos and sustained their identification with the free-love ethos and androgynous stylings of the hippie counterculture.[5] It also connected gay liberationists who were painfully isolated in rural spaces, including largely straight collectives. Troxler shared his own experiences of such in the very first issue.[6] Wittman's *RFD* writings not only expressed his sustained gay liberationist political values but also his spiritual projects, like conceiving a gay tarot.[7] *RFD* quickly won a committed, if dispersed, readership.

In 1980, a decade after the publication of "Refugees from Amerika," Milo Pyne published a manifesto of his own. Appearing in *RFD*, Pyne's piece called for a renewal of gay liberationist political values and stated the urgent need for *sanctuaries*. On the latter subject, he wrote, "We will increasingly need space to exercise our emotional, physical, and psychic beings. We also need access to land!"[8] Pyne recalls (interview, July 1, 2016) initial attempts to address such urgency earlier that spring, leading a collective project to repurpose the Appalachian farm where he lived as one of these gay liberationist sites, naming it Short Mountain Sanctuary.[9] Anthropologist Scott Lauria Morgensen has suggested that Short Mountain Sanctuary may have roots in "histories of radical southern and rural gay collectivism" but that it, like other, similar gay back-to-the-land initiatives, must be considered within colonial frames.[10] While I agree with Morgensen, I here situate Short Mountain within a different context; whereas he stresses the site's role within a developing Radical Faerie culture, I show how its early history can be understood in relation to US sanctuary movements.

In the following, I define this form of sanctuary as part of the culture of back-to-the-land gay liberation that endured in the Southeast, linking its concerns to a wider US sanctuary history. Because Wittman cast homosexuals as refugees seeking protection in a city, comparisons with the current sanctuary city movement suggest useful interpretive lenses. A. Naomi Paik shows how the latter movement has roots both in religious traditions providing short-term refuge to those the state deems criminals, and in political traditions of local movements and offices frustrating the inhumane enforcement of federal laws.[11] Both traditions involve invoking a different scope of authority against that of the state—religious authority as superior to governmental authority, or local/popular authority as exerting independence of national authority. These are strategies of liberation that often depend on setting different forms and scopes of control against one another. Further, Paik cautions the current sanctuary movement about "the contradictions of looking to the state to address the problem the state itself creates," pointing out the need to disentangle from state infrastructures—especially information networks—and to form alliances across the diverse populations in need of sanctuary.[12]

Gay liberationists were fundamentally critical of the system, making their sanctuary practices a case study for movement efforts that look *away* from the state. I argue that the back-to-the-land gay liberationism that emerged around the circulation of *RFD*, rather than engaging institutional authority, drew upon religious and political modes of resistance that relied on decentralized organization, obscurantist networking practices, and politically strategic affect to defy state surveillance. Its orientation was geared, however, toward the rural rather than the urban. With its back-to-the-land ethos, it looked to the rural as a vantage to counter the policing and economic dependency experienced in the gay ghetto, and leveraged wilderness to imagine space at the edges of state control. Access to the rural, then, figured centrally as these gay liberationists' means to exceed the city, confound state intelligence, and improvise sanctuary at the domestic peripheries of police reach.

To trace sanctuary practices within this movement, I first show how southeastern gay liberationists were embedded in the *RFD* network from its very beginning—especially in Appalachia—connected by rural sanctuary practices of collective defense and what they called "faggot spirituality." Second, I describe the experiences of terror in the late 1970s that made sanctuary an exigency before tracing how, in 1978 and 1979, gatherings at Running Water Farm in North Carolina led to the realization of a Southeastern Network of rural and urban collectives that took up the editorial reins of *RFD* and improvised regional forms of earlier sanctuary practices. Finally, I show how Short Mountain Sanctuary emerged from this Southeastern Network, mobilizing for sanctuary at the edges of the state—in terms of rural orientations, regional geopolitical scales, and politically crucial affective registers.

"Only Raising Flowers": The Mountain South, Rural Collective Defense, and Faggot Spirituality

Milo Pyne, inspired by his rural experiences with gay liberationists in the Venceremos Brigades, which collaborated with revolutionary Cuba, moved to Short Mountain in Tennessee in 1973. He went with a lover named Peter and several men and women from the rural North Carolina Tick Creek Collective after that group's house burned down.[13] Pyne was at the 1974 Midwest Gay Pride where Scofield proposed *RFD*, and he recalls (interview, July 1, 2016) collaborating with fellow native North Carolinian Troxler on the serial, contributing an illustration to the Fall 1975 issue. John Harris (later Gabby Haze) and his lesbian wife, Merrill Mushroom, lived very close to Short Mountain, at Dry Creek, with their adoptive children. Gay liberationist Harris met Pyne when he struck up a conversation about *RFD*.[14]

The mountain South figured prominently in the wider back-to-the-land movement, which also included gay liberationists, from early on. Historian John Alexander Williams has described 1970s Appalachia as a unique magnet for poverty warriors, civil rights activist veterans, counterculturists, and politicized locals.[15] The countercultural element around Short Mountain was particularly strong. Nearby was The Farm, the Tennessee intentional community founded in 1971 by Stephen Gaskin and about three hundred fellow hippies from San Francisco.[16] As Harris commented on the area, "Some of it was gay, most of it was straight—all of it was drug related at some level. We wondered, Is it going on everywhere? Is there madness happening in every little nook and cranny or are we sort of this special place?"[17] Given how concentrated the counterculture was in Appalachia, such nonconformist rural pockets were a new, but not altogether rare, phenomenon in the region.

In fact, as cultural historian Scott Herring has pointed out, by 1976, *RFD* readers in other places like Massachusetts began to self-consciously adopt a "lovely hillbillies" aesthetic to differentiate themselves from the dominant stylistics of urban gay cultures.[18] For those who dreamed of leaving the gay ghetto, this new aesthetic suggested a mountain South setting. They did not envision mere bucolic escape, though. As Herring has further shown, *RFD* was heavily influenced by lesbian publications like *Country Women* and the rural collectives they represented; he further maintains that these cultures "do not fall under the rubric of a conventional and racist 'white flight' from the city since they are literally 'flights' from racially normative metropolitan gay culture," implying further that these rural dwellers hoped the country would facilitate their activism.[19]

Part of the lesbian feminist activism of the time was what Emily Hobson has called "collective defense." She uses this term to refer to how radical lesbian collective households adapted black liberationist strategies to lend "support for armed resistance and the underground. . . . They also lived collective defense through their shared households, which sheltered both political fugitives . . . and more ordinary women escaping domestic violence."[20] As a means of both supporting the underground by providing safe passage for fugitives and of protecting women from violence in their homes, collective defense was a practice of sanctuary.

Although Hobson anchors her history in the Bay Area, Appalachia also figured importantly in networks of collective defense. Both Hobson and James T. Sears tell how radical Susan Saxe, hunted by the FBI for her part in stealing sensitive federal wartime documents and for robbing a bank to secure finances for the Black Panthers, took refuge in a network of lesbian collective households, including a pivotal one in Lexington, Kentucky. Saxe's ultimate capture led to the 1975 sentencing of the "Lexington 6." Further south, in Atlanta, in 1973, the FBI arrested former Weather Underground member and cofounder of the Atlanta Lesbian Feminist Alliance (ALFA) Vicki Gabriner for passport fraud while she was staying in a lesbian collective household.[21] Gabriner, like Pyne, had been part of the Venceremos Brigades, and Pyne shares (interview, July 1, 2016) that his own Tick Creek collective had served as a way station for radicals and activists traveling between Atlanta and DC. The FBI also kept a watch on Pyne. Sears records how the FBI opened a file on him in 1970, but nearly five years later, in January 1975, they finally closed his case, frustrated that they could find no evidence of subversive activity and concluding that the radicals at Short Mountain were "only raising flowers and various herbs."[22]

I contend that this FBI frustration with rural surveillance reveals a back-to-the-land variation on the sanctuary strategy of collective defense. Urban surveillance strategies couldn't simply be reproduced in rural spaces. Strangers stood out in town and around the farm. Radical lesbian feminists and gay liberationists knew this. While Herring argues that the rural networks represented in *Country Women* and *RFD* were flights from urban racial normativity, I add that they were also flights from the FBI's urban surveillance of collective households described by Hobson. Further, I propose that the rustic production design that Herring finds in *RFD* and *Country Women* wasn't only part of an anti-urban aesthetic but also a complementary strategy to frustrate FBI officials tasked with quickly reviewing gay liberationist serials for sensitive information. The crude typography, unfinished sentences, purposeful misspellings, random punctuation, strikethroughs, poetic language, and portmanteau coinages that Herring analyzes would have befuddled agents sent after sensitive facts. Perhaps this is one reason why historian Douglas M. Charles didn't find *RFD* listed among the gay liberationist publications that the FBI kept an eye on. Charles does specifically comment on how the bureau found gay liberation, with its anarchistic and decentralized organizational forms, much more challenging to track than traditionally structured gay activist groups.[23] Back-to-the-land gay liberationists mobilized rural locations and obscurantist print practices to frustrate state surveillance and to expand on the sanctuary work of urban collective defense.

In the Ozarks, in Fayetteville, Arkansas, a gay liberationist collective that would call themselves the Arkansas Sissies also participated in collective defense. Formed in the winter of 1975–76, the group was enmeshed in an Ozark women's socialist feminist network whose members, as Allyn Lord and Anna M. Zajicek have shown, were significantly influenced by their positive civil rights activist experiences. Nearly half of the participants Lord and Zajicek interviewed voluntarily identified as lesbian, bisexual, or transgender.[24] The Arkansas Sissies of Mulberry House temporarily shared their lodgings with lesbians Trella Laughlin and Patricia Jackson, former Weather Underground members and future founders of the rural women's community Yellowhammer.[25] Once Laughlin and Jackson moved to the country, according to Arkansas Sissie Dimid Hayes (interview, August 3–4, 2016), Mulberry House served as a safe way station for women—several of whom were women of color—as they made their way through rural Arkansas to Yellowhammer. As another form of collective defense, Mulberry House also made plans to house a gay prisoner upon his release.[26]

On Labor Day weekend 1976, the Arkansas Sissies traveled to the Faggots and Class Struggle Conference in Oregon, a rural event documented in the pages of *RFD*. This event reflected the concerns of rural collective defense in that its location was partly chosen to elude state surveillance, as seen in the fact that, despite its site in rural Wolf Creek, a strict security practice was put in place to prevent FBI infiltration.[27]

Hobson references the faggot political culture of the Bay Area but doesn't mention its spiritual components.[28] Inspired by new Bay Area feminist witchcraft movements, many gay liberationist men rallied around the figure of the witch as a way to embody a feminist defiance of the patriarchy in its global capitalist form. Gay men didn't always call themselves witches, however, but instead reclaimed the epithets *faggot* and *fairy*, in the spirit of Arthur Evans's *Witchcraft and the Gay Counterculture*, highlighting homosexuals' history of persecution within and opposition to the rise of industrial capitalism. Evans argued that the emergence of that economic regime depended on sexual and gender conformity within the nuclear family, on the professionalization of healing practices, on the religious authority of the church, and on the centralization of political economic power in the city.[29] Evans, who moved to San Francisco in 1974 from rural Washington State, began teaching these ideas in a "Faery Circle" that met in his Haight-Ashbury apartment. He advocated the worldwide collectivization of women, homosexuals, the poor, the indigenous, and people of color under a new form of revolutionary socialism that practiced "magic" ("group song, dance, sex, and ecstacy [*sic*]") to reengage each other and the exploited natural world, to "hold themselves together and function in perfect order without prisons, mental hospitals, universities, or the institution of the state."[30] He further argued that these collectives should be prepared to use violent means themselves to resist violent attack.

Evans held that the "most favorable spot for such collective work is the countryside"; however, he recognized that not everyone could escape the city, so he recommended that rural and urban collectives network.[31] This rurally oriented spiritual-political perspective resonated with the Oregon editors of *RFD*. In the Winter 1976 issue of the magazine, they referred to themselves as mostly "faggots," defined in Evans's terms above, and documented the rural Faggots and Class Struggle Conference, including one of the event's magical rituals.[32] Roughly equating covens with collectives, Evans's faggot spirituality lent a spiritual component to the sanctuary practices of collective defense, one which was—in true liberationist form—not invested in religion as a formal institution. Its underground was not furnished by church or state but rather by a network of small, dispersed rural and urban collectives.

I argue that Evans's faggot magic and ritual should be understood as an extension of the gay liberationist antipsychiatry movement, which, as Abram J. Lewis has shown, led to many lesbian feminists and gay liberationists embracing spiritual approaches to well-being rather than purely rational ones.[33] Faggot spirituality was fundamentally political—not an individualistic, self-help form of New Age practice. In fact, magic and ritual, according to Evans, helped various liberationists bond in the alliances necessary to collectivize widely and to withdraw from the state and its institutions. And, as Bay Area Reclaiming Witchcraft founder Starhawk would later write, magic and ritual were also an affective means of conserving the revolutionary energy necessary to sustain a movement.[34] This aspect interested gay liberationists, who were told that their revolution was exhausted. Consonant with other US sanctuary histories, faggot witchcraft posed a spiritual authority that was both considered higher than government authority and intended as an alternative to other oppressive social institutions. Attendees like the Arkansas Sissies took these faggot spiritual practices home to their own networks.

The year 1976 was important for back-to-the-land gay liberation, especially in the Southeast. By that year, the rest of Pyne's Short Mountain collective had left the farm, prompting him to post an ad in *RFD*: "Flying South for the Winter? Solitary faggot needs winter guests. The other (non-gay) members of our group have left me with the goats and cow, on a beautiful middle-Tennessee mountain. Come and visit if you're passin' thru."[35] Fellow gay liberationist, Miami-born Mikel Wilson, had in 1973 bought a tiny, remote Appalachian farm of his own that was perched on the side of North Carolina's Roan Mountain. He remembers (interview, February 22, 2016) naming it Running Water Farm for the continuous flow of mountain water he routed into the kitchen sink with a black plastic pipe. Wilson read Pyne's ad in *RFD* and went to visit Short Mountain in February 1977; the two discussed how they might turn their Appalachian farms to the specific support of the gay community. In a little over a year, Running Water would host a gay liberationist men's gathering, with attendees who were well versed in the political and spiritual sanctuary practices of rural collective defense and faggot spirituality. They started to materialize a southeastern version of Evans's network, a regional underground.

Gathering the Southeastern Network: Regional Terror, Running Water, and Sissie Collectivism

In early 1976, there was really no particular rural site that served this committed function of sanctuary for a large-scale network of back-to-the-land gay liberationists. Arguably, the rural Wolf Creek, Oregon, site of the 1976 Faggots and Class Struggle Conference emerged as a West Coast example of such in that year. In the Southeast, Mikel Wilson's Running Water Farm took on that role in June 1978. Over the course of 1977, the need for lesbian and gay refuge had grown more acute as terror spiked in the wake of the Florida Save Our Children campaign.

Spokesperson Anita Bryant used her media presence in the first half of that year to stoke national homophobic fear over the prospect of homosexuals recruiting the nation's vulnerable children to their perverse lifestyle. In June, when the Save Our Children campaign succeeded by overturning Miami-Dade County's ordinance to prohibit discrimination against homosexuals, many accused Bryant of emboldening homophobic violence. For example, just two weeks after the Miami poll was closed, gay San Francisco gardener Robert Hillsborough was murdered at knifepoint, while one assailant allegedly shouted "Here's one for Anita!" Hillsborough's mother attempted to sue Bryant as responsible for her son's death.[36] Around the same time, New Orleans activists implored city officials to cancel Bryant's Crescent City show because they regarded a rash of local gay suicides as stemming from fear following Bryant's successful campaign.[37] Other cities followed Miami's lead and overturned their laws protecting homosexuals from discrimination. State Senator John Briggs in California began building on Bryant's success to launch his Proposition 6, designed to prohibit openly homosexual teachers from working in public schools. Lesbians and gay men fearfully watched the Moral Majority and the New Right rise from their stages in the political theaters of Florida and California.

In 1978, those gay liberationists embedded in southeastern back-to-the-land contexts began to question the sociopolitical orientation of West Coast *RFD* editors, articulating their own regional perspective in the process. For example, in the Spring 1978 *RFD*, the Arkansas Sissies complained of the magazine's not featuring people of color and wondered whether the increasingly San Francisco–oriented editors were concerned with regions like the Southeast, where white supremacists not only continued to perpetrate violence against people of color but also began to physically attack lesbians and gay men in public spaces.[38] In the next issue, Huntsville, Alabama, bookstore owner Clarence Englebert (later known as Clear) asked the editors to put the word *country* back in the magazine's tagline, implying that *RFD* had shifted to an urban focus that obscured the role of the rural in the publication's culture.[39] In the Fall 1978 issue, Cathy Gross (later Cathy Hope) critiqued the summer *RFD* women's issue for only engaging feminism and women in superficial ways and missing the crucial opportunity to link rural lesbians with gay men within a more thoroughly feminist editorial context.[40] Gross's letter would inspire the region's "sissies."[41]

Historian of the US Right Gillian Frank has shown how the political strategists behind Anita Bryant's campaign were also active in movements against school desegregation and the Equal Rights Amendment (ERA).[42] These southeastern letters to *RFD* editors not only reflected a concern with the increasingly urban, white, male perspective of gay liberation; they also hailed from a region where homophobia was often expressed within the framework of a white supremacy and patriarchy applied through both formal political processes and direct violence. This awareness would inflect the region's future sanctuary practices.

Atlanta hosted the 1978 Southeastern Conference for Lesbians and Gay Men. The site choice was controversial because Georgia had not ratified the ERA. Feminists were concerned about minimizing expenditure in the local economy while still hosting the conference in the state. Cathy Gross, having relocated to Atlanta from Appalachian southwest Virginia in March 1977, helped to organize the conference along with her future roommate Franklin Abbott, a young mental health professional who had attended the first two regional conferences in Chapel Hill, North Carolina. During the planning process, Abbott recalls (interview, December 14, 2015) that he voted with lesbian organizers in favor of some women-only conference sessions that focused, for example, on women's sexuality; angry gay men—outvoted—walked out of the planning session. This reflected a longer tension between the two groups.[43] For example, Saralyn Chesnut and Amanda Gable detail how, in 1972, the Atlanta Lesbian Feminist Alliance (ALFA) formed as a separate entity from the Georgia GLF, mostly over gay men's monopolizing decision-making for that year's Gay Pride Parade.[44] This friction persisted, even six years later, in planning for the Atlanta conference. This unfortunate friction agitated emotions surrounding the southern anti-ERA sentiments Frank describes; it would, however, ultimately also galvanize regional sanctuary practitioners.

The conference brought far-flung back-to-the-land gay liberationists—many of whom had previously only "met" each other through the pages of *RFD*—into a shared political space for the first time. What's more, many of these gay liberationists presented at the conference. Mikel Wilson gave a talk called "Rural Gays." Franklin Abbott delivered "Gay & Angry / Gay & Sad: The Psychological Realities of Oppression." Dimid Hayes, formerly of the Arkansas Sissies and having recently relocated to New Orleans to help form the Louisiana Sissies in Struggle (LaSIS), gave a session titled "Sissie/Queer/Effeminist/Boy Love: The Cutting Edge of the Gay Male Movement." Faygele Ben Miriam, an audacious gay liberationist activist who had met the Arkansas Sissies at the 1976 Faggots and Class Struggle Conference, had recently relocated to Efland, North Carolina, with his activist mother. In true faggot spirit, he presented on "Armed Struggle and Violence."[45]

On Sunday, April 2, during a closing feedback session, lesbian feminists confronted gay male conference leadership with how they had continually hogged microphone time and presentation space. After charging the men with working on their sexism, the women walked out of the session. Most of the men soon followed. However, a small knot of men remained, many of whom were back-to-the-land gay liberationists who had been profoundly shaped by lesbian feminism. Mikel Wilson offered Running Water for a summer solstice event for the men to work on the issues highlighted by lesbian feminist critique.[46]

There were several important ways that the first two 1978 Running Water gatherings continued the back-to-the-land gay liberationist sanctuary practices outlined earlier. First, faggot witchcraft spirituality was part of the experience. Ben Miriam and Hayes had both been at the 1976 Faggots and Class Struggle Conference and also attended the early Running Water gatherings. Hayes recalls (interview, August 3–4, 2016) that Charlie Murphy, who would record the US feminist witchcraft anthem "Burning Times," also attended, performing music from the porch of the farmhouse. Englebert remembers (interview, February 28, 2016) participating in a spiral dance, a ritual central to the Bay Area's Reclaiming Witch-craft tradition. Second, the emphatic use of the term *gathering*, rather than *confer-ence*, the word that was used in Oregon, captured the decentralized, informal struc-ture of the event. Third, the collective household necessary for collective defense and rural-urban networking was held to be important. Reflective of this value, at the very first gathering, Wilson proposed that his farm should be collectivized. Fourth, the culture's primary print platform, *RFD*, migrated to the region with Ben Miriam, from Washington. He'd been tasked with saving the struggling serial, and at the first Running Water gathering, attendees agreed to share editorial and publishing responsibility for the magazine.

In their first year, the Running Water gatherings promised the kind of refuge inspired by Evans's rural-urban faggot collectivization, by lesbian feminist collec-tive defense, and by *RFD*'s critically rustic print practices. This was especially true when the events reflected a recognizably sissie vision. The Arkansas Sissies, and their hived-off collective LaSIS, chose to embrace a *sissie* subjectivity, rather than an overtly faggot one, for several important reasons. The Arkansas Sissies had thought of themselves as *sissies* before attending the 1976 Faggots and Class Struggle Conference, as a way to reflect their genderqueer style and socialist feminist politics learned from the Ozark lesbian collectivist network in which they were originally embedded. Sissie Michael Oglesby wrote a critique of the Oregon conference from a working-class perspective that reflected this regional socialist feminist bent.[47] Fur-ther, when Bay Area gay liberationists of color critiqued the Faggots and Class Strug-gle Conference for both excluding women and rallying around a faggot figure that drew exclusively on white European experiences of colonialism, the southeastern Sis-sies agreed.[48] They preferred *sissie* because it didn't seem to carry the implicitly white associations that *faggot* or *fairy*, drawn from European folklore and history, did, and it seemed all the more important to turn from such associations, given the ubiquitous white supremacy of the Jim Crow region where they lived, and given the civil rights experience of the Ozark socialist feminists within their network. Expressing a commit-ment to cross-racial and cross-gender alliance in their sissie subjectivity, they simulta-neously clarified who should make up their southeastern sanctuary networks.

Following the first June 1978 Running Water gathering, Hayes wrote "A Letter of Action" from the New Orleans French Quarter, over a chicory coffee, and mailed it to gathering attendees. He expressed an urgency provoked by social changes "accompanied by a chaos of . . . new proportions" and a revolutionary pro-cess moving "at a greater speed than any of us cn [*sic*] be/are aware of."[49] He cited spiking fear around increased queer-bashing, striking postal workers, and Bryant's inspiring both a modern "witch hunt" and a New Right. In response to this terror, Hayes advocated collectivizing rural sites as healing spaces, as battery boosts for revolutionary energy and vision, and as refuges "needed to harbor sisters and brothers from destructive forces in the cities." Although the 1978 gatherings were attended by gay liberationist men (and a few children, including John Harris's), Hayes urged attendees to "examine the politics" inherent in thinking of the rural space as owned by young, white gay men. He called for them to actively include other "revolutionary forces" in the region—women, the young and old, transgender people, the working class, and especially, given the racist dynamics of the Southeast, people of color. For Hayes, access to such rural space was too dear to be hoarded by those with advantage.

In the Winter 1978 *RFD*, Hayes wrote the apocalyptic "Poem One, 10/18/ 1978." In it, Hayes made clear his disaffection with the state. The poem confused chronology, declaring the Orwellian, totalitarian 1984 already arrived and the 1976 "Buy—centennial" as the year the liberationist "1970s fell over dead."[50] Although "Poem One" took as a given that democracy under global capitalism was a sham, Hayes closed with a note of revolutionary threat: "(TO KNOW WHAT WE KNOW AND NOT TELL THEM IS A TERRORIST WEAPON)." In the same issue, fellow LaSIS member Robert Reich, known in the network as Stacy Brotherlover, endorsed Hayes's rural collectivist vision but expressed its political scale and form like Arthur Evans, calling for regional "Sissie Networking" of rural and urban "anarcho-effeminist" collectives. The network would allow members to move between houses in order to contribute to different political projects and to minimize waged dependency on any single local economy.[51] Short Mountain's Milo Pyne, who traveled with Englebert to New Orleans to help with this *RFD* issue, contributed a map of the Sissie Network. In true "anarcho-effeminist" form, it pictured just the southeastern region, with no political borders and no names of states, only dots for known sissie collectives and lines for rivers. Tellingly, the names for the saltwater areas surrounding the region were written in Spanish, evoking Pyne's—and US gay liberation's—Cuban Venceremos history and suggesting the Sissie Network's understanding of region and the rural through a transnational lens.[52] For the sissies, collectivism constantly had to imagine ways to skirt the closets posed by state borders. A regional scale not only included both rural and urban collectives but suggested ways that subnational and international borders might be straddled. They were mapping a complex, regional underground in counterpoint to the state.

More tragedy would addle this sissie momentum, though. In the time between writing and publishing the Winter 1978 *RFD*, Harvey Milk was assassinated in San Francisco. The news hit the network hard. The winter was a bleak one. The tiny, mountainous Running Water was almost impossible to reach in winter. To fill the void after the two earlier 1978 gatherings, in February 1979 both New Orleans and Atlanta hosted urban events. Wilson moved to Atlanta that winter, forming a cultural link between Running Water and the Georgia capital. In the Spring 1979 *RFD*, Wilson despaired over the fate of the Appalachian farm but resolved to return, to grow it as the "Running Water Healing Center."[53]

The healing function loomed large for the Atlanta–Running Water axis. Following the murder of Milk, it seemed the times demanded it. Also, in Atlanta, gay liberation fixed on psychological concerns early. Formed in 1971, the Georgia GLF wrote in its statement of purpose that "the term [*gay ghetto*] applies to gay people in a psychological rather than a physical sense."[54] In Atlanta, the gay male leadership from which ALFA splintered included vocal representation by gay religious groups: Catholic Dignity, Episcopalian Integrity, and Lutherans Concerned. This phenomenon lent the culture a pastoral air. Franklin Abbott, central to Atlanta gatherings, shares (interview, December 14, 2015) that he was a mental health professional and had worked with Atlanta lesbian therapist Jane Gavin to establish a gay center and helpline named Tempo.

In the Spring 1979 *RFD*, published from Atlanta, Abbott reflected on the winter gathering in his city: "The city-country analysis that gaymen in the Southeast are developing appears to recognize the need for balancing the formal and the spacious. The country focus, the space and anarchy of the Running Water experiences, and the deliberate setting aside of space by urban gaymen's support circles were all essential in the unfolding of the Atlanta weekend."[55] Drawing upon Buddhism and Taoism, Abbott contended that "in quietly being together, we were healing ourselves and healing each other. The dis-ease we often feel from isolation / competition / imbalance was reduced, leaving us space to explore new possibilities of being together." In Abbott's case, this therapeutic focus did not mean abandonment of radical political action. He ended a poem commemorating the first Running Water gathering by claiming that the experience had rendered him "a better lover / my gentleness refined, aligned / and dangerous."[56] However, Abbott considers (interview, December 14, 2015) his own contribution to the network to be a poetic, vision-based, and therapeutic one, while he lauded LaSIS for giving the regional movement a radical political practice.

Through their *RFD* editorial collaborations, New Orleans's LaSIS and Tennessee's Short Mountain formed another axis in the network. When Short Mountain took the magazine's editorial reins for the Summer 1979 issue, an even more firmly regional gay liberationist political perspective emerged. For one, the issue's two main feature articles were by women. Even though, given the culture's deep debts to lesbian feminism, this move shouldn't have seemed radical, Running Water gatherings—formed out of a charge from lesbian feminists for gay men to pursue separate space to work on their sexism—had so far included only men and their children. Also, since the unfocused Summer 1977 women's issue, which Cathy Gross had critiqued, there had been little effort to prioritize women's voices in *RFD*.

Short Mountain's Summer 1979 issue featured June Boyd writing about her experiences as an incarcerated black woman within a prison system that functioned as part of a white supremacist state, and anarcho-lesbian feminist Kathy Fire critiquing the nuclear power industry.[57] Although Boyd was incarcerated in Muncie, Indiana, her piece complemented the *RFD* series "Brothers behind Bars," which networked imprisoned and free gay liberationists, and by foregrounding prison writing, Boyd implicitly invited readers to map prisons to stress the fact that many *RFD* readers were, in fact, in prisons in the Southeast—in, for example, Memphis, Atlanta, and Appalachian Tennessee. The Short Mountain editors annotated Fire's article with the comment, "Our layout headquarters is in a little old log cabin up in a beautiful holler. We have electricity here, a necessity for a typewriter of this kind. We burn precious few watts, but we are tied in to TVA's nuclear expansion program nonetheless. We are in the heart of an area destined for development, exploitation, and internal colonialism." The text was accompanied by a map of the Southeast with a big inverted triangle bearing a caption: "The biggest power project ever undertaken in America is centered in Middle Tennessee's 'Electric Triangle.'"[58] This issue stressed ways by which the state made the region an instrument of domination and exploitation.

This editorial shift conceived the rural differently: from a space with the capacity to frustrate urban-based state surveillance to a geography uniquely exploited within the political economy via state-funded enterprises like the prison and energy industries. Importantly, the Short Mountain editors' invoking "internal colonialism" further defined their political view as informed, whether directly or indirectly, by black liberation. Hobson has shown how Bay Area gay liberation and lesbian feminism learned from the Black Panthers' concept of internal colonialism.[59] Also, in 1978, Appalachian studies groundbreaker Helen Matthews Lewis had published her analysis of Appalachia as subject to internal colonialism, her own theories influenced by her reading of Frantz Fanon.[60] This Summer 1979 issue of *RFD* focused its back-to-the-land gay liberationist critique more firmly in the Southeast than it had previously. The editors refined their concept of sanctuary to one taking an active political interest in the rural places where sanctuary was performed.

The two axes in the Southeastern Network took on different roles over the course of that summer. Ben Miriam reported that, at the June 1979 gathering, it was decided, after much debate, that Running Water would be a "specifically faggot space; children welcome."[61] Although this decision reflected a continued commitment on the part of gay male attendees to take space and time to work on their sexism, it also coincided with Short Mountain editors' decision to centralize lesbian feminist voices in *RFD*. Hayes's argument in his "Letter to Action," to actively include women (and others) in the sanctuary provided by Running Water, was therefore not realized at the time. A New Orleans sanctuary would be difficult to pull off. Into the summer of 1979, the sissies there contended with police harassment, as they were arrested multiple times on manufactured charges of nudity in view of a public school.[62] The network needed another rural space for sanctuary of the kind Hayes described, but this need became harder to articulate as a national gay rights movement emerged in the wake of Milk's death.

Fairy Tales: Placing Sanctuary in 1980, and Beyond

Two relevant national events occurred in the second half of 1979. One took place over Labor Day weekend: the first Spiritual Conference for Radical Fairies held in Benson, Arizona, at a rural spiritual retreat called Desert Sanctuary.[63] The event was organized by West Coast gay liberationist leaders interested in connecting spirituality to their politics, among them Harry Hay, the cofounder of the Mattachine Society, founded in 1950. The conference shared commonalities with both the Faggots and Class Struggle Conference and the Running Water Farm gatherings in that all three concerned themselves with the intersections of gay liberation, political spirituality, and rural events. Unlike Running Water, the Arizona event drew over two hundred attendees from all over the nation, in part driven there by fears stemming from the recent assassination of Milk and from the upcoming election in 1980. Several from the Southeastern Network attended, inspired by the numbers and comparable liberationist vision. In fact, the LaSIS-Short Mountain editors of *RFD*, back in New Orleans that fall, devoted most of the magazine's pages to documenting the desert event. Their editorial note proclaimed that *RFD* was "now a fairy journal" and referred to the "fairies of LaSIS."[64] However, the editors also riffed on the *RFD* acronym, naming the issue "Returning Forest Darlings," thereby emphasizing that the issue also marked a return from the desert to the work of the Southeastern Network.

The second event was the October 1979 March on Washington for Lesbian and Gay Rights. Ben Miriam, who attended a Philadelphia planning conference for the march, reported that several "felt the conference to be dominated by the New York/San Francisco axis" and "felt it necessary to help form a hinterlands caucus, representing not only rural and small town folk, but even those from big cities other than N.Y. and S.F."[65] *RFD* published a letter from "19 Lesbians and Gay Men from Tennessee," which, among other critiques, recommended rescheduling the march for 1980, implying the event should be framed less as a ten-year Stonewall anniversary than as an intervention on the 1980 presidential elections.[66] LaSIS attended the event, but Sears tells us that a Phillip Pendleton marched with the sissies and commented, "No one I knew went to lobby Congress the next day. Our goal was to overthrow the government, not enter into dialogue with it!"[67] The Southeastern Network's response to the national march indicated that they hewed both to the rural and anti-state components of their sanctuary practice even as the national gay rights movement amplified; however, they also saw a place for themselves in the larger gay liberationist scale which the Radical Fairy conference suggested. It was within this context that formal regional sanctuary practice emerged.

At the 1979 Southeastern Conference for Lesbians and Gay Men in Chapel Hill, Milo Pyne announced the Short Mountain Reinhabitation project, to begin in the spring of 1980. Among the seven who answered his call and came to work on the project were Cathy Gross and Dimid Hayes. With a lesbian feminist resident, Gross and Hayes remember (interview, August 5, 2018), the eight jokingly referred to themselves as "Snow White and the Seven Dwarves" and worked to ready the Short Mountain farm as a place for residence and gathering. Back in New Orleans, with the help of Stacy Brotherlover's accounting background, LaSIS took on fundraising and bookkeeping duties for the project, making Short Mountain the first step toward realizing the sissie networking that they had written of nearly two years before. Looking back, Gross and Hayes remember naturally coming to associate the word *sanctuary* with what they were doing. They held their first gathering on May Day 1980. When several women critiqued the phallic maypole at the heart of the ritual, Gross improvised by linking arms with fellow resident Crazy Owl, replacing the symbolic phallus with the literal bodies of a lesbian feminist and a gay liberationist who had together labored to build the sanctuary. Although Gross and Hayes stayed at Short Mountain for less than six months, their brief residence reflected the sissie practice of serial commitment to collective projects and to circulation within the underground.

In the Fall 1980 issue of *RFD*, Milo Pyne published his "A Faeryist Not-Manifesto." Appearing a decade after Wittman's "Refugees from Amerika," it called for a revival of gay liberationist politics and stated the urgent need for sanctuaries. Like Wittman, Pyne emphasized the importance of alliance with the liberation movements of women and people of color. As examples of such support, he referenced regional gay liberationists' participation in the anti-Klan rallies following the 1979 Greensboro Massacre, carrying signs reading "QUEERS AGAINST RACISM," and he urged extending the work of the "dyke affinity group" called the Spiderworts, who were arrested for occupying the Virginia North Anna nuclear plant. Pyne worried that the national gay rights movement was forgetting the wider and longer-term goals of liberation, which dedicated itself to the overturning of colonialism in all its forms, internal and international.

I argue, though, that Pyne's manifesto registered a twist on the regional concept of sanctuary that preceded it. The first aspect of that twist involved the affective and strategic dimensions of what it might mean to associate sanctuary with a fairy subjectivity, rather than a faggot or sissie one alone. Clearly, the 1979 Arizona conference prompted southeastern gay liberationists to try the word on; however, I read Pyne's use of the word "faeryist" in the title to signal both a place within the wider Radical Faerie culture anchored in the West as well as a regional uniqueness rooted in sissie interpretations. In his manifesto, Pyne invoked sanctuary in the terms of the fairy tale, associating both with wild environments: "We must create sanctuaries for ourselves, for the elves and gnomes, for the trees and flowers, birds, salamanders,

The fairies are the friends of the faggots. They help each other whenever they can. The fairies do not live among the men. They live in trees and caves and bushes. They come out at night to dance and sing. The men know that there are fairies but are not sure if they have seen one or not. Only the faggots have seen them for sure. Sometimes the fairies dance and sing for the faggots and sometimes the faggots dance and sing for the fairies and sometimes, the best times, they dance and sing together.

mitchell/asta

Figure 1. Organizers of the summer 1979 Running Water Farm gathering illustrated their circulated mailing list with an excerpt from Mitchell and Asta's *Faggots & Their Friends between Revolutions*, articulating a relationship between the work of rural sanctuary and liberationist militancy. Running Water Farm mailing list (June 15–17, 1979). Conference—Radical Faeries—"Gatherings" at Running Water, 1979–1981 (Box 1, Folder 6), Gay Spirit Visions records, W127, Archives for Research on Women and Gender, Special Collections and Archives, Georgia State University, Atlanta.

frogs and little furry critters. If the planet dies, we will bear witness and sing the death song. If a species is extinguished, we will avenge it by our love. We must develop and perform ceremonies to strengthen Gaia and confound her enemies— put a hex on TVA."[68] He sounded an ecofeminist and bioregional conservationist note, joining it to Evans's faggot witchcraft. What is also noteworthy, though, is how Pyne conceived magic as a means not only of forming bonds with nature and fellow liberationists, as Evans understood its function, but also to *confound* the state (in this case, the Tennessee Valley Authority, or TVA).

Rural means of confusing the state had been a part of back-to-the-land gay liberation's strategy for years, but doing so in the register of the fairy tale was rather new. Short Mountain Sanctuary residents' ironically identifying with the Snow White story fit that pattern. An announcement for the summer 1979 Running Water gathering included an image and quote (fig. 1) from *The Faggots & Their Friends between Revolutions* (1977) by Larry Mitchell (author) and Ned Asta (illustrator), portraying a circle of dancers in a forest clearing, with a winged figure flying above; the quote read, "The fairies are the friends of the faggots. They help each other whenever they can. The fairies do not live among the men. They live in trees and caves and bushes."[69] Associating fairies with remote, mysterious wilderness uniquely positioned them to provide sanctuary to their faggot friends engaged on the front lines of the revolution. LaSIS furthered this complementarity between the militant faggot and the sanctuarian fairy and wrote in the Summer 1981 *RFD* that "fairies can vanish into the woodwork of corporate paneling or forest trees, leaving hets to figure it out for themselves. Of course Fairies always have to be ready to step in whenever hets begin to endanger our Mother, the Earth."[70] The early southeastern sense of the fairy role was of rural gay liberationists practiced at strategies of confusion, obscurantism, and evasion and situated in the wilderness as keepers of sanctuary for faggot revolutionaries.

A second aspect of the Short Mountain twist on sanctuary involved how Pyne thought of gay liberation in relation to land movements. At the Labor Day 1980 Radical Faerie gathering in Colorado, when Harry Hay urged the attendees to join in establishing rural gay land trusts, someone from Short Mountain shouted that this work was already under way in Tennessee.[71] In his manifesto, Pyne called on gay liberationists to support anticolonial sovereignty movements, specifically mentioning Puerto Rico, US indigenous land movements, Chicana territories at the Mexican border, and New Afrika. Such support begs the question as to what degree those in the Southeastern Network imagined their own sanctuaries as parallel autonomous territories to the US state.[72] I further wonder whether the work of rural *reinhabitation* meant the advent of a more concentrated focus on the *dwelling* of sanctuary stewards, a focus which risked losing sight of highly mobile revolutionaries' need for sanctuary as they circulated through the rural-urban underground.

Certainly, the Southeastern Network didn't achieve all its loftiest goals in terms of sanctuary. For example, Clear Englebert admitted as early as fall 1981 his own "cautionary feelings about the gatherings" due to his sense that their largely white, male culture did not fully interrogate its racism and sexism.[73] Women, such as Gross, were crucial to Short Mountain's formation; in the following years, they remained important to the sanctuary, but their numbers within the culture were relatively small. It also remains unclear how well gathering organizers actively facilitated access to their rural sanctuaries for those who understandably saw its backroads as dangerous routes. For example, Douglas Caulkins mentions an attendee at a 1991 Gay Spirit Visions event (a rural North Carolina gathering culture that succeeded Running Water's) whose black friend grew fearful as they wound deeper into the rural landscape that hosted the event.[74] Planners' vision to the contrary, sanctuary wasn't always evenly accessible.

However, the emergence of Tennessee's Short Mountain Sanctuary from back-to-the-land gay liberationism and southeastern sissie networking signals for historians of sanctuary movements the importance of exploring the tensions between sanctuary as both political practice and place, as short-term tactic (refuge) and longer-term vision (sovereignty). In asking serious questions about the relationship between faggots, sissies, and fairies, these regional gay liberationists worked to theorize the different necessary roles in a sanctuary movement that sought to look away from the capital.

What the Southeastern Network improvised echoed the concerns of A. Naomi Paik for contemporary sanctuary movements in terms of urging them to turn away from the neoliberal state, to withdraw from its infrastructure, and to form alliances across the varied subjectivities in need of refuge. They also drew on a combination of political and spiritual resources, which, as Paik shows, is also typical of the contemporary sanctuary movement. And they continued to address Wittman's concerns with the compromised citizenship lesbians and gay men held, especially when fixed in urban gay "ghettos."

By the summer of 1979, the Southeastern Network had envisioned a sanctuary practice rooted in rural collective defense and in a regional sissie variation on the rural-urban networking of faggot spirituality. Hayes's "A Letter to Action" and Brotherlover's "Sissie Networking" posed the rural-urban network clustered around Running Water gatherings as the circulation system for an underground that could provide refuge for diverse groups in urgent need of sanctuary during the ascendance of the New Right, but which could also nominally mitigate dependence on the state and local economies. This sanctuary format also redefined the collective— away from a model of permanent commitment and more toward that of a serial group marriage by which liberationists changed collectives based on the projects they wanted to complete in a season's stay.

Pyne's map of southeastern sissie networking erased state borders both to prioritize the natural environment and to imagine regional sanctuary transnationally. In the Southeast, this meant turning away from urban centers elsewhere in the country to orient toward a "deeper south," toward the Caribbean and the Venceremos experiences in Cuba, which had already inspired and threatened their gay liberationist revolutionary spirit.[75] Part of this deeper south commitment meant confronting the white supremacist and patriarchal forces sewn into the formal political and social structures of the US Southeast. For Short Mountain, it also meant contending with the internal colonialism that targeted the region's rural areas in the forms of state-backed prison and energy industries, especially in Appalachia. And later, at Short Mountain Sanctuary, its response to internal colonialism included an ecofeminist protection of, and identification with, wilderness, expressed by the trying on of fairy subjectivity.

Finally, the early Running Water gatherings foregrounded the affective elements crucial for collectivizing, for networking sites and alliances, and for sustaining revolutionary energy. Born of a lesbian feminist charge for gay liberationist men to work on their sexism, the gatherings featured men's practice with care labor—with listening, ceding space, lending support, and providing childcare. In their practice of spiritual ritual, as defined by West Coast witchcraft traditions, they forged bonds, celebrated sexuality, and maintained political fire. Such practices echo gay Venceremos veteran Allen Young's claim that gay liberation might offer something unique to revolution: ways of "dealing with the politics of personal relations, and as such [be] the path of personal fulfillment and joy."[76] Within this context, we can also understand how the erotic enabled alliance and therefore, as Abbott poetically asserted, how being a better lover made one both gentle *and* dangerous. Such convictions reflected lesbian feminist thought of the time, particularly Audre Lorde's theory of the erotic, first presented at a conference on women's history in 1978.[77]

These were the components of their planned system of sanctuary built on the principles of lesbian feminist collective defense and faggot spirituality—but oriented rurally, calibrated to a regional scale, and attuned to affective concerns. If, for many of these gay liberationists, their early 1970s Venceremos Brigade experiences shaped their sense of revolution, it is telling, then, to recognize that, roughly ten years later, they applied their sanctuary practice to the aid of gay Cuban refugees detained during the 1980 Mariel boatlifts. An update appeared in the same Fall 1980 issue as Pyne's manifesto, asking readers to shelter any of the roughly six hundred lesbian and gay Cuban refugees—many surely with interests in and skills for rural living—who were detained at the Fort Chaffee military base in rural Arkansas.[78] Although I can't say how many of these lesbian and gay Marielitos might have entered the southeastern sissie network and found homes in its forests or hills, I can say that the suggestion itself rested on a decade's practice of regional back-to-the-land, gay liberationist sanctuary.

Jason Ezell is an assistant professor and the instruction and research coordinator at Loyola University New Orleans's Monroe Library. His research focuses on LGBTQ+ cultural and political history, critical rural studies, and affect.

Notes

1. Wittman, "Refugees from Amerika."
2. Luther Hillman, *Dressing for the Culture Wars*; Stryker, *Transgender History*.
3. Sears, *Rebels, Rubyfruit, and Rhinestones*; the magazine's quoted dedication is from the cover of *RFD* 3 (Spring 1975).
4. Sears, *Rebels, Rubyfruit, and Rhinestones*, 146.
5. Stryker, *Transgender History*.

6. Troxler, "A Rejection."
7. Wittman, "Towards a Gay Tarot."
8. Pyne, "A Faeryist Not-Man-ifesto," 58.
9. Primary research such as this and other oral history interviews come from my dissertation, "Between F° Words."
10. Morgensen, "Arrival at Home," 72.
11. Paik, "Abolitionist Futures."
12. Paik, "Abolitionist Futures," 19.
13. Lekus, "Queer Harvests"; Sears, *Rebels, Rubyfruit, and Rhinestones*.
14. Sears, *Rebels, Rubyfruit, and Rhinestones*.
15. Williams, *Appalachia: A History*.
16. "The Beginning."
17. Sears, *Rebels, Rubyfruit, and Rhinestones*, 144.
18. Herring, *Another Country*, 90.
19. Herring, *Another Country*, 88.
20. Hobson, *Lavender and Red*, 43.
21. Sears, *Rebels, Rubyfruit, and Rhinestones*, 196.
22. Quoted in Sears, *Rebels, Rubyfruit, and Rhinestones*, 348.
23. Charles, *Hoover's War on Gays*.
24. Lord and Zajicek, *The History of the Contemporary Grassroots Women's Movement*. This link between civil rights experience and sexual identity may reflect what historian John Howard argued in *Men Like That*, namely that the conservative coding of civil rights activists as perverse resulted in a heightened politicization of sexual identity in the Southeast.
25. Lord and Zajicek, *The History of the Contemporary Grassroots Women's Movement*; Stephen Vider discusses Mulberry House in his overview of gay liberationist collective households, "'The Ultimate Extension of Gay Community.'"
26. Williams, personal journal.
27. "Sum-Up," 9–10.
28. Hobson, *Lavender and Red*, 74–75.
29. Evans, *Witchcraft and the Gay Counterculture*.
30. Evans, *Witchcraft and the Gay Counterculture*, 148–49. Evans joined a wider set of politicized witchcraft traditions in the 1970s Bay Area, which included Starhawk's ecofeminist *Reclaiming Witchcraft*. Starhawk was trained in the Anderson Feri tradition of witchcraft, which, by its emphasis on feminist ecstasy rather than feminine fertility, was attractive to those with nonconforming sexualities.
31. Evans, *Witchcraft and the Gay Counterculture*, 148.
32. "RFD Collective Statement," 4; Elliot, "Bread & Roses Revisited," 7.
33. Lewis, "'We Are Certain of Our Own Insanity.'"
34. Starhawk, *The Spiral Dance*.
35. Pyne, "Flying South for the Winter?," 44.
36. Clendinen and Nagourney, *Out for Good*.
37. Bryant, "Playboy Interview."
38. Arkansas Sissies, letter to the editors, 4. This letter cited KKK attacks on lesbian and gay bars. The Arkansas Sissies also attended a rally for Dessie Woods, a black Georgia woman jailed for killing her would-be rapist, according to Dennis Williams's personal journal, 1977–78.
39. Englebert, letter to the editor.

40. Gross, letter to the editor.

41. Gross's letter is cited in several of the sissie statements in "Sissie."

42. Frank, "'The Civil Rights of Parents.'"

43. For more on Georgia's role in regional lesbian and gay activist organizing, see Sears, *Rebels, Rubyfruit, and Rhinestones.*

44. Chesnut and Gable, "'Women Ran It.'"

45. Third Southeastern Conference for Lesbians and Gay Men, conference pamphlet.

46. Adding a religious tenor to this offer, Abbott describes Wilson as "one of the wild creatures who had come down to the conference." "Mikel was a weaver. He wove all his own clothes. He had a long beard. He wore a tunic that he had woven out of rough wool and carried a staff, and looked like an Old Testament prophet." Franklin Abbott, interview.

47. Oglesby, "A Critique of the Conference."

48. Williams, personal journal.

49. Hayes, "A Letter of Action."

50. Hayes, "Poem One."

51. Brotherlover, "Sissie Networking." For more on effeminism, see Dansky, Knoebel, and Pitchford, "The Effeminist Manifesto."

52. Lekus argues in "Queer Harvests" that such decentralized, often rural gay collectives were the most immediate manifestation of gay liberationist Venceremos experiences in the United States. In the 1980s, Pyne, and others in the network and in *RFD*, engaged with Central American culture and politics in ways which support Hobson's argument in *Lavender and Red* for a longer gay liberation committed to transnational political activity, especially in Central America.

53. Wilson, "A Dreamer's Reality."

54. Cutler, "Statement of Purpose of the Georgia GLF."

55. Abbott, "Space for Support." The portmanteau term *gaymen* was used in the region to sometimes refer to gay men of a liberal rather than liberationist political bent and other times as a word for male gay liberationists who did not identify as sissies.

56. Abbott, "Ascent, Lament, and Admonition."

57. Boyd, "June Boyd: A Black Strong Woman"; Fire, "Nuclear Realities, Part One."

58. *RFD* editorial comment.

59. Hobson, *Lavender and Red.*

60. Lewis, Johnson, and Askins, *Colonialism in America*; and Lewis, *Helen Matthews Lewis.*

61. Running Water Farm Gathering flier (for September 21–23, 1979).

62. "LaSIS Update."

63. For a description of the event, see Timmons, *The Trouble with Harry Hay.*

64. *RFD* editorial note.

65. Ben Miriam, *RFD* National March update.

66. "19 Lesbians and Gay Men from Tennessee," 3.

67. Sears, *Rebels, Rubyfruit, and Rhinestones*, 306.

68. Pyne, "A Faeryist Not-Man-ifesto," 5.

69. Mitchell and Asta, *The Faggots & Their Friends*; Running Water Farm mailing list.

70. LaSIS, "On the Question of Names," 16.

71. Timmons, *The Trouble with Harry Hay*, 275.

72. Morgensen has called critical attention to how Radical Faerie sanctuaries risk a queer reproduction of settler colonialism in "Arrival at Home" and *Spaces between Us.*

73. Englebert, "Profiles and Interviews."

74. Caulkins, "Running Water Farm."
75. This places this southeastern back-to-the-land gay liberationist history in dialogue with other such transnational LGBT+ histories focused on the Caribbean and Central America, such as those of Hobson, Lekus, and Julio Capo Jr.'s *Welcome to Fairyland*. The phrase "deeper south" comes from Lekus's essay on the gay Cuban Venceremos experience.
76. Young, "The Cuban Revolution and Gay Liberation," 207. For another view on how black liberation offered such tools to gay liberation, see Ongiri, "Prisoner of Love."
77. Lorde, "The Uses of the Erotic."
78. "Sponsoring Cuban Refugees Update"; I learned of these Fort Chaffee refugees' difficult experiences from Edwin Unzalu's undergraduate thesis, "The Cuban Exodus of 1980."

References

Abbott, Franklin. "Ascent, Lament, and Admonition." In *Mortal Love: Selected Poems*. Liberty, TN: RFD Press, 1999.

Abbott, Franklin. Interview by Wesley Chenault, Atlanta, GA, September 30, 2011. Social Change Collection. Special Collections and Archives, Georgia State University, Atlanta.

Abbott, Franklin. "Space for Support." *RFD* 19 (Spring 1979): 7.

Arkansas Sissies. Letter to the editor. *RFD* 15 (Spring 1978): 4.

"The Beginning." *The Farm Community*, November 14, 2018. http://thefarmcommunity.com /the-beginning/.

Ben Miriam, Faygele. *RFD* National March Update. *RFD* 19 (Spring 1979): 4.

Boyd, June. "June Boyd: A Black Strong Woman." *RFD* 20 (Summer 1979): 4.

Brotherlover, Stacy (Robert Reich). "Sissie Networking." *RFD* 18 (Winter 1978): 20.

Bryant, Anita. "Playboy Interview." Interviewed by Ken Kelley. *Playboy*, May 1978, 73–96.

Capo, Julio, Jr. *Welcome to Fairyland: Queer Miami before 1940*. Chapel Hill: University of North Carolina Press, 2017.

Caulkins, Douglas B. "Running Water Farm." 2010 GSV Letters and Magazine Articles, Gay Spirit Visions Records, Archives for Research on Women and Gender, Special Collections and Archives, Georgia State University, Atlanta.

Charles, Douglas M. *Hoover's War on Gays: Exposing the FBI's 'Sex Deviates' Program*. Lawrence: University Press of Kansas, 2015.

Chesnut, Saralyn, and Amanda C. Gable. "'Women Ran It': Charis Books and More and Atlanta's Lesbian-Feminist Community, 1971–1981." In *Carryin' On in the Lesbian and Gay South*, edited by John Howard, 241–84. New York: New York University Press, 1997.

Clendinen, Dudley, and Adam Nagourney. *Out for Good: The Struggle to Build a Gay Rights Movement in America*. New York: Simon and Schuster, 1999.

Cutler, William. "Statement of Purpose of the Georgia GLF." *Gay Good Times*, newspaper clipping, March 8, 1971. Atlanta Lesbian Feminist Alliance Papers, Box 15, Gay Liberation Front, Folder 36, David M. Rubenstein Rare Book and Manuscript Collection, Duke University.

Dansky, Steven, John Knoebel, and Kenneth Pitchford. "The Effeminist Manifesto." In *We Are Everywhere: A Historical Sourcebook for Gay and Lesbian Politics*, edited by Mark Blasius and Shane Phelan, 435–38. New York: Routledge, 1997.

Elliot, Jai D. "Bread & Roses Revisited." *RFD* 10 (Winter 1976): 7.

Englebert, Clarence (Clear). Letter to the editor. *RFD* 16 (Summer 1978): 3.

Englebert, Clarence (Clear). "Profiles and Interviews: A Visit with Clear Englebert in S.E. Tennessee." *RFD* 28 (Fall 1981): 50–52.

Evans, Arthur. *Witchcraft and the Gay Counterculture.* Boston: Fag Rag Books, 1978.

Ezell, Samuel Jason. "Between F° Words: Rural & Gay Liberationist Refrains in the Southeast, 1970–1981." PhD diss., University of Maryland, College Park, 2017.

Frank, Gillian. "'The Civil Rights of Parents': Race and Conservative Politics in Anita Bryant's Campaign against Gay Rights in 1970s Florida." *Journal of the History of Sexuality* 22, no. 1 (2013): 126–60.

Gross, Cathy (Hope). Letter to the editor. *RFD* 17 (Fall 1978): 10.

Hayes, Dimid. "A Letter of Action" (unpublished). Personal collection of Dimid Hayes.

Hayes, Dimid. "Poem One, 10/18/1978." *RFD* 18 (Winter 1978): 7.

Herring, Scott. *Another Country: Queer Anti-Urbanism.* New York: New York University Press, 2010.

Hobson, Emily K. *Lavender and Red: Liberation and Solidarity in the Gay and Lesbian Left.* Oakland: University of California Press, 2016.

Howard, John. *Men Like That: A Southern Queer History.* Chicago: University of Chicago Press, 1999.

LaSIS. "On the Question of Names." *RFD* 27 (Summer 1981): 14–16.

"LaSIS Update." *RFD* 20 (Summer 1979): 3.

Lekus, Ian. "Queer Harvests: Homosexuality, the U.S. New Left, and the Venceremos Brigades to Cuba." *Radical History Review* 89 (2004): 57–91.

Lewis, Abram J. "'We Are Certain of Our Own Insanity': Antipsychiatry and the Gay Liberation Movement, 1968–1980." *Journal of the History of Sexuality* 25, no. 1 (2016): 83–113.

Lewis, Helen Matthews. *Helen Matthews Lewis: Living Social Justice in Appalachia.* Lexington: University Press of Kentucky, 2012.

Lewis, Helen Matthews, Linda Johnson, and Donald Askins. *Colonialism in Modern America: The Appalachian Case.* Boone, NC: Appalachian Consortium Press, 1978.

Lord, Allyn, and Anna M. Zajicek. *The History of the Contemporary Grassroots Women's Movement in Northwest Arkansas, 1970–2000.* Fayetteville: University of Arkansas Press, 2000.

Lorde, Audre. "Uses of the Erotic: The Erotic as Power." In *Sister Outsider,* 53–59. Freedom, CA: Crossing Press, 1984.

Luther Hillman, Betty. *Dressing for the Culture Wars: Style and the Politics of Self-Presentation in the 1960s and 1970s.* Lincoln: University of Nebraska Press, 2015.

Mitchell, Larry, and Ned Asta. *The Faggots & Their Friends between Revolutions.* New York: Calamus Books, 1977.

Morgensen, Scott Lauria. "Arrival at Home: Radical Faerie Configurations of Sexuality and Place." *GLQ: A Journal of Lesbian and Gay Studies* 15, no. 1 (2009): 67–96.

Morgensen, Scott Lauria. *Spaces between Us: Queer Settler Colonialism and Indigenous Decolonization.* Minneapolis: University of Minnesota Press, 2011.

"19 Lesbians and Gay Men from Tennessee" (letter). *RFD* 20 (Summer 1979): 3.

Oglesby, Michael. "A Critique of the Conference." *RFD* 10 (Winter 1976): 18–19.

Ongiri, Amy Abugo. "Prisoner of Love: Affiliation, Sexuality, and the Black Panther Party." *Journal of African American History* 94, no. 1 (2009): 69–86.

Paik, A. Naomi. "Abolitionist Futures and the U.S. Sanctuary Movement." *Race and Class* 59, no. 2 (2017): 3–25. doi.org/10.1177/0306396817717858.

Pyne, Milo. "A Faeryist Not-Man-ifesto." *RFD* 25 (Fall/Winter 1980): 56–58.

Pyne, Milo. "Flying South for the Winter?" *RFD* 10 (Winter 1976): 44.

"RFD Collective Statement." *RFD* 10 (Winter 1976): 4.

RFD editorial comment. *RFD* 20 (Summer 1979): 16.

RFD editorial note. *RFD* 22 (Winter 1979): inside cover.

Running Water Farm Gathering flier (for September 21–23, 1979). Conference—Radical Faeries—"Gatherings" at Running Water, 1979–1981 (Box 1, Folder 6), Gay Spirit Visions records, W127, Archives for Research on Women and Gender, Special Collections and Archives, Georgia State University, Atlanta.

Running Water Farm mailing list (June 15–17, 1979). Conference—Radical Faeries—"Gatherings" at Running Water, 1979–1981 (Box 1, Folder 6), Gay Spirit Visions records, W127, Archives for Research on Women and Gender, Special Collections and Archives, Georgia State University, Atlanta.

Sears, James T. *Rebels, Rubyfruit, and Rhinestones: Queering Space in the Stonewall South.* New Brunswick, NJ: Rutgers University Press, 2001.

"Sissie." *RFD* 18 (Winter 1978): 4–5.

"Sponsoring Cuban Refugees Update." *RFD* 25 (Fall/Winter 1980): 5.

Starhawk. *The Spiral Dance: A Rebirth of the Ancient Religion of the Great Goddess.* New York: Harper, 1979.

Stryker, Susan. *Transgender History.* Berkeley, CA: Seal Press, 2008.

"Sum-Up." *Morning Due: A Journal of Men against Sexism* 2, no. 6 (1976): 4–10. Special issue: A Conference Report: Faggots and Class Struggle. https://itwascuriosity.files.wordpress.com/2012/12/conference-report-faggots-and-class-struggle.pdf.

Third Southeastern Conference for Lesbians and Gay Men, conference pamphlet. Atlanta Lesbian Feminist Alliance Papers Box 16, Southeast Gay Coalition, Folder 3. David M. Rubenstein Rare Book and Manuscript Library, Duke University.

Timmons, Stuart. *The Trouble with Harry Hay: Founder of the Modern Gay Movement.* New York: Allyson Books, 1990.

Troxler, Allan. "A Rejection." *RFD* 1 (Fall 1974): 15.

Unzalu, Edwin. "The Cuban Exodus of 1980: The Stories and News Coverage of the Undesirables." Undergraduate honors thesis, Loyola University New Orleans, 2017. http://www.louisianadigitallibrary.org/islandora/object/loyno-etd%3A243.

Vider, Stephen. "'The Ultimate Extension of Gay Community': Communal Living and Gay Liberation in the 1970s." *Gender and History* 27, no. 3 (2015): 865–81.

Williams, Dennis (Melba'son). Personal journal, 1977–78 (unpublished), personal collection of Dimid Hayes.

Williams, John Alexander. *Appalachia: A History.* New edition. Chapel Hill: University of North Carolina Press, 2002.

Wilson, Mikel. "A Dreamer's Reality." *RFD* 19 (Spring 1979): 5.

Wittman, Carl. "Refugees from Amerika: A Gay Manifesto." *History Is a Weapon*, November 14, 2018. www.historyisaweapon.com/defcon1/wittmanmanifesto.html.

Wittman, Carl. "Towards a Gay Tarot." *RFD* 2 (Winter 1974): 32–37.

Young, Allen. "The Cuban Revolution and Gay Liberation." In *Out of the Closets: Voices of Gay Liberation*, edited by Karla Jay and Allen Young, 206–7. 20th anniversary ed. New York: New York University Press, 1992.

From Sanctuary to Safe Space

Gay and Lesbian Police-Reform Activism in Los Angeles

Treva Ellison

In this article, I historicize gay police-reform activism in Los Angeles to outline the production of safe space from a politics of sanctuary, following A. Naomi Paik's articulation of a politics of sanctuary as indexing a range of antiviolence efforts that challenge the bounds of citizenship using civil disobedience, advocacy, and legal and policy activism.[1] Sanctuary politics deform and reform dominant boundaries of belonging in order to lodge a demand for inclusion that requires dominant structures, paradigms, and practices of governance to qualitatively change. In that sense, sanctuary politics can be understood as a trajectory of antiviolence organizing, and gay and lesbian police reform can be read as an instantiation of sanctuary politics. Considering gay and lesbian police-reform politics in Los Angeles offers a radical approach to the history of sanctuary that opens the space to think across the disciplinary and discursive bounds that often separate historiographies of antiviolence organizing from what is more normatively understood as "the sanctuary movement." In the first part of this article, drawing from sanctuary literature, I will demonstrate how gay and lesbian police-reform activists enacted a politics of sanctuary by (1) protesting laws deemed unjust, using the moral authority of religious institutions to intervene in common sense or public discourse;[2] (2) building identity-based advocacy institutions that protect and define an injured group;[3] (3) devising mechanisms

Radical History Review

Issue 135 (October 2019)   DOI 10.1215/01636545-7607845

© 2019 by MARHO: The Radical Historians' Organization, Inc.

95

to subvert the legal system and coming up with protection systems;[4] and (4) creating territory within the material and political landscape of Los Angeles.[5]

Thinking about a politics of sanctuary in relationship to gay and lesbian police-reform efforts is informed by both the historical and ethnographic work done on the sanctuary movement and abolitionist historiographies of antiviolence activism that consider how the production of relational differential value flows through identity-based and neighborhood politics.[6] Relational differential value as a concept asks us to consider how social value is contoured through the expansion of criminalization and punishment. Racism, or "the state-sanctioned and/or extralegal production and exploitation of group-differentiation vulnerability to premature death,"[7] and race, the political, ethical, legal, and symbolic arsenal produced through racism, are the primary methods of producing social value. In her study of racialization, criminality, and the production of social value in US politics and culture, Lisa Marie Cacho argues that recuperating social value in US political and juridical discourse *requires* the reproduction of disavowed otherness, a condition of being surplus to legality and legal protection. Disavowed otherness highlights how the re-articulation of social deviance through violence and punishment acts a mechanism of class composition through the terms of racial capitalism.[8] Relational differential value as a concept outlines how claims for rights and political protection are subtended by both criminalization and the preservation of group difference as an undergirding ideology of social and spatial organization. Dynamic abolitionist approaches have to continually reckon with relational differential value when interfacing with juridical power. How do we craft political demands for protection and safety that do not condemn others to vulnerability to premature death? How do we use state capacity without reconstructing racial enclosures?[8]

Sanctuary politics have historically functioned to define and criticize premature death and name and challenge the systems that support it. When sanctuary politics are transcoded into safe space, however, the impetus to protect people from extralegal and state-sanctioned vulnerability to premature death becomes entwined with the reproduction of relational differential value.[9] There are several moves that highlight the transformation of a politics of sanctuary into the production of safe space. I will highlight three of these moves: the move from networks of struggle to resegmented populations, the move from spaces of dependence to racial enclosures, and the move from analogized suffering to protected status. In the second part of this essay, I will show how these moves are evinced in the trajectory of gay and lesbian police-reform efforts in Los Angeles in the context of the transition from military Keynesianism to post-Keynesian militarism.

Rather than offering a normative history of gay police-reform activism or the sanctuary movement in Los Angeles, which have both already been done, my approach expands our understanding of the interplay between neighborhood politics, policing, and the reterritorialization of the welfare state. The reterritorialization of the welfare state at the national and county levels works alongside LAPD (Los Angeles Police Department) community-policing strategies to entwine the politics of solidarity with the impetus to articulate oneself as a minoritized group. The effect of this is the preservation of race as a mode of sociospatial differentiation and the preservation of the discretionary power of the police. Systems of relational differential value adapt to and incorporate oppositional strategies of power into their domains. As racial capitalism innovates, so too must abolitionist strategies meant to oppose the violent imposition of relational differential value.

The Sanctuary Politics of Gay and Lesbian Police Reform

Police targeting of gay and lesbian people began to increase in Los Angeles in 1950. Efforts to contain gay and lesbian sociality were often headed by the LAPD's vice squad, which before the 1950s refined its tactics of violence, harassment, and abuse in what is now known as South Central throughout the late 1930s and 1940s, when Black migration to Los Angeles rose dramatically.[10] LAPD vice squad officers often made arrests based on the penal codes for lewd vagrancy, sex perversion, and an constellation of prostitution-related penal codes: offering, solicitation, and facilitation.[11] The earliest attempt to address antigay policing, the Citizens' Committee to Outlaw Entrapment (CCOE), was started by members of the Los Angeles chapter of the Mattachine Society in the spring of 1952, in response to increased arrests in parks and clubs for lewd vagrancy and LAPD vice squad entrapment tactics, after Mattachine member Dale Jennings was arrested for lewd vagrancy in MacArthur Park. Mattachine members created the CCOE as the public face of the campaign to raise awareness and funds for Jennings's legal defense. Jennings refused to accept a plea bargain and admitted to being a homosexual but refused to admit that he had committed a crime. After the jury remained deadlocked for ten days, the judge dismissed the charges. This was an unprecedented victory, especially in the homophobic climate of the 1950s that linked homosexuality to the threat of communism. Mattachine published news of the legal victory, emphasizing that the victory was not just for homosexuals but for "all citizens interested in equal justice under the law."[12] The society made connections between antigay and racist policing, citing a case of LAPD vice officers shooting teenager William Rubio in the course of trying to entrap Rubio and four of his friends in a public restroom.[13] As news of the legal victory grew, Mattachine ranks quickly swelled. However, rumors that the five founders had communist ties and complaints of the secrecy of the organizational structure forced the founders and member John Gruber out of the organization.[14] The excision of these members ended the tentative relationship with the Civil Rights Congress that CCOE had been building around the issue of police harassment. The fragmentation of Mattachine around communism, and anticommunism in general, stymied the development of antiracism in gay and lesbian politics and an organized gay and lesbian left until the mid-1970s. Anticommunism also forestalled the development of gay and lesbian organizing in response to policing until the late 1960s. The general trajectory of gay and lesbian police reform from the late 1960s onward reflects what has already been documented in historical accounts of gay and lesbian organizing against criminalization in the United States between the late 1960s and 1980s.[15] This literature emphasizes that gay and lesbian activist efforts addressed at policing often evolved in proximity and coalition with antiracist social movements, and eventually taper off between the late 1970s and 1980s as social attitudes and local and national policing priorities change.

Stonewall-era efforts at police reform in Los Angeles grew in response to LAPD raids, harassments, and murders. Gay and lesbian Angelenos formed spaces of dependence, or "those more-or-less localized social relations upon which we depend for the realization of essential interests,"[16] to create sanctuary for gay and lesbian life. These organizations included US Mission, a gay religious service organization founded in 1962; Homophile Effort for Legal Protection (HELP), an AAA-style bail and bar protection service established in 1968 that grew to address police harassment of gay bars, particularly venues that catered to the leather community; Gay Liberation Front, the Los Angeles chapter of the national organization established in 1969; Gay Community Alliance (GCA), a fraternal political lobby and direct action caucus established in 1971; and the Gay Community Services Center, established in 1969, now the LA Gay and Lesbian Center, one of the oldest and largest LGBT nonprofit organizations in the world. No single gay and lesbian police-reform organization can claim responsibility for a decisive victory against LAPD vice policing. Instead, gay and lesbian activists decriminalized gay and lesbian identity by enacting a politics of sanctuary that included (1) protesting laws deemed unjust, using the moral authority of religious institutes to intervene in common sense or public discourse; (2) building identity-based advocacy institutions and defining and articulating an identity-based group that was being targeted by the state; (3) devising mechanisms to subvert the legal system, coming up with protection systems; and (4) creating gay territory within the material and political landscape of Los Angeles.

Protesting Laws Deemed Unjust and Abuses of Power, Using the Moral Authority
of Religious Institutions and the Trope of Innocence to Intervene in Common
Sense or Public Discourse

We can witness how these organizations formed spaces of dependence in the way they responded to spectacular acts of violence such as the murders of Howard Efland, a Jewish gay man who was beaten to death by vice cops in 1969, and Larry Laverne Turner, a Black, gender-nonconforming person who was shot and killed by undercover LAPD vice officers in 1970, on the anniversary of Efland's murder.[17] These two murders were galvanizing events that brought gay and lesbian activists together around the issue of police reform.

Hours after Larry Laverne Turner was pronounced dead, 200 to 250 protestors, unaware of Turner's murder and led by several gay and lesbian organizations including Gay Liberation Front, US Mission, and Metropolitan Community
Church, marched from Civic Center Plaza to the downtown LAPD headquarters,
demanding government intervention into vice policing. The mobilization was
planned to commemorate Efland's 1969 murder. After Turner's murder was made
public, the Reverend Robert Humphries of US Mission reached out to Turner's
family and held a special memorial service for Turner (as he had done for Efland),
which Turner's family attended. US Mission also held a service for Efland, whose
family denied that he was gay and obfuscated how he died at the service they held
for him. Humphries claimed Turner as a "homosexual brother" in printed materials
like flyers and press releases. In both public statements and press releases from US
Mission, the critique of criminalization focused on the uniqueness of sexual difference and the narrative of victimless crimes. "His only crime was love," was repeatedly invoked by Rev. Bob Humphries in public speeches and press statements made
about both Turner and Efland.[18]

US Mission used its designation as a religious institution to argue that antigay
vice policies reflected only a subset of religious beliefs and thus violated their right
to religious freedom as a queer-friendly church.[19] US Mission contributed to police-
reform efforts by raising public awareness around the deaths of several gay and
queer people who were murdered by the LAPD between 1969 and 1971. US Mission issued press releases for each murder, narrating the events surrounding the
deaths. Activists used testimony in order to expose the violence of LAPD vice
policing and also to highlight the paradigm of erasure that circumscribed anti-
queer police violence. US Mission couched its critique of vice policing in the rhetoric of self-expression and individual rights. It deployed refuge as an outward-facing
narrative to appeal to people who fell outside the purview of family-oriented social
services. US Mission also worked to transform everyday homophobia by writing and
publishing gay religious tracts for public dissemination. To US Mission, vice policing
worked to socially stigmatize gays and lesbians and alienate them from civil society.
Alienation from civil society, in Humphries's view, increased gay and lesbian people's vulnerability to poverty and antisocial behavior. For US Mission, ending vice
policing was the first step in creating an environment where gays and lesbians had
the freedom of self-expression and could therefore pursue self-actualization without
social ostracism. US Mission's work made a decisive connection between the politics
of sanctuary and the infrastructure and tax status of religious organizations.

While gay liberal organizations were beginning to focus their efforts against
policing in Hollywood, and after setting up their call line, Gay Liberation Front
(GLF) members began to receive complaints about homophobic policing in the
Rampart division and began to organize there in addition to Hollywood. To commemorate the LAPD murders of Howard Efland, LaVerne Turner, and Virginia

Gallegos, GLF organized a march on March 7, 1971, asking participants to bring a small tin can and pencil to make noise as a part of an exorcism, designed to levitate the Rampart division police station "at least several feet in the air."[20] Marchers walked from MacArthur Park to the Rampart station in a procession, carrying floral wreathes and a pig's head on a silver platter.

Gay Community Alliance (GCA) used direct protest to challenge the LAPD more than any other gay police-reform organization. Members claimed Hollywood as gay territory, frequently using Hollywood High as a rallying point for marches and rallies against LAPD vice policing. When GCA was first founded, they worked with Homophile Effort for Legal Protection (HELP) to compile information on police harassment of gay people and gay establishments. GCA members sought to increase police accountability to the gay community by regularly attending LAPD Police Commission meetings and filing grievances at those meetings based on the information they collected. In October 1973, GCA's persistence paid off when the Los Angeles Police Commission ruled that it would now schedule special meetings, open to the public, where a group spokesperson could file grievances on behalf of individual members of that group. The ruling, supported by Mayor Tom Bradley, was described by David Glascock, former GCA president, as "a victory for all minorities with gay liberation in the vanguard."[21] By 1972, GCA boasted of "having involved over 4000 gay people in the Los Angeles area in politics,"[22] in a letter campaign aimed at building relationships with local and national politicians. In the letter, GCA members distanced themselves from the more confrontational gay liberationist crowd: "Though we oppose anti-homosexual policies by every appropriate means, we are not inflexibly anti-police or anti-establishment."[23] GCA eschewed nonprofit status and service provision so it could focus on political campaigning, but it relied on the Metropolitan Community Church for hosting all of its public events, meetings, and forums.

Building Identity-Based Political Advocacy Institutions to Protect a Defined Group That Was Being Targeted by the State
US Mission was started by members of a gay religious coterie called Order of the Androgyne, headed primarily by white gay men including Morris Kight and Pat Rocco. Kight's and Rocco's involvement is notable because Kight was a founding member of Gay Liberation Front Los Angeles, and both Kight and Rocco were a part of the formation of the Gay Community Services Center. By 1970, US Mission was expanding its aid program into San Francisco. After 1972, US Mission recedes as a visible presence in the struggle to reform vice policing in Los Angeles. However it provided a vital organizational hub in the beginnings of gay organizing around vice policing in Los Angeles at a time when other gay liberal organizations and containers for organizing, like the Gay Community Services Center, were still in their formative stages.

Gay Community Alliance (GCA) was founded in 1971 out of frustration over the consistent failure of the Brown Bill, which would have legalized all consenting adult sexual behavior. GCA members sought to create a group focused solely on building gay political power. They defined the scope of their work early on, saying that they were "Activist, Political, Male-Oriented, Educational, Local, and Fraternal."[24] In their call to action, members write, "GCA is Male-Oriented. Focusing on the pressing legal and political needs of male homosexuals and seeking a social atmosphere liberating to males, but GCA is sympathetic to the separate problems of Gay Women and Transsexuals."[25] GCA started a political forum in 1971, inviting city and state politicians and lawyers to dialogue with the gay public about gay civil rights, and educating members about their rights and what to do in case of arrest. Because it eschewed nonprofit status, GCA was able to lobby for political candidates. For the 1973 city elections, GCA endorsed Tom Bradley for mayor, Burt Pines for city attorney, and Robert Stevenson for city council in District 13. GCA also endorsed a slate of candidates for the Board of Education and Board of Trustees in City Council District 3. Both HELP and GCA supported Pines for city attorney and vetted him through the GCA political forum. Pines was an attractive candidate to gay liberal organizations because he promised to minimize prosecution of nonviolent sex crimes arrests if elected. Once elected, Pines did in fact go on record and say that he planned to shift the priorities of the city attorney's office in relation to gay-related arrests.[26] While it had a short organizational lifespan, GCA formed an ardent force of nonviolent direct action against the LAPD that often worked in conjunction with organizations like HELP and the Gay Community Service Center, which focused more on building membership and service provision in the early 1970s. Incomplete records make it difficult to know how many members GCA had at its height, although undated membership rosters list forty different names and addresses. Gay Community Alliance devoted a significant amount of time to building gay political power.

After Pines's 1973 election, LAPD arrests for lewd conduct, sex perversion (fellatio), and sodomy did decrease, from 3,783 arrests in 1973 to 2,950 arrests in 1974. The dispositions of sex crimes arrests also became less severe, as felony dispositions decreased from 304 to 277 between 1973 and 1974. Sex crimes arrests continued to decrease throughout the 1970s and rise again in the 1980s. However, for any given year between 1970 and 1990, prostitution arrests always exceeded sex crimes arrests, particularly in Hollywood, as gay and lesbian organizations began to claim West Hollywood and Hollywood as "Gay LA." Furthermore, in the years leading up to Pines's election to city attorney, arrests for sex crimes downtown exceeded arrests in Hollywood (734 and 400, respectively). It is only after 1973, as Hollywood was being territorialized as a gay district, that arrests for sex crimes in Hollywood exceeded sex crimes arrests in the downtown and Rampart divisions.

By 1973, after two years of existence, the Gay Community Services Center (GCSC) had at least thirteen ongoing daily social service programs, including emergency and temporary housing, a venereal disease clinic, a women's health clinic, couples and individual counseling, drug and alcohol counseling, employment and job training programs for women and trans people, a "Systems Assistance Project" or reentry program for formerly incarcerated people that included job training and welfare counseling, and a program for gay and lesbian runaways who found themselves stranded in Hollywood. Gay and lesbian police-reform activists relied on the language of racialized and gendered risk and precarity secured through the protected categories that emerged from the 1964 Civil Rights Act to argue for funding dollars.

Gay police-reform organizations were able to convince everyday people, other organizations, and city officials that gays and lesbians formed a unique cluster of risk and reward that should be included in the political and economic milieu of community and nonprofit governance. As a result, some of these organizations, like US Mission and the GCSC, now the Los Angeles Gay and Lesbian Center, were able to build themselves into large, long-standing institutions. Other organizations, like HELP and GCA, rose and fell as internal organizational goals became less clear. The demands, framing, and internal struggles of these organizations illustrate how policing forced people to posit the connections between race, gender, and sexuality and struggle over the meaning and function of gay and lesbian identity and politics.

Devising Mechanisms to Subvert Legal Systems, Coming up with Protection Systems
In August 1968, LAPD vice officers raided the Patch, a gay bar in Wilmington near Los Angeles Harbor, demanding to see identification and arresting patrons. Bar owner Lee Glaze took to the stage and encouraged patrons to resist the LAPD's tactics, saying, "It's not a crime to be in a gay bar."[27] A rally ensued, with patrons chanting, "We're Americans, too!"[28] Patrons then proceeded to march to the Harbor Division police station after obtaining flowers from a local florist, also a patron of the Patch, demanding the release of all those arrested. After the raid on the Patch, several patrons, frustrated with the lack of momentum and political action around police entrapment, formed Homophile Effort for Legal Protection (HELP) in 1970. HELP was an AAA-type service for gay men, gay and lesbian bars, and increasingly members of and bars associated with the leather community. The bail service included a twenty-four-hour call line, bail service, and legal referrals. The annual rate for individual HELP membership in 1971 was $15. The benefits of membership included twenty-four-hour free legal advice on any subject, and immediate bail for any misdemeanor charges and/or the felony charges of oral copulation or sodomy. Bail was required to be repaid by the individual to HELP at a rate of 10 percent per week, interest free. If an individual member was arrested in a member establishment, then bail was provided for free. Later on, HELP members amended membership rules and created two forms of individual membership: general

membership ($10 annual fee) and voting membership ($60 annual fee). Meeting minutes from March 28, 1973, indicate that HELP membership reached an all-time high that year, with 750 paid members.[29] HELP also organized the Tavern and Guild Association; bars and taverns could pay a membership fee of $60 that included free legal assistance for issues like licensing and permits and legal assistance for any bar patron arrested in the establishment, even if the individual was not a HELP member. The bar membership also designated the owner or manager as an individual member and covered up to four on-duty employees. For a fee of $100, bars and taverns could enjoy all of the above benefits plus coverage for up to nine on-duty employees.[30]

When HELP first began offering these services, it had six member establishments, and by the beginning of the next year, bar and tavern membership had grown to include fifty different establishments, as well as several organizational affiliates. HELP's protection strategy paid off, for example, in August 1972, when the Black Pipe, a newer leather bar, was raided by the police. HELP mobilized its attorneys and bondsmen and had all twenty-one arrestees bailed out immediately and, eventually, twenty of the twenty-one exonerated of all charges.[31] HELP subsequently filed a $100,000 lawsuit against the LAPD for damages, arguing the arrests jeopardized the "reputation and standing of the conservative legal aid organization, resulting from the false arrests of many persons."[32] HELP organized gay and/or gay-friendly attorneys to offer discounted legal services for people arrested for sex crimes. HELP quoted the market rate for a lewd conduct defense at $800 to $1,200. With a HELP membership, however, the price was reduced to $150 to $300. What HELP sought to do was consolidate gay capital and leverage it to train the legal system to decriminalize gays by making sure that gays arrested for particular sex crimes offenses didn't spend significant time in jail or go bankrupt defending themselves. The offenses included PC 286, Sodomy; PC 288(a), Oral Copulation; PC 314, Lewd or Obscene Conduct; PC 647(a), Solicitation of Lewd Conduct. Although membership did entitle one to bail assistance for any misdemeanor, HELP's focus on sex crimes automatically streamlined their audience to focus on white gay men. Lesbians, and women in general, were more often arrested for prostitution-related codes, which HELP organizing left untouched, than for the collection of penal codes described as sex crimes. Incomplete records make it difficult to estimate how many bails and legal references HELP arranged during the peak of its years of activity, 1970–74, but scattered records from a few months in 1971 show at least sixty individual cases from the months of October, December, April, and May combined. HELP did negotiate with the LAPD at times, especially on the issue of "own recognizance" release for misdemeanor sex crime bookings. Organizers put a majority of their capacity into building a base of gay capital that could be leveraged to meet the needs of individuals and businesses on a case-by-case basis.

HELP innovated strategies of advocacy and expansive networks of protection and support as it tried to turn bars and clubs into sanctuaries for nonnormative economies of desire. Although HELP operated primarily on volunteer labor, the organization was led by a board, and leadership was composed mostly of white men and sometimes white women. The leadership diversified throughout the 1970s, and HELP was slightly more multiracial by the late 1970s, near its official end in 1980.[33]

Creating Gay Territory within the Material and Political Landscape of Los Angeles
The passage of AB489, the consenting adult sex bill, in 1975, a version of the Brown Bill introduced in 1970, repealed the legal ban against sodomy. This caused a pause in direct confrontations and organizing between gay and lesbian police-reform groups and the police. By 1975, GCA, HELP, and the Gay Liberation Front were inactive. The radical survival programs developed by the Gay Liberation Front had been incorporated by Kight and GSCS co-director Donald Kilhefner into the service provision work of the Gay Community Services Center. The passage of the Brown Bill marked the ascendancy of certain gay male leaders into municipal governance and the territorialization of West Hollywood and Hollywood as "Gay LA." In 1975, the Gay Community Services Center moved from its Westlake office to Hollywood, in a decisive move by Morris Kight to make the area the new "epicenter" of gay Los Angeles, and because Westlake had increased crime and poverty that was distasteful to leadership.[34] The conditions of white flight that lessened the area's appeal to Kight set the stage for the area to become predominantly Central American, Cuban, and South American by 1980.[35]

In January 1975, former Gay Community Alliance president David Glascock was hired by District 3 county supervisor Ed Edelman to work at Edelman's new West Hollywood branch office specifically on issues impacting gays and lesbians. Estimating that between sixty thousand and one hundred thousand gays and lesbians lived in District 3, Supervisor Edelman saw himself as ahead of the curve on gay and lesbian issues. He remarked, "Other than City Atty. Burt Pines, I'm one of the first public officials to seek representation in the gay community. This large segment has *unique* problems which have been neglected" (emphasis mine).[36] While many gay police-reform organizations did not have long organizational life spans, they created a space of dependence that successfully inserted gay activists into the city's political infrastructure.

Activists learned throughout the tail end of the 1970s that the Brown Bill was not as effective as they hoped, since the LAPD mostly used the lewd conduct penal code to criminalize gay people and places. A year after the Brown Bill had gone into effect, sex crimes arrests increased from 2,580 arrests in 1976 to 2,858 in 1977, with 50 percent of that increase being in the Hollywood police division, although the number of felony dispositions of these arrests decrease. Gay liberal organizations had effectively dented city council's support for LAPD Police Chief Ed Davis and for vice policing, and had helped elect the more gay-friendly city attorney Burt Pines. Gay liberal organizations had also made political inroads with Lieutenant Governor Mervyn Dymally toward overturning the lewd conduct code. However, police harassment and entrapment of gays continued, because lewd conduct hinged on the LAPD's discretionary power to discern gay and lesbian sociality as lewd in spite of the Brown Bill's passage in the 1975–76 legislative session as A.B. 489. In 1978, GCSC organizational files show that the board began circulating a memo to try to bring together a coalition of organizations to address the homophobic tenor of vice policing that continued despite A.B. 489's passage. By this time, LAPD Chief Ed Davis had retired and was replaced by Daryl Gates, who quickly became critiqued for his aggressive policing tactics, particularly against Black and Latino young people, increasingly labeled as gang members. Although the Civil Service Commission removed the ban on homosexuality in the requirements to be a police officer, there had still been no movement by LAPD officials to hire gay and lesbian police officers.

The Los Angeles Gay and Lesbian Police Task Advisory Force (Task Force) took up this issue as a central concern in its organizing, along with education and training of LAPD officers on gay and lesbian issues. The Task Force formally began in August 1981, after several members gave testimony in front of the Police Commission, reiterating the longtime demands of gay liberal police-reform activists: the designation of a gay community police liaison, reform of vice policing, and hiring of gay and lesbian police officers. Daryl Gates acquiesced to some of these demands and appointed officer Ken Hickman as liaison. The Task Force was member driven but led by cochairs Jim La Maida and lesbian activist Ivy Bottini. The group had monthly general meetings and working committees that met as needed. The Task Force acted as the political bargaining unit for the gay and lesbian community, especially as other organizations disintegrated. Its primary goal was to get official recognition from the LAPD as the political voice of the gay and lesbian community, and then use that status to implement departmental reforms. The Task Force was officially recognized by the LAPD on April 14, 1982. Task Force members used the LAPD liaison, Ken Hickman, as a conduit to channel complaints about police harassment of gays and lesbians directly to the LAPD administration. They collected complaints from gay and lesbian people and businesses, held public forums, and in turn addressed complaints received by the LAPD that might heighten policing of the gay and lesbian nightlife crowd. For example, in 1983, Task Force members began an alley patrol with the purpose of reducing complaints to the LAPD from property owners and residents near West Hollywood area bars. In June 1983 they began to pass out leaflets that read: "We all know that gay sex is wonderful. It just should not be happening in the backyards of residential neighborhoods. We would appreciate your cooperation in making social contact in a safe and suitable place."[37] The Task Force's tenuous relationship with the LAPD encouraged Task Force members to forward a model gay consumer who could enjoy the nightlife but also had access to housing or real estate in order to keep sex off the streets. The LAPD liaison also tacitly encouraged the Task Force not to work in coalitions with "other" groups working on police reform, in this case antiracist and Black- and Latino-led organizations.[38] The Task Force assented to this demand and continued to push for recruitment of gay and lesbian officers and gay and lesbian liaisons at each of the eighteen police divisions, and for participation from Task Force members in LAPD officer training. They hoped that having openly gay and lesbian officers would intervene in the LAPD's discretionary use of the lewd conduct code to criminalize gays and lesbians. Gates agreed to the inclusion of Task Force members in sensitivity training right away. Members began to develop their own training program called "Gay and Lesbian Cultural Awareness Training for Law Enforcement."[39] The group was eventually destroyed by infighting that ended in all the people-of-color organizations being expelled from the Task Force at an April 1989 meeting, in front of LAPD representatives.[40]

In their efforts to reform the LAPD, gay and lesbian activists intervened in the 1973 election that reorganized the city's political landscape. Both Efland and Turner, whose deaths sparked outrage and organizing, were killed in Central and South Central Los Angeles, places that gay organizing and protest gradually retreated from between 1970 and 1980. Gay police-reform activism entwined sexuality as an *identity category* into liberal praxis through the production of space. The leveraging of political power through service provision, exemplified by US Mission, HELP, and GCSC, created a sociospatial narrative for the public, city officials, and other gays and lesbians to understand gays and lesbians as constituting an oppressed minority group targeted for a victimless crime. For example, a favorable *Times* article on the issue of decriminalizing consensual adult sexual behavior reads: "Aside from an occasional clash with Chief Davis—to which the Gay Libbers apply the maximum dramatic flair—the Gay community also is involved in a number social programs as staid and respectable as the Salvation Army."[41] Similarly, US Mission's service programs were lauded by the likes of Tom Bradley, Dianne Feinstein, Pete Wilson, and Governor Deukmejian.[42]

Reviewing some of the early grants that the GCSC applied for reveals its astute understanding of the spatial, racialized, and gendered politics of precarity. For example, in 1975, the GCSC applied to the Echo Park/Silver Lake Regional Drug Coalition for a grant to start a detoxification and residential treatment center. The proposal justified the need for the grant based on the precarity of people residing within the catchment area.[43] The proposal lists high rates of substance abuse, a large Latino population, some of the highest suicide rates in Los Angeles County, low median family income levels compared to the whole county, a high concentration of people with mental illnesses, and a high infant mortality rate as characterizing features of the population living in the catchment area. While gays and lesbians were fighting to make sexual difference a legible category in city politics, it was the racialized, gendered, and classed categories of precarity that activists used to script themselves into the nonprofit service provision, which provided organizations with increased fiscal stability and social legitimacy. While activists reorganized the meaning of sexual and gender deviance through an identity politics of sanctuary, their efforts were drawn into the production of safe space. When federal voluntary sector funds fell through at the end of the 1980s, GCSC became more reliant on private funding and began to act as a force of redevelopment.[44]

The Production of Safe Space

Gay and lesbian police-reform activism in Los Angeles does not simply end in the 1980s. Gay and lesbian activists, along with other activists, are scripted into the reterritorialization of the welfare state and therefore into discourses of relational differential value and the life cycles of criminalization that rely on the coordination of the administrative and disciplinary capacities of the state and ruling class. Gay and lesbian police reform in this instance moved from a politics of sanctuary to a politics of safe space. The production of safe space demonstrates how activists were scripted into the project of community policing and underscores the importance of abolitionist approaches to criminalization that also work against the "impossible politics of difference." Rather than a repudiation of identity politics, this account shows both how identity politics expose the limits of the social and spatial categories meant to keep people in place, and how the territorialization of identity can become sequestered into the reproduction of the administrative and disciplinary capacities of the state and ruling class.

Christina Hanhardt offers the concept of safe space to index how the placemaking efforts of LGBT activists confronted neoliberal transformations in welfare state and carceral state governance at both the municipal and federal scale.[45] Value becomes important as identity-based groups' desire for safety and protection gets fashioned into a proxy for social value, which gets recruited into schemes of renewing urban land (value) as a proxy for redistributing capital, land, and power to working-class people. Gay street patrols in 1970s New York, for example, first began in response to homophobic attacks, but then became complicit in neoliberal quality-of-life policing strategies that targeted youth of color, including queer and trans youth of color, to clear the land and make it safe for a middle-class, consumptive, and largely white gay and lesbian gentry.[46]

Safe spaces are often conceived through a politics of sanctuary as creative interventions crafted by everyday people to sustain movement culture or to respond to the cycles of violence of racial capitalism. Safe space underscores how neoliberal capital's speculative violence attempts to delink representation, recognition, affective connection, awareness, and "consciousness raising" from any substantive and durable redistributions of money or property that might abolish the relational differential value that circumscribe the world we live in.[47]

Gay and lesbian police-reform activism is also shaped by what geographer Ruth Wilson Gilmore has termed a shift from military Keynesianism, or a mode of state capacity in which the profits from war making are channeled into the development of a welfare state, to post-Keynesian militarism, a mode of state capacity centered on the preservation of warfare as a mode of accumulation coupled with the planned abandonment of welfare state infrastructure and focus on work and personal responsibility.[48] Planned abandonment of social services did not just look like simply getting rid of them completely but also transferring the responsibility of administering them to other entities, often those looking to create refuge through a politics of grassroots self-determination. By 1982, 56 percent of social services provision was being delivered by voluntary sector organizations, 4 percent by the private sector, and 40 percent by official state entities.[49] The contradiction of organized efforts for safety, sanctuary, and refuge in this era is that through the reterritorialization of welfare state governance, spaces of refuge can also be secure spaces for surplus racial capital and for the renewal of state capacity, the ability of the state to act as the state. Safe spaces expand through the aegis of the reterritorialization of welfare state governance and in concert with community policing throughout the 1960s and 1970s. Safe space is a neoliberal strategy of racial enclosure, one that encloses collective strategies of providing mutual aid in the racializing terms of group difference, population, and risk management.

Gay and lesbian police-reform organizations were conditioned by neoliberal transformations at several spatial scales. Sexual liberalism flourished throughout the late 1950s and 1960s. Legal victories at the close of the 1950s around homosexual free speech (*ONE Inc. v. Olesen*, 1958) and around what counts as obscene (*Roth v. United States* and *Alberts v. California*, 1957) supported the multiplication of sexual subcultures by removing content restrictions on publications that were circulated via mail. This was important then and now, as the archive that informs this article relies heavily on newsletters and newspapers that circulated through the mail. In Los Angeles however, sexual liberalism that was enforced federally by the Supreme Court was met locally with a police crackdown on obscenity, public nudity, and lewd behavior. It is important to recognize that policing preserves the social relations of racial capitalism via racial-sexual management even during periods of social and political liberalism.

While gay police reform was getting off the ground organizationally in 1969, the LAPD and the FBI were waging a war on the Black Panther Party (BPP) in Los Angeles. Between 1968 and 1969, LAPD officers shot and killed at least four Panthers, raided the Black Panther Party office at 41st and Central (blocks away from where Larry LaVerne Turner was murdered by the LAPD) several times, drew guns on children in the BPP childcare program on the grounds of investigating a landlord nuisance complaint, and raided the BPP breakfast program in Watts under a directive from the FBI to destroy BPP survival programs. This war on the Black Panthers culminated in a December 8, 1969, shootout between BPP members and four hundred LAPD officers. The fact that GLF's survival programs, modeled on the Panther's survival programs, became enshrined in the milieu of voluntary sector governance vis-à-vis the Gay Community Services Center while those of the Panthers were systematically destroyed underscores how relational differential value is coordinated between the administrative and disciplinary capacities of the state and ruling class.[50] Dismantling of the Black Panther Party in Los Angeles was as much about disciplining blackness as it was about disciplining politics in general by directing it into racializing forms that governments could regulate and control.[51] Gates's response to the Task Force also exemplifies how community policing developed in the 1970s and 1980s in the LAPD as a neoliberal strategy of racial enclosure. While LAPD Chief William Parker (1950–65) preferred a top-down style of policing, his successors, such as Thomas Reddin and Ed Davis, while iron-fisted with the gay and lesbian community, evolved the velvet glove approach of the LAPD. Reddin expanded the Community Relations Department from a staff of four to over one hundred after the Watts uprising. By 1971, LAPD had over seventy-one community relations programs including youth programs, storefront substations, citizens' watch groups, and programs for formerly incarcerated people. During Ed Davis's tenure as chief, he expanded community policing through the Basic Car Plan, which divided the city into ninety-five subdistricts and assigned a permanent police car and officer to each subdistrict. Davis's tenure also saw the development of a team-policing experiment in the Black and Latino Oakwood community in Venice.[52] Davis also authorized the formation of the Community Resources against Street Hoodlums (CRASH) unit, which became vital in the criminalization of Latino immigrants in Los Angeles during the 1990s. CRASH, which was originally devised to target Black youth in South Central, was repurposed in the late 1990s to criminalize and deport Latino youth, in spite of Special Order 40, a mandate made in 1979 by the LAPD and Los Angeles City Council that police officers not question people for the sole purpose of determining or obtaining that person's immigration status. Special Order 40 was supposed to prevent the LAPD from operating as immigration enforcement agents but was constantly flouted and LAPD continued to collaborate with INS (now ICE) to identify and criminalize immigrants after Special Order 40 was drafted.

The mayoral administration of Tom Bradley from 1973 to 1993 marked the beginning of a period of reform liberalism in city politics. Bradley's tenuous political bloc, however, tempered his ability to adequately redistribute wealth and resources by shifting city budget priorities. Instead, Bradley's strategy was to leverage outside funding to fund social services and reinvest in South Central, and then foster longer term economic growth and jobs through redeveloping downtown and creating pathways for foreign investment by assembling a pro-business city hall.[53] Within the first month of Bradley's election, he successfully lobbied for a leftover half-million dollars in US Department of Health, Education and Welfare funds and used it as seed money for the development of the City Volunteer Corps through a grant from federal ACTION funds, and for local job-training programs through a grant from the US Department of Labor. By fiscal year 1978, grants to the city totaled $412.7 million, up from $99.1 million in fiscal year 1972, the year before Bradley's election. Federal grants became the means to deliver on campaign promises made to poor people, without upsetting the business alliance through increased taxation. The LAPD budget peaked during the Sam Yorty mayoral administration at 22 percent of the total budget in 1972. Bradley was able to rein in the LAPD budget by 17 percent, but he did so primarily by capping police pensions and limiting equipment purchases, not by significantly decreasing or limiting the number of sworn officers.[54]

At the federal level, the Bradley administration's ability to fund social services through contingent and external funding sources was enhanced by the general revenue sharing program. General revenue sharing (GRS) was a funding scheme developed by US Keynesian economist Walter Heller and signed into law by President Nixon in October 1972. Through the GRS program, federal tax dollars were distributed to state and local governments to fund programs or cover budget deficits. The GRS program lasted until 1986, and during that time, $85 billion in federal revenues was distributed to states and municipalities. It is in this context that gay liberal institutions used service provision as a tactic to incorporate themselves into the political milieu of city and county politics. The GRS program and Bradley's enthusiasm for a "self-help" approach to funding social services created an opportunity for community organizations to boost their organizational capacity with federal funding. The trade-off was that funding guidelines required community organizations to adopt a professional structure. For example, to be eligible for GRS funds through Los Angeles County, organizations had to provide a mission statement, organizational bylaws, a description of the organization's structure, an organizational history, and an itemized budget describing how funds would be spent. Organizations also had to explain how their work addressed federally defined high-need or high-risk service areas and/or populations. The pressure to narrate and organize identity through the rhetoric of population and geographic computations of risk tends toward reifying race as a sociospatial mode of territorialization.[55]

While War on Poverty programs invited community organizations to participate in shaping community development, tax revolts and the shift in state capacity toward post-Keynesian militarism evinced by federal programs like GRS pitted community organizations against municipalities over distribution of limited funds. While the federal government did mandate specific service areas and at-risk populations, Los Angeles City Council was able to successfully funnel federal grants into every council district in spite of federal regulations and restrictions.[56] Mayor

Bradley, who was leveraging GRS funds to deliver on campaign promises, had planned to redistribute the majority of GRS money among city and county governmental agencies. Gay Community Services Center director Donald Kilhefner found this out and helped to organize the Community Coalition for Equitable Revenue Sharing, a coalition of three hundred Los Angeles area community organizations, each representing a particular group or population. In 1972 the coalition successfully lobbied the Bradley administration to distribute GRS funds to community organizations as well as governmental agencies. While this coalitional work is a testament to how organized people can shift city politics, we should be wary of the ways that such coalitional models reified the fragmentation of geographies of struggle into service delivery zones, which themselves only reflected and naturalized the history of racist spatial development in Los Angeles.

Police pressure from LAPD chief Daryl Gates for the Task Force to distance itself from race-based groups marks the limit of identity politics in the context of neoliberal governance. Gates's play to court the gay and lesbian community at a time when he was receiving harsh criticism from antiracist and progressive groups over the 1979 murder of Eulia Love over a $22 unpaid gas bill and LAPD choke hold deaths typifies how inclusion is leveraged to channel dissent into manageable forms. It is in this light that we should understand the often lauded Special Order 40 measure, which was crafted by Gates in 1979. Special Order 40 amended the LAPD training manual to state that LAPD officers would not initiate police action for the sole purpose of obtaining someone's citizenship status, nor would they notify immigration enforcement of having arrested an undocumented person unless that person was being arrested for multiple misdemeanors, a "high grade" misdemeanor or felony, or being arrested for a second time. This policy, which was praised as a sanctuary measure,[57] was offered as a strategy of counterinsurgent governance to appease a faction of the growing dissent to LAPD brutality,[58] similarly to how the Task Force was given a special status in relationship to the LAPD to prevent members from aligning themselves politically with the growing Coalition Against Police Abuse (CAPA). Gates was able to effectively leverage the police department's discretionary power to channel networks of struggle over police power into manageable sociospatial forms that were inherently racialized and/or territorial.

In this account we can witness safe space develop as a strategy of counterinsurgent governance in the shift from post-Keynesian militarism in the late sixties to neoliberalism by the mid-seventies. The trajectory of gay and lesbian police reform evinces several moves in the production of safe space from a politics of sanctuary. First, the move from networks of struggle to resegmented populations can be seen in the general trajectory of reform efforts beginning with the Citizen's Committee to Outlaw Entrapment, which drew from material connections with antiracist and labor organizing, and ending with GCSC's police task force, which drew primarily from strategic partnerships with and representation from within other identity-based formations. Also, the Gay Community Alliance's and HELP's insistence on single-issue politics that affected mostly gay men created semiprotected statuses and zones of decriminalization that were tenuous at best. While gay police reform created a cultural shift, it did not displace police discretionary power, which enabled Davis to instruct LAPD officers to approach gay culture as lewd and vagrant. By 1975, people like Efland and Turner, whose murders galvanized gay and lesbian police reform, were not any less legally vulnerable to police abuse than they had been in 1969 and 1970, or than they are now. The LAPD still uses lewd conduct codes in undercover stings and mass arrests of LGBT people.

The spatial clustering of organizations and protest in West Hollywood and Hollywood began as an effort to create a space of dependence. Over time the production of safe space turns gay neighborhoods into racial enclaves in which racialization forms the criteria of difference that guides the exercise of police discretionary power. We see these organizations each become racial enclaves as they are drawn into the reterritorializing welfare state and into the work of community policing. The trajectory of gay and lesbian police reform addressed only a subset of the penal codes used to criminalize gender and sexual nonconformity, making police reform only reflective of the people who had the power to spatially imbricate their visions and versions of identity and politics. The move from analogized suffering to protected status is witnessed in the general way that gay and lesbian police-reform activists often analogized police violence in relationship to racialized people and places, but then also articulated gay and lesbian identity through the trope of innocence, arguing that they were not the *real* criminals and were targets of discrimination and thus eligible for protection as a minority group. LGBT people didn't gain official protected federal status until more than a decade later, but these organizers used political pluralism as a strategy to gain provisional protection through electoral politics, political bargaining, and protest. They also accomplished this by distancing their legislative activism from sex work, despite that fact the prostitution arrests always exceeded lewd conduct, sodomy, and oral copulation arrests. This was and remains specifically impactful on sex workers, despite how instrumental anti–sex work codes continue to be for criminalizing LGBT people.[59] Organizers also encouraged gays and lesbians to privatize their sexual practices. In the move from analogized suffering to protected status, the discretionary power of the police is implicitly reified around the racialized enclaves of political activism. What scholars and writers who study past and present sanctuary movements have narrated as an overreliance on liberal strategies was not just a poor choice but a flexible cultural project of neoliberal racial capitalism designed to securitize sanctuary.[60]

Treva Ellison is an abolitionist scholar and artist who works as an assistant professor of geography and women's, gender, and sexuality studies at Dartmouth College. Treva is currently completing their manuscript "The Promise of Black Gender: Black Life, Transgender Geographies, and Carceral Biopower in Postwar Los Angeles."

Notes

1. Paik, "Abolitionist Futures and the US Sanctuary Movement."
2. On protesting laws deemed unjust as a sanctuary strategy that is supported by the infrastructure and moral authority of the church, see Kotin, Dyrness, and Irazábal, "Immigration and Integration"; Freeland, "Negotiating Place, Space, and Borders"; Hamilton and Chinchilla, *Seeking Community in a Global City*, 223–24; Zilberg, "Disquieting Complicities," 13; Yukich, "Constructing the Model Immigrant"; and Zilberg, *Space of Detention*, 25–30.
3. On building advocacy organizations and networks that protect and define an injured group as a sanctuary movement strategy, see Chinchilla and Hamilton, "Changing Networks and Alliances in a Transnational Context"; Nicholls, "Forging a 'New' Organizational Infrastructure"; Terriquez, "Intersectional Mobilization, Social Movement Spillover"; Loyd and Burridge, "La Gran Marcha"; Stuelke, "The Reparative Politics of Central America Solidarity Movement Culture"; and Pastor, "How Immigrant Activists Changed LA."
4. Subverting the legal system and legal protections as a sanctuary strategy: Perla and Coutin, "Legacies and Origins of the 1980s US-Central American Sanctuary Movement"; Loyd and Burridge, "La Gran Marcha"; and Gonzales, "The 2006 Mega Marchas in Greater Los Angeles."
5. On spatial imbrication and territorialization as a sanctuary strategy, see Perla and Coutin, Legacies and Origins of the 1980s US-Central American Sanctuary Movement"; Nicholls, "Forging a 'New' Organizational Infrastructure"; Chinchilla and Hamilton, "Changing Networks and Alliances in a Transnational Context"; Hamilton and Chinchilla, *Seeking Community in a Global City*, 61–68, 121; and Cruz, "Little San Salvador," 71.
6. Hanhardt, *Safe Space*; Escobar, *Captivity beyond Prisons*, 173; Richie, *Arrested Justice*; Lee, *Building a Latino Civil Rights Movement*; Pulido, "Geographies of Race and Ethnicity II"; and Cacho, *Social Death*.
7. Gilmore, *Golden Gulag*, 28.
8. Cacho, *Social Death*, 8–15.
9. Sexton, "People-of-Color-Blindness"; Stuelke, "The Reparative Politics of Central America Solidarity Movement Culture," 774; Yukich, "Constructing the Model Immigrant."
10. Hernández, *City of Inmates*, 158–94.
11. Ellison, "Towards a Politics of Perfect Disorder," 53–55.
12. "An Open Letter to Friends of the Citizens' Committee to Outlaw Entrapment," 1952 Press Release, Citizen's Committee to Outlaw Police Entrapment, Box 1:14, Mattachine Society Project Collection, Coll2008–016, ONE National Gay and Lesbian Archives, Los Angeles, California.
13. Hobson, "Policing Gay LA," 119.
14. Faderman and Timmons, *Gay LA*, 113–14.
15. Knopp, "Social Theory, Social Movements and Public Policy"; Stewart-Winter, *Queer Clout*; Agee, "Gayola."
16. Cox, "Spaces of Dependence, Spaces of Engagement," 2.
17. *Los Angeles Free Press*, March 20, 1970, "Larry LaVerne Turner," ONE Subject File collection, Coll2012–001, ONE National Gay and Lesbian Archives, Los Angeles, California; Undated Press Release on Howard Efland's murder, United States Mission Collection, Coll2012.125, ONE National Gay and Lesbian Archives, Los Angeles, California.

18. US Mission Press Releases, 1970, "Dover Hotel," ONE Subject File collection, Coll2012–001, ONE National Gay and Lesbian Archives, Los Angeles, California.

19. Don Jackson, "Crusade against Vice (Officers): Illegal Entrapment of Gays Charged," *Los Angeles Free Press*, August 13, 1971.

20. "Watch LAPD, GLF Is Going to 'Magick' You," *The Advocate* (Los Angeles, CA), March 3, 1971; and "GLF Gives LAPD a Lift," *The Advocate*, March 31, 1971.

21. "LA Gays Gain Police Board Ear," *The Advocate*, October 24, 1973, 1.

22. Letter to Senator George McGovern, dated January 7, 1972, inviting him to come to address GCA members in Los Angeles. In the letter, President David Glascock promises McGovern an audience of at least eight hundred people. Gay Community Alliance Collection, Coll2011–045, ONE National Gay and Lesbian Archives, Los Angeles, California.

23. Letter to Senator George McGovern, January 7, 1972, Gay Community Alliance Collection, Coll2011–045, ONE National Gay and Lesbian Archives, Los Angeles, California.

24. "An Invitation to Participate," May 10, 1971, Gay Community Alliance Collection, Coll2011–045, ONE National Gay and Lesbian Archives, Los Angeles, California.

25. "Statement of Purpose and Call to Action," March, 2, 1971, Gay Community Alliance Collection, Coll2011–045, ONE National Gay and Lesbian Archives, Los Angeles, California.

26. "Pines to Minimize Prosecutions for Activity in Gay Bars," *Los Angeles Times*, April 22, 1974.

27. Faderman and Timmons, *Gay LA*, 157.

28. Faderman and Timmons, *Gay LA*, 158.

29. Meeting Minutes, March 28, 1973, Box 4:1, Homophile Effort for Legal Protection, Incorporated (HELP, Inc.), Records, Coll2008–052, ONE National Gay and Lesbian Archives, Los Angeles, California.

30. HELP Inc. Newsletter 1:1, September 1970, Box 4:2, Homophile Effort for Legal Protection, Incorporated (HELP, Inc.), Records, Coll2008–052, ONE National Gay and Lesbian Archives, Los Angeles, California.

31. Ima Freeman, "Help Line," Box 4:6, Homophile Effort for Legal Protection, Incorporated (HELP, Inc.), Records, Coll2008–052, ONE National Gay and Lesbian Archives, Los Angeles, California.

32. *Drummer* volume 2:3, November 15, 1972, Box 4:5, Homophile Effort for Legal Protection, Incorporated (HELP, Inc.), Records, Coll2008–052, ONE National Gay and Lesbian Archives, Los Angeles, California.

33. Letter to State of California officially disbanding HELP, 1980, Box 1:1, Homophile Effort for Legal Protection, Incorporated (HELP, Inc.), Records, Coll2008–052, ONE National Gay and Lesbian Archives, Los Angeles, California.

34. Kenney, *Mapping Gay LA*, 86–87.

35. Hamilton and Chinchilla, *Seeking Community in a Global City*, 61.

36. Ray Zeman, "Edelman Hires Assistant to Work in Gay Community," *Los Angeles Times*, January 10, 1975, 29.

37. "Gay and Lesbian Police Advisory Task Force Media Watch," July 27, 1983, Gay and Lesbian Police Advisory Task Force (Los Angeles) Collection, Coll2011–049, ONE National Gay and Lesbian Archives, Los Angeles, California.

38. Meeting Minutes, September 10, 1981, Gay and Lesbian Police Advisory Task Force (Los Angeles) Collection, Coll2011–049, ONE National Gay and Lesbian Archives, Los Angeles, California.

39. "Gay and Lesbian Cultural Awareness Training for Law Enforcement," Undated Materials, Gay and Lesbian Police Advisory Task Force (Los Angeles) Collection, Coll2011–049, ONE National Gay and Lesbian Archives, Los Angeles, California.

40. Lloyd Jordon, "Policing the Task Force," *BLK: National Black Lesbian and Gay Newsmagazine*, issue 6 (May 1989): 8–12, 10.

41. Dave Smith, "Homosexual Groups Push Fight for Liberalized Morals Laws," *Los Angeles Times*, January 24, 1971, A1.

42. "Gay? Homeless?" (United States Mission Promotional Brochure), United States Mission Collection, Coll2012.125, ONE National Gay and Lesbian Archives, Los Angeles, California.

43. Echo Park/Silverlake Region Drug Coalition, Detoxification and Residential Treatment Project Funding Proposal, 1974, Box 6:1, L.A. Gay and Lesbian Center records, Coll2007–010, ONE National Gay and Lesbian Archives, Los Angeles, California, 6.

44. Ian M. Baldwin, "Family, Housing, and the Political Geography of Gay Liberation in Los Angeles County"; Kenney, *Mapping Gay LA*, 86–87.

45. Hanhardt, *Safe Space*.

46. Hanhardt, "Butterflies, Whistles, and Fists"; and Manalansan, "Race, Violence, and Neoliberal Spatial Politics in the Global City."

47. Stuelke, "The Reparative Politics of Central America Solidarity Movement Culture," 774.

48. Gilmore, "Globalisation and US Prison Growth."

49. Salamon, "Of Market Failure, Voluntary Failure, and Third-Party Government."

50. Paik, *Rightlessness*.

51. Joassart-Marcelli and Wolch, "The Intrametropolitan Geography of Poverty and the Nonprofit Sector in Southern California," 77–79.

52. Platt et al., "The Iron Fist and the Velvet Glove," 65–68.

53. Sonenshein, *Politics in Black and White*, 158.

54. Sonenshein, *Politics in Black and White*.

55. On the evolution of the discourse of population, see Foucault, *Security, Territory, Population*. On race, criminality, and the making of population statistics, see Browne, "Race and Surveillance"; and Muhammad, "Where Did All the White Criminals Go?" On the racist underpinnings of population discourse, see Gannett, "Racism and Human Genome Diversity Research"; and Roberts, *Fatal Invention*.

56. Sonenshein, *Politics in Black and White*, 164–69.

57. Bratton, "The LAPD Fights Crime, Not Illegal Immigration."

58. Maya, "To Serve and Protect or to Betray and Neglect," 1662. Maya notes that at the time Special Order 40 was passed, the LAPD was also facing a lawsuit from two Latino residents who had been falsely arrested on suspicion of being undocumented. Special Order 40 was passed to cover up the fact that, until then, it was LAPD policy to arrest people on noncriminal charges in order to turn them over to the Immigration and Naturalization Service (INS).

59. Jackson and Heineman, "Repeal FOSTA and Decriminalize Sex Work."

60. Loyd and Burridge, in "La Gran Marcha," emphasize how some of the liberal framings coming from the immigrant rights movement, like being tax-paying citizens, were

reactions to false ideas like the idea that immigrants do not pay taxes. This account asks us to think about the kinds of organizational models and infrastructures for sustaining organizations that concretize these framings as asymmetric power relations.

References

Agee, Christopher. "Gayola: Police Professionalization and the Politics of San Francisco's Gay Bars, 1950–1968." *Journal of the History of Sexuality* 15, no. 3 (2006): 462–89.

Baldwin, Ian M. "Family, Housing, and the Political Geography of Gay Liberation in Los Angeles County, 1960–1986," unpublished, 2016.

Bratton, William. "The LAPD Fights Crime, Not Illegal Immigration." *Los Angeles Times*, October 27, 2009.

Browne, Simone. "Race and Surveillance." In *Routledge Handbook of Surveillance Studies*, edited by Kirstie Ball, Kevin D. Haggerty, and David Lyon, 72–79. New York: Routledge, 2012.

Cacho, Lisa Marie. *Social Death: Racialized Rightlessness and the Criminalization of the Unprotected*. New York: New York University Press, 2012.

Chávez, Karma R. "From Sanctuary to a Queer Politics of Fugitivity." *QED: A Journal in GLBTQ Worldmaking* 4, no. 2 (2017): 63–70.

Chinchilla, Norma, and Nora Hamilton. "Changing Networks and Alliances in a Transnational Context: Salvadoran and Guatemalan Immigrants in Southern California." *Social Justice* 26, no. 3 (1999): 4–26.

Cox, Kevin R. "Spaces of Dependence, Spaces of Engagement and the Politics of Scale, Or: Looking for Local Politics." *Political Geography* 17, no. 1 (1998): 1–23.

Cruz, Marcelo. "Little San Salvador: Identity of Places/Places of Identity in an Innercity Enclave of Los Angeles, California." *Journal of Latino/Latin American Studies* 2, no. 1 (2006): 62–83.

Ellison, Treva C. "Towards a Politics of Perfect Disorder: Carceral Geographies, Queer Criminality, and Other Ways to Be." PhD diss., University of Southern California, 2015.

Escobar, Martha D. *Captivity beyond Prisons: Criminalization Experiences of Latina (Im)migrants*. Austin: University of Texas Press, 2016.

Faderman, Lillian, and Stuart Timmons. *Gay LA: A History of Sexual Outlaws, Power Politics, and Lipstick Lesbians*. New York: Basic Books, 2006.

Foucault, Michel. *Security, Territory, Population: Lectures at the Collège de France, 1977–78*. New York: Palgrave Macmillan, 2007.

Freeland, Gregory. "Negotiating Place, Space, and Borders: The New Sanctuary Movement." *Latino Studies* 8, no. 4 (2010): 485–508.

Gannett, Lisa. "Racism and Human Genome Diversity Research: The Ethical Limits of 'Population Thinking.'" *Philosophy of Science* 68, no. S3 (2001): S479–92.

Gilmore, Ruth Wilson. "Globalisation and US Prison Growth: From Military Keynesianism to Post-Keynesian Militarism." *Race and Class* 40, no. 2–3 (1999): 171–88.

Gilmore, Ruth Wilson. *Golden Gulag: Prisons, Surplus, Crisis, and Opposition in Globalizing California*. Berkeley: University of California Press, 2007.

Gonzales, Alfonso. "The 2006 Mega Marchas in Greater Los Angeles: Counter-Hegemonic Moment and the Future of El Migrante Struggle." *Latino Studies* 7, no. 1 (2009): 30–59.

Hall, Stuart. "Race, Articulation, and Societies Structured in Dominance." In *Black British Cultural Studies: A Reader*, edited by Houston A. Baker, Jr., Manthia Diawara, and Ruth H. Lindeborg, 16–60. Chicago: University of Chicago Press, 1996.

Hamilton, Nora, and Norma Stoltz Chinchilla. *Seeking Community in a Global City: Guatemalans and Salvadorans in Los Angeles*. Philadelphia: Temple University Press, 2001.

Hanhardt, Christina B. "Butterflies, Whistles, and Fists: Gay Safe Streets Patrols and the New Gay Ghetto, 1976–1981." *Radical History Review*, no. 100 (2008): 61–85.

Hanhardt, Christina B. *Safe Space: Gay Neighborhood History and the Politics of Violence*. Durham, NC: Duke University Press, 2013.

Hernández, Kelly Lytle. *City of Inmates: Conquest, Rebellion, and the Rise of Human Caging in Los Angeles, 1771–1965*. Chapel Hill: University of North Carolina Press, 2017.

Hobson, Emily. "Policing Gay LA: Mapping Racial Divides in the Homophile Era, 1950–1967." In *The Rising Tide of Color: Race, State Violence, and Radical Movements across the Pacific*, edited by Moon-Ho Jung, 188–212. Seattle: University of Washington Press, 2014.

Jackson, Crystal A., and Jenny Heineman. "Repeal FOSTA and Decriminalize Sex Work." *Contexts* 17, no. 3 (2018): 74–75.

Joassart-Marcelli, Pascale, and Jennifer R. Wolch. "The Intrametropolitan Geography of Poverty and the Nonprofit Sector in Southern California." *Nonprofit and Voluntary Sector Quarterly* 32, no. 1 (2003): 70–96.

Kenney, Moira. *Mapping Gay LA: The Intersection of Place and Politics*. Philadelphia: Temple University Press, 2001.

Knopp, Lawrence. "Social Theory, Social Movements and Public Policy: Recent Accomplishments of the Gay and Lesbian Movements in Minneapolis, Minnesota." *International Journal of Urban and Regional Research* 11, no. 2 (1987): 243–61.

Kotin, Stephanie, Grace R. Dyrness, and Clara Irazábal. "Immigration and Integration: Religious and Political Activism for/with Immigrants in Los Angeles." *Progress in Development Studies* 11, no. 4 (2011): 263–84.

Lee, Sonia Song-Ha. *Building a Latino Civil Rights Movement: Puerto Ricans, African Americans, and the Pursuit of Racial Justice in New York City*. Chapel Hill: University of North Carolina Press, 2014.

Loyd, Jenna M., and Andrew Burridge. "La Gran Marcha: Anti-racism and Immigrants' Rights in Southern California." *ACME: An International E-Journal for Critical Geographies* 6, no. 1 (2007): 1–35.

Manalansan, M. F. "Race, Violence, and Neoliberal Spatial Politics in the Global City." *Social Text* 23 (2005): 141–55.

Maya, Theodore W. "To Serve and Protect or to Betray and Neglect: The LAPD and Undocumented Immigrants." *UCLA Law Review* 49 (2001): 1611.

Muhammad, Khalil Gibran. "Where Did All the White Criminals Go? Reconfiguring Race and Crime on the Road to Mass Incarceration." *Souls* 13, no. 1 (2011): 72–90.

Nicholls, W. J. "Forging a 'New' Organizational Infrastructure for Los Angeles' Progressive Community." *International Journal of Urban and Regional Research* 27, no. 4 (2003): 881–96.

Paik, A. Naomi. "Abolitionist Futures and the US Sanctuary Movement." *Race and Class* 59, no. 2 (2017): 3–25.

Paik, A. Naomi. *Rightlessness: Testimony and Redress in US Prison Camps since World War II*. Chapel Hill: University of North Carolina Press Books, 2016.

Pastor, Manuel. "How Immigrant Activists Changed LA." *Dissent* 62, no. 1 (2015): 55–63.

Perla, Hector, Jr., and Susan Bibler Coutin. "Legacies and Origins of the 1980s US-Central American Sanctuary Movement." In *Sanctuary Practices in International Perspectives: Migration, Citizenship, and Social Movements*, edited by Randy K. Lippert and Sean Rehaag, 75–91. New York: Routledge, 2013.

Platt, Tony, Jon Frappier, Gerda Ray, Richard Schauffler, Larry Trujillo, Lynn Cooper, Elliot Currie, and Sidney Harring. *The Iron Fist and the Velvet Glove: An Analysis of the US Police*. San Francisco: Crime and Social Justice Associates, 1982.

Pulido, L. "Geographies of Race and Ethnicity II: Environmental Racism, Racial Capitalism and State-Sanctioned Violence." *Progress in Human Geography* 41, no. 4 (2017): 524–33.

Richie, Beth. *Arrested Justice: Black Women, Violence, and America's Prison Nation*. New York: New York University Press, 2012.

Roberts, Dorothy. *Fatal Invention: How Science, Politics, and Big Business Re-create Race in the Twenty-First Century*. New York: New Press, 2011.

Salamon, Lester M. "Of Market Failure, Voluntary Failure, and Third-Party Government: Toward a Theory of Government-Nonprofit Relations in the Modern Welfare State." *Journal of Voluntary Action Research* 16, no. 1–2 (1987): 29–49.

Sexton, Jared. "People-of-Color-Blindness: Notes on the Afterlife of Slavery." *Social Text* 28, no. 2 (2010): 31–56.

Sonenshein, Raphael. *Politics in Black and White: Race and Power in Los Angeles*. Princeton, NJ: Princeton University Press, 1993.

Stewart-Winter, Timothy. *Queer Clout: Chicago and the Rise of Gay Politics*. Philadelphia: University of Pennsylvania Press, 2015.

Stuelke, Patricia. "The Reparative Politics of Central America Solidarity Movement Culture." *American Quarterly* 66, no. 3 (2014): 767–90.

Terriquez, Veronica. "Intersectional Mobilization, Social Movement Spillover, and Queer Youth Leadership in the Immigrant Rights Movement." *Social Problems* 62, no. 3 (2015): 343–62.

Yukich, Grace. "Constructing the Model Immigrant: Movement Strategy and Immigrant Deservingness in the New Sanctuary Movement." *Social Problems* 60, no. 3 (2013): 302–20.

Zilberg, Elana. "Disquieting Complicities: The Double Binds of Anthropology, Advocacy, and Activism." *Journal of Contemporary Ethnography* 45, no. 6 (2016): 716–40.

Zilberg, Elana. *Space of Detention: The Making of a Transnational Gang Crisis between Los Angeles and San Salvador*. Durham, NC: Duke University Press, 2011.

Sanctuary Squats

The Political Contestations of Piazza Indipendenza Refugee Occupiers

Carla Hung

We were on the move, running and caught somewhere between the water cannons and the police on foot, their batons raised and ready. We were trying to help those who had fallen, trying to salvage the pieces of luggage soaking and dirty, hoping that documents delicately placed between layers of baby clothes would stay dry. We were trying to figure out what the next step would be. The occupiers were being evicted from the formerly abandoned eight-story office building in Piazza Indipendenza they had called home for roughly four years. This prominent five-hundred-person "squat" was occupied by individuals and families from the Horn of Africa, primarily Eritreans, who had obtained some form of internationally recognized refugee status and right of residency in Italy.

In the wee hours of the morning on August 24, 2017, the call went out to friends, activists, and journalists. "They're evicting us, there are water cannons [*idranti*], hurry, come quick." As dawn broke, I got off the tram at Rome's main train station, Termini, and heard chanting in the near distance. As I got closer I could hear Habtom's outcries reverberate. He was visibly shivering, his flannel shirt soaking wet, but his voice carried. Water cannons towered above, advancing and retreating, as the group of Eritrean, Ethiopian, and Somali occupiers, the majority of whom had some kind of refugee status, did the same. Their shouts seemed unable to penetrate the monstrous water cannons, easily mistakable for tanks, that were made to

Radical History Review
Issue 135 (October 2019)   DOI 10.1215/01636545-7607872
© 2019 by MARHO: The Radical Historians' Organization, Inc.

shove them further and further back and out. Habtom told me that they woke up to torrents of water in their faces some forty minutes earlier.

The water cannons would punctuate the day, coming back to hose down women and disabled occupiers who were intentionally holding the front lines in order to leverage vulnerability as a form of protection. They hoped that public outcry would come to their aid. All the while, photojournalists frantically photographed the scene, negotiating delusions of Pulitzer Prize grandeur with the preservation instinct to keep their equipment dry and intact. The police had their own camera crew. They were quick to circulate footage of a refugee occupier throwing a gas canister (hitting no one in particular) in the scuffle that ensued after the water cannons were deployed. For days to come, news outlets would cycle through these images and debate whether the eviction was warranted or excessively violent.

As night fell, we reconvened around big pots of spiced meat called *zignyi* that people in the Habesha, or Horn of Africa, community had made in their restaurants or houses.[1] They brought the pots out to the street to feed those who had spent the day confronting the police, in hopes of providing some nourishment and reprieve for those dragged away from their homes. We sat on the sidewalk eating in this impromptu enclave, an improvised sanctuary of sorts, as police cars drove by assessing the situation, making their presence known.

The crowd swelled after the meeting with housing and immigration NGOs and community organizations in the nearby municipal building ended. Those participating decided that women and children could go to a bare-bones temporary homeless shelter called the Sala Operativa Sociale (SOS) run by the municipality, while everyone else would stay with Baobab Experience, a volunteer organization that provides legal and medical assistance to transit migrants (those who have yet to start asylum applications or are having trouble with the process) living in the streets of Rome. Those evicted would discover that staying with Baobab would mean sleeping on the concrete outside the Tiburtina station. They would join transit and clandestine migrants trying to get around fingerprint surveillance in order to leave Italy and apply for asylum or find work in another country of the European Union (EU).[2] "There isn't even cardboard," those returning from Baobab said. Many of those evicted were not in transit; they had been living in Rome for over a decade.

After a long day full of state violence, community care, and confusion, it was unclear who was left to appeal to. One woman began to laugh. "What a nice shower we all got today." Others were more imploring: "Why would they say that they can host us when they cannot?" "It would be better not to pretend that there is a place for us." Being sent to Baobab reminded some of those evicted that the border management system was why they lived in occupations: "They won't delete our fingerprints and they force us to stay here but what is here for us?" That night, the city was dead set on getting these refugee occupiers out of Rome's city center, and so those evicted turned back to their community and temporarily found sanctuary in other squats.

Political Contestations of Refugee Occupiers

This article details the political contestations of refugee occupiers after they were violently evicted from their home, colloquially called Piazza Indipendenza. Participant observation as an activist and friend of Eritrean refugees during the time of their eviction by the municipal state brought to light the way refugee occupiers both demand rights to subsidized housing and care for each other. This article details how refugees confront the discriminatory distribution of integration resources in Italy by establishing autonomous structures, like housing occupations of abandoned buildings, to both approximate their entitlement to subsidized housing and assert their rights. I argue that, for Eritrean refugee occupiers, it is the Habesha community itself that provides the most reliable form of care, shelter, and protection, such that migrant-occupied squats act as sites of sanctuary.[3]

Occupying housing is not simply an act of necessity; it is a political act to advocate for housing rights. Activists involved in the housing occupation movement generally operate in reference to an *autonomismo* politics of engaged withdrawal.[4] Autonomists are critical of state structures and work to build alternative social arrangements to provide for the needs of the community. Autonomist squatters come from a political tradition willing to undermine the legitimacy of the state when providing care for marginalized people is considered illegal. The Piazza Indipendenza occupation is unique within the context of housing activism in Rome because the occupiers were refugees or individuals with some form of recognized international protection, all from the Horn of Africa. Being both refugees and from a former Italian colonial region, these Eritrean refugees occupy two persecuted subject positions. As refugees, they sought asylum in defiance of legal regimes that persecute or criminalize unjustly. In Italy, these Eritrean refugees turn to housing occupations as they face forms of discrimination oriented around marginalizing poor and foreign others.

Legally contestable practices that provide shelter to persecuted persons have historically been recognized as institutions of sanctuary (for instance, the sanctuary practices in Europe during the high Middle Ages, and the New Sanctuary Movement that burgeoned in the United States). A definitive feature of sanctuary is that it invokes a higher power (whether international law in the case of political asylum, or divine justice in the case of religious/Christian sanctuary) to protect someone from suffering the consequences of a crime that should no longer be considered as such. I thus turn to the practice and literature of sanctuary in order to attend to the interplay between protection, persecution, and criminality at work when refugees, from a place that was formerly colonized, occupy housing in Rome. I argue that while refugee occupiers do not use the ethico-political language of sanctuary to define the care practices of sheltering members of their community, the concept of sanctuary helps interpret the kinds of political and legal contestations undergirding forms of shelter and care in the Habesha refugee community in Rome. Since squats are not recognized religious spaces they are arguably more vulnerable to state intervention than sanctuaries, particularly through evictions. Despite the fact that these spaces are not immune to state violence, these sanctuary squats act as shelters for the persecuted from which to contest repressive governmental policies.

The Ethical Imperative of Sanctuary

Sanctuaries are places where creatures can seek shelter from persecution. While the institution of sanctuary morphs in relation to the sociohistorical context in which it is practiced, it is defined as a holy place in which one can seek refuge or safety. Across numerous sanctuary practices, the most robust codification of the institution of sanctuary for which records exist is found in the ecclesiastic laws of the high Middle Ages. In these sanctuaries, Jews and avowed criminals (fugitive slaves, debtors, thieves, and murderers) could seek protection from corporal and capital punishment as arrangements were made for their exile. However, refuge here was contingent on either conversion to Catholicism, penance, and/or penalty. With the rise of centralized power territorialized in the secular nation-state, the practice of sanctuary became reinterpreted as a means of fostering impunity for criminals and an infringement on sovereign jurisdiction. It was effectively abolished by the eighteenth century.[5]

Practices of providing shelter or legal support to protect persecuted people are being revived in the New Sanctuary Movement, a revival of the US sanctuary movement of the 1980s that opposed deportations of Salvadoran and Guatemalan migrants. Members of the sanctuary movement invoked not only divine justice but also contemporary refugee law to recast deportees as refugees and implicate the US government in contributing to the political conflict these asylum seekers were fleeing (by providing the Salvadoran and Guatemalan governments with funds, training, and arms, for example).[6] The churches and secular institutions that were part of the sanctuary movement contested the legitimacy of immigration law and US foreign policy by sheltering migrants with deportation orders. In the 2000s, the New Sanctuary Movement (NSM) revived this practice of shelter, which is currently being resuscitated in response to the increased deportations ordered by recent US presidential administrations. The NSM, at its most political, shelters undocumented migrants with deportation orders in defiance of Immigration and Customs Enforcement (ICE) officials. By emphasizing that people in sanctuary have a right to an asylum hearing and detailing the dangers they may face once deported, the NSM works to undermine ICE's claims that migrants in sanctuary are criminals who violated US laws and must be deported. Choosing holy sites, mainly churches, as sanctuaries sends the message that disregard for the political sovereignty of the US government in these spaces is not an evasive act to foster impunity for criminal actions but an ethical act to care for the stranger.[7]

Sanctuary movements tend to seek sacred spaces as forms of shelter. Here shelter is provided in the name of divine justice, which is understood to entail ethical and moral commitments that exceed the terrestrial laws of a political entity like the nation-state. While housing occupations are not conceived of as sacred spaces, they pose a similar concern for state jurisdiction and sovereignty. Occupiers defy laws against illegal squatting in order to enable a neglected community to care for itself.

In Rome, housing activists respond to the lack of affordable housing through an autonomist politics of engaged withdrawal. Engaged withdrawal is organized around creating autonomous spaces to both provide for the needs of the community and practice horizontal forms of self-governance.[8] These movements often oppose the hierarchical way the state both distributes resources and selectively represents certain, often privileged, segments of its constituency. Engaged withdrawal refuses to acknowledge the legitimacy of a state when it marginalizes certain factions of society. This refusal is accomplished by building alternative forms of governance and withdrawing into autonomous enclaves, such as housing occupations, where horizontal forms of representation are put into practice. These occupations are like sanctuaries in that they understand themselves to be apart from the purview of the state. Occupations differ from sanctuaries in that they are not considered to be holy. But in the same way that sanctuaries became conceived of as infringing on state sovereignty, the state considers providing shelter in these spaces to be illegal. In these occupied sites, as in sanctuaries, the sovereign legitimacy of a state to deem forms of care and shelter illegal is contested as unjust.

Engaged Withdrawal

Housing occupations are places of solidarity building to mobilize collective forms of engagement with the state and advocate for a more equitable distribution of state resources and representation. For decades, activists in Rome have organized housing occupations in order to increase access to the right to housing, a right enshrined in the Italian constitution.[9] Housing occupations are also established to address the lack of affordable housing in Rome, a result of mismanagement of public housing and real estate speculation. Most housing occupations are oriented around advocating for the state to recognize occupiers' rights to public housing; in so doing, occupiers intentionally seek abandoned, government-owned or requisitioned buildings to occupy.[10]

The occupied building in Piazza Indipendenza, for example, was once the headquarters of Federconsorzi, a state-run agency that provided financial services to Italy's farmers. The company was cooperatively owned until corruption scandals led to its liquidation in 1991, when the headquarters was sequestered by the state.[11] While ownership of the building passed through the hands of real estate speculators, it lay abandoned until 2013, when the housing rights organization Blocchi Precari

Metropolitani (BPM) organized its occupation in conjunction with a number of refugees and immigrants from the Horn of Africa.[12] Once the initial threat of eviction subsided and the occupation was established, BPM left the governance of the building to the Habesha community who lived there. A committee was formed of elected representatives from the varying groups, often determined by ethnic or religious affiliation, to manage the building. This committee was tasked with organizing guard duty and collecting dues for maintenance (cleaning supplies, locks, and interfaces through which to siphon electricity, television, and water), as well as mediating disputes (since, as one occupier put it, "you obviously can't call the police to come").

Occupied housing committees also work toward transforming these buildings considered the property of the state in a way that makes them not only inhabitable but compliant with housing code. Doing so enables these spaces to gain recognition as legal residences by the government, effectively doing the work of the state to provision public housing resources for themselves. Recognition of occupations as legal residences not only secures occupiers permanence in their self-made yet state-owned homes, but it also affords occupants access to health care services as well as the ability to renew legal documents that require proof of a valid address. For refugees and immigrants with permanent residency status, a formal address is the most important element for integration, because in order to qualify for naturalization as an Italian citizen you need a state-recognized residence to demonstrate that you have lived for ten consecutive years on the territory.

The committees of housing occupations also organize occupiers to participate in protests and solidarity building oriented around advocating for housing reform. Residents in certain occupations are obligated to take turns protesting in order to be in good standing as a housing occupier. The political work of occupation engages with the state to advocate for a more equitable distribution of resources. It also withdraws from the state into autonomous forms of self-governance that undermine the legitimacy of state sovereignty when state actors and institutions neglect and marginalize vulnerable members of the community. This contestation of state sovereignty thus mirrors defining aspects of sanctuary as seen in the NSM and the asylum system, where sheltering deportees is not only about withdrawing into sanctuaries. The New Sanctuary Movement is also oriented around engaging with the state to reconsider the right of residency for those in sanctuary. Like many practitioners of the New Sanctuary Movement, who actively took part in state-sanctioned legal hearings on behalf of individuals in sanctuary, housing occupiers are similarly oriented toward engaging with the state to advocate on behalf of those marginalized for their reintegration into society. While housing activists often advocate on behalf of refugees, occupied housing movements are predominantly oriented around horizontal forms of governance to enable refugee occupiers to advocate for themselves. This emphasis on promoting occupier-led initiatives through activist-organized and migrant-run movements perhaps marks a divergence from certain sanctuary movements that tend to rely on the integrity of religious figures or congregations to vouch for those in sanctuary.

From Immigrant Back to Asylum Seeker

Occupying creates space in a situation of severe resource scarcity, especially for underserved and marginalized sectors of society. The majority of individuals in housing occupations in Rome are immigrants, which is indicative of the inadequate, corrupt, and racist ways the state distributes resources.[13] Violent evictions reveal forms of marginalization that usually appear, if at all, as mere negligence. Evictions force negotiation between occupiers and state officials when public outcry over the spectacle of neglect can be leveraged in order to advocate for housing integration. Indeed, the state considered the demands of the displaced refugee occupiers in the aftermath of the Piazza Indipendenza eviction. While evictions are critical political moments, neglecting to provide refugee occupiers with alternatives after an eviction merely leads occupiers to cycle through other housing occupations—vulnerable to repeated evictions as they turn to more precarious forms of squatting.[14]

Many of the Piazza Indipendenza residents had bounced between occupations and were cautiously optimistic that they might be relocated when the police first came to evict them. Many were once part of the Ponte Mammolo occupation, a tented squat that had established itself on a large, grassy triangular area on the outskirts of Rome in the Trieste neighborhood, whose street names "Ethiopia," "Libya," and "Asmara" pay homage to past colonial exploits. When Ponte Mammolo was evicted, two years earlier in the summer of 2015, occupiers slept outside for months, protesting with Italian housing activists. These protests led to roundtables with elected officials, which resulted in negotiations with municipal officers and access to public housing vouchers. These vouchers are part of a neoliberal-style program in which the municipality pays private homeowners the rent of the few voucher holders selected from the ever-increasing pool of people eligible for public housing. Despite having vouchers, it was difficult for many of these Eritrean refugees to find a homeowner willing to rent to them, since Rome lacks adequate antidiscrimination laws, and homeowners can freely specify if they do not want to rent to "blacks" or "foreigners." Many of the occupiers of the Ponte Mammolo squat who were given vouchers retreated to other community occupations, including Piazza Indipendenza, while they tried to find an undiscriminating landlord with a rental that met the stringent facility standards imposed by the city.

Only two years had passed between the two evictions and yet, in this small span of time, the municipal government's willingness to negotiate and offer alternatives drastically changed. After the Piazza Indipendenza eviction there were no vouchers and no recognition of the squat as a residency. Representatives from the municipal government were willing to offer only 107 beds for women with children in asylum reception centers (SPRAR) located on the outskirts of

Rome in Torre Maura e Boccea. The nearly five hundred residents evicted from Piazza Indipendenza elected representatives among themselves to explain why these were not viable options for them, but most of what they said in their brief encounters with municipal officials fell on deaf ears.

Many occupiers were concerned that they were not offered the kinds of government-subsidized housing options that other squatters had been offered in the past, but merely space in temporary asylum reception centers for those deemed vulnerable instead. These were the only structures that were available, or so the municipal representatives claimed. Temporary asylum reception centers in Rome are provisioned through another neoliberal program in which private real estate owners contract with the municipality to turn buildings into spaces for refugee reception.[15] This setup is arguably more lucrative for real estate owners than public housing for a number of reasons, primarily because a portion of the funds come from the EU and because an owner can host more people in smaller spaces.[16] However, from the perspective of the refugee occupiers, it was almost as if the expansion of a more robust infrastructure of asylum reception had the effect of pulling recognized refugees away from the housing rights Italian citizens are entitled to and treating them instead as newly arrived asylum seekers despite their permanent residency status.

The dormitories that the municipal officials made available to those deemed vulnerable were used for political asylum applicants who did not have legal recognition as refugees and who had just arrived on the territory. Treating the occupiers of Piazza Indipendenza on a par with asylum seekers and not as permanent residents meant that the state could significantly diminish the kinds of resources that those evicted would otherwise have access to—creating more barriers to their integration. This move included refugees in a way that insisted on their difference, not as potential/future citizens entitled to rights but as foreigners to be contained in reception centers and evicted from places within the community. What the eviction of Piazza Indipendenza made clear is that Rome's municipal government is shifting away from informal tolerance of occupations as makeshift solutions to the systemic problem of public housing in the city, and toward increased evictions. If this continues, many immigrant occupiers will lose their homes before getting the chance to be recognized as citizens of the country where they have lived, albeit on the margins, for over a decade. Whereas recognizing occupations as legal residencies or relocating occupiers to public housing would enable refugee integration as citizens after ten years, evicting refugee occupiers exacerbates the exclusion of refugees from becoming enfranchised and entitled to greater rights.

Evicted from Eternity

In the days following the eviction, thousands of people came out to protest, with the refugee occupiers from Piazza Indipendenza leading on the front lines. Signs and rallying cries against xenophobia and for the right to housing and refugee integration filled the air and carried across to the ears, and perhaps chagrin, of the tourists and police officers lining the street that led from the Colosseum to Piazza Venezia. People filled the street of the Imperial Forums, the same street where nearly one hundred years earlier 5,500 homes were demolished by the Fascist regime to make their violent claim to authority and power spectacularly manifest in time for the October 1922 March on Rome.[17]

It seemed fitting to protest the marginalization of these refugee occupiers from Piazza Indipendenza upon the now invisible ruination of homes that were demolished to better display the Roman Forums on the way to the Colosseum. It was through these kinds of forced evictions that Rome was transformed from a city with multiple foci into one with a single city center, oriented around the office of Mussolini, the Fascist leader, with Piazza Venezia at its fulcrum. The forcible relocation of the city's poor inhabitants to the periphery made spatially legible the hierarchy of class and power during the Fascist era. This Fascist remodeling and marginalization, or "glorious cleansing," of the urban poor from the city center to the periphery, enabled the unearthing and magnificent reconstruction of the ruins of the Roman Forums. Showcasing the relics of ancient Rome was an integral part of visibly manipulating history in a way that portrayed the Fascist state model as the inevitable outcome of Italy's history, a direct revival of the glory of the Roman Empire.[18] Our march down Via dei Fori Imperiali was a staged interruption on this street where nowadays tourists and Italians alike promenade in bucolic revelry of ancient Rome. It aimed to draw attention to forms of marginalization that continue to persist in the city.[19] We protested against evictions and reasserted that immigrants and the urban poor have as much, if not more, right to the eternal city of Rome as anyone else.

As the sun began to set on the Palatine Hill, Italians who came out in solidarity with the occupiers retreated to their homes, while those evicted refused to leave. They demanded an audience with the mayor, Virginia Raggi, whose office in Palazzo Senatorio was situated at the heart of the city, thanks in part to Mussolini's urban reconstruction projects. In front of Trajan's Column, in arguably the most visible part of the city center, the evicted Eritreans made their encampment and waited for the mayor's response. From here, an occupier and good friend, Simon, pointed to the municipal building kitty-corner to where we were. I followed his finger to the balcony; that is where Mussolini declared Eritrea an Italian colony, he tells me.[20] "Look at us now, you know when the Italians were in Eritrea they wouldn't let Eritreans live in Asmara? Our fathers were not allowed to walk on the main Harnet Avenue but forced to walk in the streets with the horse shit. Here, they won't even let us live on the sidewalk."[21] Simon laughed as I looked down at the pile of horse shit that the police on horseback, assigned to monitor the protest, had left at our feet. I looked up and saw occupiers hanging a banner between two trees: "VIA

Figure 1. WE ARE REFUGEES (NOT) TERRORISTS!!! banner in Piazza Venezia.

CURTATONE 3/PIAZZA INDIPENDENZA, SIAMO RIFUGIATI(NON)TER-RORISTI!!!" (3 CURTATONE STREET/INDEPENDENCE SQUARE, WE ARE REFUGEES (NOT) TERRORISTS) (fig. 1). The night hung heavy with the specter of how the Fascist Italian state experimented with forms of discrimination through spatial exclusion in the colonies before implementing these same techniques back home in Italy.[22]

Despite being able to secure an audience with municipal officials, the refugee occupiers of Piazza Indipendenza were not provided with any housing alternatives—they no longer qualified for public housing because they had illegally squatted. For decades, housing occupations were tolerated in Rome, even by right-wing governments responsible for liberalizing the real estate market and dismantling the Fair Rent Act (Law no. 392/1978). These governments selectively choose whether or not to enforce laws. For example, Law no. 80, passed on May 23, 2014, makes it illegal for squatters to qualify for public housing; if they are caught, they're removed from the waiting list. Although this wasn't enforced in 2015 during the Ponte Mammolo eviction, when occupiers received housing vouchers, it was being invoked now.

The characterization of refugee occupiers as criminal squatters ricocheted in the media through rhetorical slights of hand that made a point to mention migrants alongside terrorist activity, particularly in right-wing media outlets. This was what slogans like "we are refugees not terrorists" were responding to. After the eviction, right-wing media published article after article accusing the squat of harboring transit migrants, or dangerously riotous individuals who would throw gas canisters and Molotov cocktails at the police, or economic exploiters who made a profit on rent. Three occupiers were arrested on charges of resisting arrest, and footage from police surveillance on the scene replayed images of one or two refugee occupiers throwing gas canisters (otherwise used for cooking) in the scuffle with police.[23] These legal and rhetorical forms of criminalization divest the act of occupation of its political intent. Representing refugee occupiers and their attempts to shelter and care for themselves as parasitic and criminal consequently frees the municipality from its obligation to provide refugees with adequate access to the social welfare services they would otherwise be entitled to. Occupying housing through *autogestione* or

Figure 2. Women and disabled refugee occupiers holding down the front lines against police water cannons during the Piazza Indipendenza eviction in Rome, Italy, on August 24, 2017. Angelo Carconi/AP.

self-organization is increasingly understood by state officials as being at odds with state attempts to combat security threats with increased surveillance.

On the other side of the political spectrum were scenes of police officers caught on camera saying, "Make them disappear, if any of them run break their arms." Scenes replayed in the news and on social media of water cannons knocking Habesha women off their feet while a disabled man on crutches struggles to stand against torrents of water that left broken noses and full body bruises in its wake. These scenes portrayed the refugee occupiers not only as vulnerable but also as victims of excessive force used by the police.[24] Placing those seen as vulnerable, like women with children and the disabled, on the front lines is a tactic often used by occupiers to protect the group as a whole. This tactic creates a spectacle aimed at inciting a public outcry, making visible what social neglect and marginalization would rather push to the periphery. The photograph above (fig. 2) is one of the few from that day that capture women and the disabled defiant in front of water cannons before being knocked to the ground.

Refugees are familiar with being portrayed as victims of persecution because it is part of how political asylum claims are adjudicated. This is mirrored in liberal sanctuary movements that often portray those in sanctuary as upstanding migrants whose only crime is crossing a border, a crime that shouldn't be conceived of as such, especially when their right to an asylum hearing is unjustly ignored. The righteousness of the person in sanctuary is invoked to legitimize the nebulous legal line of sanctuary's noncompliance with state security officials. Contemporary sanctuary practices diverge from their medieval counterparts in that they refuse to harbor avowed criminals. They have instead taken on the logic of the political asylum system that harbors those who are victims of persecution—not because of a criminal action they have done but of who they are. Refugees are understood internationally to be victims of repressive regimes in their country of origin that unjustly categorized them as criminals. The ingenuity of the sanctuary movement however, is that it also implicated asylum-granting countries (namely, the United States) in contributing to the conflict that persecuted refugees from San Salvador and Guatemala. While refugee occupiers in Italy cannot be said to experience a form of persecution akin to enforced lifelong military conscription or torture, denouncing asylum-granting countries for lack of integration resources to adequately shelter refugees has been used as a legally valid argument to justify refugees seeking asylum in other EU countries further north.

Fortress Europe

The porous borders of the European Union were initially created to facilitate the steel and coal trades, but soon the Schengen laws allowed European citizens to freely cross national borders as if they were moving through domestic territory. The movement of non-European citizens, however, is heavily regulated by comparison. These regulations are codified in the Dublin Protocols, whereby asylum seekers are required to apply for asylum in the first country of their arrival in the EU. These regulations were established to discourage country choosing and to keep the practice of asylum a practice of seeking protection not opportunity. However, the regulation of internal borders, coupled with the fact that migrants have few (if any) legal means to arrive to asylum-granting countries, means that Europe's frontier countries (Italy included) receive the majority of asylum claims. As a result, frontier countries like Italy and Greece are under greater strain to adequately provide resources for asylum and refugee reception. Asylum seekers traveling through Italy and Greece have invoked this inadequacy to successfully lodge asylum claims in other European countries further north.

In the hallmark case of *M.S.S. v. Belgium and Greece* from 2011, for example, demonstrating the inadequacies of the asylum reception system in Greece justified asylum seeking in Belgium instead.[25] The logic of this case posits that Greece can no longer be considered a country of asylum if it provides insufficient resources there for asylum adjudication and refugee integration. The EU has attempted to offer more financial support for the reception of asylum seekers in countries of first arrival, as well as to institutionalize responsibility sharing of refugee integration across the EU through relocation programs like that of European Asylum Support Office (EASO). It has thus become harder for defense attorneys to argue, on behalf of their intrepid clients under threat of deportation back to Italy, that access to Italian integration resources were inadequate.

During the protests, after the evictions, and in the deliberations about what issues to bring up in municipal negotiations, refugee occupiers repeatedly demanded that their fingerprints be deleted. If the municipal government was going to renege on its recognition of them as refugees and treat them like asylum seekers instead, then they should have the right to seek asylum elsewhere, or so the logic went. They called for the deletion of fingerprints because it is through fingerprint surveillance that European officials track the movement of asylum seekers, registering their country of first arrival and deporting them back to those countries when they try to claim asylum or are found without a right of residency in other parts of the EU. When refugee occupiers call for the cancelation of their finger-prints, they accuse the Italian government of failing to be an asylum-granting coun-try able to ensure that refugees receive their right to adequate integration resources. Refugees protesting against fingerprint surveillance also express frustration with the inequities of the Dublin laws that force them to stay in frontier countries of first arrival, while EU citizens are allowed freer movement in the Eurozone. It is not uncommon for border patrol agents to enforce this inequality through racial or class profiling, by only asking Black passengers, or passengers with shabby-looking luggage, or none at all, for their documents on Europe's transnational trains.

Many of those living in the Piazza Indipendenza occupation professed some pride in having chosen to stay in Italy. Others do not choose to stay in Italy but are constrained to, despite having family members, often wives and children, living in other EU countries. These, often fathers, can only visit their families for a maximum of three months at a time. Often, they only stay for the couple of days they can take off work—perpetually stuck in the predicament of having to sacrifice being present for their family in order to provide them with financial support. Those overstaying this allotment of time run the risk of being deported back to Italy, where they would subsequently face a five-year embargo on their travel out of the country. Housing occupations are attractive options for those who only need housing for a few inter-spersed months of the year or for those looking to cut corners in order to send more money to those they care for. Deleting their fingerprints would allow these refugees to seek asylum in other EU countries, where many already have family ties and potential work opportunities.

Suffice it to say that refugee occupier demands to have more expansive rights to free movement through the EU also fell on deaf ears. The eviction quickly destroyed much of the work that those living in Piazza Indipendenza had done to build a life in the diaspora. Many not only lost their homes but their jobs as well. Many employers fired them because they couldn't understand why their wages weren't enough to live in a legally sanctioned home and so suspected them of crim-inal proclivities. After the eviction, the majority of these refugee occupiers sought solace in other, often more precarious, housing occupations with dubious structural integrity, farther out on the outskirts of town.

Sanctuary Squats

Evictions do a funny thing to one's sense of time. In an hour, you can lose your home. In a few days, life on the streets starts to get to you. In a week, you can find yourself in another housing occupation, further marginalized, on the outskirts of the city, feeling like you lost a decade of your life. In a month, you can give up trying to fight back. And yet, the threat of eviction is always on the horizon, ever present, ever possible.

In the end, Piazza Indipendenza occupiers sought solace within their own community, in the remaining occupations that are increasingly under threat of eviction. Evictions are moments when the spectacle of state violence provides a forum through which migrants can draw attention to the obscured forms of state neglect that led them to occupy the building in the first place. This publicity thus positions them to be better able to advocate for recognition of their right to affordable housing and international protection. But what happens when the public is no longer sympathetic? As rising populist movements in Italy gain votes by scapegoating refugees and migrants, the public offers little sympathy and little outcry over migrant evictions.

Drawing parallels between sanctuary practices and housing occupations encourages us to reconsider the illegality of housing occupations and the criminalization of refugee occupiers. Housing occupations are interventions that attempt to build alternative forms of community in a context of resource scarcity. If criminalizing these practices functions not to integrate refugees into society but marginalize them further, then perhaps squatting is a crime that should no longer be considered as such.

In DIY refugee-occupied places, people can become proprietary about the resources they've invested to make their space inhabitable. But often, these are places where people share what little they have with those who are in need of that little, making a life for themselves as they are made to wait and work for change. These squats are not sacred spaces, but they are sanctuaries where the illegality of sheltering and caring for those perennially marginalized is cause for contestation.

Carla Hung is a postdoctoral researcher at Arizona State University. Her dissertation, "The Politics of Asylum among Eritrean Refugees in Italy," investigates how hospitality among Eritreans is criminalized by Europe's border security system. Her ethnographic work focuses on the intersections between migration studies, humanitarianism, and postcolonial studies.

Notes

1. "Habesha" is a term for the highland-living ethnic groups that span both Eritrea and Ethiopia whose language derives from Ge'ez (Tesfagiorgis, *Eritrea*, 210). The major part of the diasporic community in Rome with whom I conducted ethnographic research defined themselves as part of the Habesha community, even though there were always exceptions with people who were Afar or Bilen, etc. Reference to the term "Habesha" serves as a sometimes clumsy shorthand to highlight the community of Ethiopian, Eritrean, and even Somali individuals from different ethnic groups that live together in these contested diasporic spaces.

2. The transit migrants who tend to be part of the Baobab crowd have generally been found to be in violation of the Schengen laws that regulate movement within the European Union. Often, these transit migrants have been sent back to Italy because their fingerprints were originally registered there as the first asylum granting country of arrival, and the Dublin Regulations necessitate that they must therefore apply for asylum in Italy. Upon return, many have trouble inserting themselves into overcrowded

reception centers and thus find themselves living on the street while they wait for a decision to be made on their asylum request or while they try to organize a way to leave the country again. Others still are asylum seekers who have received a negative decision on their asylum application and are effectively undocumented or clandestine.

3. In Italy, reference is made to the term "occupation" when speaking about an illegally occupied space used for housing; whereas the colloquial English term "squat" is rarely used. Use of the term "occupation" in Rome complicates the illegality of occupying abandoned state-owned structures by contextualizing these acts within a political history of struggle for housing rights, as well as in a social history of establishing "social centers" to encourage autonomous or alternative ways of life to flourish apart from those established by mainstream capitalism. Throughout the text, I have elected to strategically use both terms, "occupation" and "squat," in order to underscore differing perspectives. Mudu, "Ogni Sfratto Sarà una Barricata."

4. Virno, "Virtuosity and Revolution."

5. Shoemaker, *Sanctuary and Crime in the Middle Ages*; Rosenwein, *Negotiating Space*; Sassen, *Territory, Authority, Rights*.

6. Coutin, *The Culture of Protest*.

7. Coutin and Perla, "Legacies and Origins of the 1980s US–Central American Sanctuary Movement"; Chinchilla, Hamilton, and Loucky, "The Sanctuary Movement and Central American Activism in Los Angeles"; Wiltfang and Cochran, "The Sanctuary Movement and the Smuggling of Undocumented Central Americans into the United States"; Crittenden, *Sanctuary*; Michels and Blaikie, "'I Took Up the Case of the Stranger'"; Hondagneu-Sotelo, *God's Heart Has No Borders*; and Terry and Jiménez, "The New Sanctuary Movement."

8. Virno, "Virtuosity and Revolution," 196–97; Berardi, *After the Future*; Graeber, *Fragments of an Anarchist Anthropology*, 60; and Procupez, "The Need for Patience."

9. See Articles 2, 3, and 47, subsection 2 of the Italian Constitution enacted in 1947. Senato della Repubblica, 1947, *Costituzione della Repubblica Italiana*.

10. Squatting Europe Kollective, *The Squatters' Movement in Europe*; Marinaro and Thomassen, *Global Rome*; Mudu, "Patterns of Segregation in Contemporary Rome"; Armati, *La Scintilla*; and Belloni, "Learning How to Squat."

11. "Le speculazioni immobiliari."

12. "Lo sgombero e il destino del palazzo di via Curtatone."

13. Arjona, *La città meticcia*; Vereni, "Liminal Cosmopolitanisms."

14. López, "The Squatters' Movement in Europe"; Manjikian, *Securitization of Property Squatting in Europe*; Neuwirth, *Cities*; Vasudevan, "The Autonomous City."

15. "Rapporto sulla protezione internazionale in Italia 2017."

16. "Ecco quanto spende l'Italia per i migranti."

17. Cervelli, "Rome as a Global City."

18. Cervelli, "Rome as a Global City," 49; Gentile, *Fascismo di pietra*; Baxa, *Roads and Ruins*; Arthurs, *Excavating Modernity*; Agnew, "The Impossible Capital"; Painter, *Mussolini's Rome*; and Herzfeld, *Evicted from Eternity*.

19. Cannata, Carloni, and Castronovi, *Le periferie nella città metropolitana*; Daolio, *Le lotte per la casa in Italia*; Insolera, *Roma moderna*; and Tozzetti, *La casa e non solo*.

20. In Piazza Venezia on May 9, 1936, Mussolini took to the balcony and declared that Italy finally had its empire now that Ethiopia was under Italian sovereignty.

21. Harnet Avenue was once called Viale Mussolini, "Harnet" meaning "independence" in Tigrinya, the official state language of Eritrea.
22. Makki, "Imperial Fantasies, Colonial Realities"; Pankhurst, "Italian Settlement Policy in Eritrea"; Taddia, "Constructing Colonial Power"; Ben-Ghiat and Fuller, *Italian Colonialism*; Palumbo, *A Place in the Sun*; and Mesghenna, *Italian Colonialism*.
23. Progetto Melting Pot Europa, "Pena sospesa per i rifugiati condannati in seguito agli sgomberi di Piazza Indipendenza."
24. "Sgombero dei rifugiati a Roma"; and "Italy: Police Beat Refugees."
25. Clayton, "Asylum Seekers in Europe"; Mallia, "Case of *M.S.S. v. Belgium and Greece*"; Moreno-Lax, "Dismantling the Dublin System"; *M.S.S. v. Belgium and Greece*; and "Case of *M.S.S. v. Belgium and Greece* European Court of Human Rights."

References

Agnew, John. "The Impossible Capital: Monumental Rome under Liberal and Fascist Regimes, 1870–1943." *Geografiska Annaler: Series B, Human Geography* 80, no. 4 (1998): 229–40.

Arjona, Ángeles. *La città meticcia: Riflessioni teoriche e analisi di alcuni casi europei per il governo locale delle migrazioni*. Milan: Franco Angeli, 2007.

Armati, Cristiano. *La Scintilla: Dalla Valle Alla Metropoli, Una Storia Antagonista Della Lotta per La Casa*. Rome: Fandango libri, 2015.

Arthurs, Joshua. *Excavating Modernity: The Roman Past in Fascist Italy*. Ithaca, NY: Cornell University Press, 2013.

Baxa, Paul. *Roads and Ruins: The Symbolic Landscape of Fascist Rome*. Toronto: University of Toronto Press, 2010.

Belloni, Milena. "Learning How to Squat: Cooperation and Conflict between Refugees and Natives in Rome." *Journal of Refugee Studies* 29, no. 4 (December 1, 2016): 506–27.

Ben-Ghiat, Ruth, and Mia Fuller. *Italian Colonialism*. New York: Palgrave Macmillan, 2016.

Berardi, Franco. *After the Future*. Baltimore, MD: AK Press, 2011.

Cannata, B., S. Carloni, and A. Castronovi. *Le periferie nella città metropolitana*. Rome: Ediesse, 2008.

"Case of *M.S.S. v. Belgium and Greece* European Court of Human Rights." *International Journal of Refugee Law* 23, no. 2 (2011): 288–403.

Cervelli, Pierluigi. "Rome as a Global City: Mapping New Cultural and Political Boundaries." In *Global Rome: Changing Faces of the Eternal City*, edited by Isabella Clough Marinaro and Bjorn Thomassen, translated by Isabella Clough Marinaro, 48–61. Bloomington: Indiana University Press, 2014.

Chinchilla, Norma Stoltz, Nora Hamilton, and James Loucky. "The Sanctuary Movement and Central American Activism in Los Angeles." *Latin American Perspectives* 36, no. 6 (2009): 101–26.

Clayton, Gina. "Asylum Seekers in Europe: *M.S.S. v Belgium and Greece*." *Human Rights Law Review* 11, no. 4 (2011): 758–73.

Coutin, Susan Bibler. *The Culture of Protest: Religious Activism and the U.S. Sanctuary Movement*. Boulder, CO: Westview Press, 1993.

Coutin, Susan Bibler, and Hector Perla. "Legacies and Origins of the 1980s US-Central American Sanctuary Movement." In *Sanctuary Practices in International Perspectives: Migration, Citizenship, and Social Movements*, edited by Randy K. Lippert and Sean Rehaag, 91–109. New York: Routledge, 2013.

Crittenden, Ann. *Sanctuary: A Story of American Conscience and the Law in Collision*. New York: Weidenfeld and Nicolson, 1988.

Daolio, Andreina, ed. *Le lotte per la casa in Italia: Milano, Torino, Roma, Napoli*. Milan: Feltrinelli, 1974.

"Ecco quanto spende l'Italia per i migranti: E quanto contribuisce l'Unione europea." *Eunews*, June 11, 2018. www.eunews.it/2018/06/11/quanto-spende-italia-migranti-unione-europea /106009.

Gentile, Emilio. *Fascismo di pietra*. Rome: Laterza, 2007.

Graeber, David. *Fragments of an Anarchist Anthropology*. Chicago: Prickly Paradigm Press, 2004.

Grazioli, Margherita. "From Citizens to Citadins? Rethinking Right to the City inside Housing Squats in Rome, Italy." *Citizenship Studies* 21, no. 4 (2017): 393–408.

Herzfeld, Michael. *Evicted from Eternity: The Restructuring of Modern Rome*. Chicago: University of Chicago Press, 2009.

Hondagneu-Sotelo, Pierrette. *God's Heart Has No Borders: How Religious Activists Are Working for Immigrant Rights*. Berkeley: University of California Press, 2008.

Insolera, Italo. *Roma moderna: Da Napoleone I al XXI secolo*. Turin: G. Einaudi, 2011.

"Italy: Police Beat Refugees during Eviction." Human Rights Watch, August 25, 2017. www.hrw .org/news/2017/08/25/italy-police-beat-refugees-during-eviction.

"Le speculazioni immobiliari di Idea-Fimit dietro allo sgombero e alle violenze di piazza Indipendenza." *Business Insider Italia*, August 31, 2017. it.businessinsider.com/le -speculazioni-immobiliari-di-idea-fimit-dietro-allo-sgombero-e-alle-violenze-di-piazza -indipendenza/.

"Lo sgombero e il destino del palazzo di via Curtatone." *Il Manifesto*, August 26, 2017. ilmanifesto.it/lurgenza-dello-sgombero-e-il-destino-del-palazzo-di-via-curtatone/.

López, Miguel A. Martínez. "The Squatters' Movement in Europe: A Durable Struggle for Social Autonomy in Urban Politics." *Antipode* 45, no. 4 (2013): 866–87.

Makki, Fouad. "Imperial Fantasies, Colonial Realities: Contesting Power and Culture in Italian Eritrea." *South Atlantic Quarterly* 107, no. 4 (2008): 735–54.

Mallia, Patricia. "Case of *M.S.S. v. Belgium and Greece*: A Catalyst in the Re-thinking of the Dublin II Regulation." *Refugee Survey Quarterly* 30, no. 3 (2011): 107–28.

Manjikian, Mary. *Securitization of Property Squatting in Europe*. New York: Routledge, 2013.

Marinaro, Isabella Clough, and Bjorn Thomassen. *Global Rome: Changing Faces of the Eternal City*. Bloomington: Indiana University Press, 2014.

Mesghenna, Yemane. *Italian Colonialism: A Case of Study of Eritrea, 1869–1934: Motive, Praxis, and Result*. Lund, Sweden: University of Lund, 1988.

Michels, David H., and David Blaikie. "'I Took Up the Case of the Stranger': Arguments from Faith, History and Law." In *Sanctuary Practices in International Perspectives: Migration, Citizenship, and Social Movements*, edited by Randy K. Lippert and Sean Rehaag, 28–42. London: Routledge, 2013.

Moreno-Lax, Violeta. "Dismantling the Dublin System: *M.S.S. v. Belgium and Greece*." *European Journal of Migration and Law* 14, no. 1 (2012): 1–31.

M.S.S. v. Belgium and Greece. Application no. 30696/09, European Court of Human Rights Grand Chamber, January 21, 2011.

Mudu, Pierpaolo. "Ogni Sfratto Sarà una Barricata: Squatting for Housing and Social Conflict in Rome." In *The Squatters' Movement in Europe: Commons and Autonomy as Alternatives to*

Capitalism, by Squatting Europe Kollective, edited by Claudio Cattaneo and Miguel A. Martínez, 136–64. London: Pluto Press, 2014.

Mudu, Pierpaolo. "Patterns of Segregation in Contemporary Rome." *Urban Geography* 27, no. 5 (2006): 422–40.

Neuwirth, Robert. *Shadow Cities: A Billion Squatters, A New Urban World*. London: Routledge, 2016.

Painter, Borden. *Mussolini's Rome: Rebuilding the Eternal City*. New York: Macmillan, 2005.

Palumbo, Patrizia. *A Place in the Sun: Africa in Italian Colonial Culture from Post-Unification to the Present*. Berkeley: University of California Press, 2003.

Pankhurst, Richard. "Italian Settlement Policy in Eritrea and Its Repercussions, 1889–1896." *Boston University Papers in African History* 1 (1964): 1–19.

Procupez, Valeria. "The Need for Patience: The Politics of Housing Emergency in Buenos Aires." *Current Anthropology* 56, no. S11 (2015): S55–65.

Progetto Melting Pot Europa (blog). "Pena sospesa per i rifugiati condannati in seguito agli sgomberi di Piazza Indipendenza." www.meltingpot.org/Pena-sospesa-per-i-rifugiati -condannati-in-seguito-agli.html (accessed October 7, 2018).

"Rapporto sulla protezione internazionale in Italia 2017." Anci, Caritas Italiana, Cittalia, Fondazione Migrantes, Servisione Centrale Dello Sprar, UNHCR, October 2017. www .unhcr.it/wp-content/uploads/2017/10/Rapporto_2017_web.pdf.

Rosenwein, Barbara H. *Negotiating Space: Power, Restraint, and Privileges of Immunity in Early Medieval Europe*. Ithaca, NY: Cornell University Press, 1999.

Sassen, Saskia. *Territory, Authority, Rights: From Medieval to Global Assemblages*. Princeton, NJ: Princeton University Press, 2006.

Senato della Repubblica. *Costituzione della Repubblica Italiana* (1947). www.senato.it /documenti/repository/istituzione/costituzione.pdf.

"Sgombero dei rifugiati a Roma, è crisi di gestione non di immigrazione." UNICEF, agosto 2017. www.unicef.it/7713/sgombero-dei-rifugiati-a-roma-crisi-di-gestione-non-di-migranti .htm.

Shoemaker, Karl. *Sanctuary and Crime in the Middle Ages, 400–1500*. New York: Fordham University Press, 2011.

Squatting Europe Kollective. *The Squatters' Movement in Europe: Commons and Autonomy as Alternatives to Capitalism*, edited by Claudio Cattaneo and Miguel A. Martínez. London: Pluto Press, 2014.

Taddia, Irma. "Constructing Colonial Power and Political Collaboration in Italian Eritrea." In *Personality and Political Culture in Modern Africa*, edited by Melvin E. Page, Stephanie F. Beswick, Tim Carmichael, and Jay Spaulding, 23–36. Boston: African Studies Center, Boston University, 1998.

Terry, Diana, and Nicolás A. Jiménez. "The New Sanctuary Movement." *Hispanic* 20, no. 8 (2007): 42.

Tesfagiorgis G., Mussie. *Eritrea*. Africa in Focus. Santa Barbara, CA: ABC-CLIO, 2010.

Tozzetti, Aldo. *La casa e non solo: Lotte popolari a Roma e in Italia dal dopoguerra a oggi*. Rome: Editori Riuniti, 1989.

Vasudevan, Alexander. "The Autonomous City: Towards a Critical Geography of Occupation." *Progress in Human Geography* 39, no. 3 (2015): 316–37.

Vereni, Piero. "Liminal Cosmopolitanisms: Identity Strategies and Categorization of Culture and Class in Multi-Ethnic Squats in Rome." *Anuac* 4, no. 2 (2016): 130–56.

Virno, Paolo. "Virtuosity and Revolution: The Political Theory of Exodus." In *Radical Thought in Italy: A Potential Politics*, edited by Paolo Virno and Michael Hardt, 189–212. Minneapolis: University of Minnesota Press, 1996.

Wiltfang, Gregory L., and John K. Cochran. "The Sanctuary Movement and the Smuggling of Undocumented Central Americans into the United States: Crime, Deviance, or Defiance?" *Sociological Spectrum* 14, no. 2 (1994): 101–28.

Freedom to Move, Freedom to Stay, Freedom to Return

Freedom to Return

A Transnational Roundtable on Sanctuary Activism

Sunaina Maira

This roundtable focuses on the concept of sanctuary in different national contexts of migrant solidarity activism, putting into conversation activists in the United States, Europe, and Australia. This transnational forum is based on interviews I did individually in 2017 with sanctuary and Palestine solidarity activists in the San Francisco Bay Area (Lara Kiswani and Sagnicthe Salazar); in London with an activist from the UK organization Right to Remain (Lisa Matthews); and with activists from a *sans-papiers* solidarity organization in Basel, Switzerland (Fabrice Mangold, Olivia Jost, Jana Haeberlein, Claudia Berger). These interviews were part of pilot research that I did in the context of growing public interest in sanctuary activism in the United States in the era of President Donald J. Trump, and my own desire to learn from experiences of migrant solidarity organizing in Europe. This dialogue also draws on a sanctuary activism workshop I co-organized in San Francisco in October 2017. "Community and Movement Defense in the Trump Era" involved forty community activists from different organizations in the Bay Area, the US–Mexico border, as well as from Europe and Australia (including Kiswani, Salazar, Haeberlein, Maurice Stierl from Germany, and Charandev Singh from Australia). It included a prominent faith leader of the US sanctuary movement from Arizona (Rev. John Fife); Oakland activists from the abolitionist organization Critical

Radical History Review
Issue 135 (October 2019)   DOI 10.1215/01636545-7607884
© 2019 by MARHO: The Radical Historians' Organization, Inc.

Resistance;[1] and a Syrian activist based in Switzerland (Osama Abdullah), who participated virtually as he was denied a US visa after Trump's travel ban. The San Francisco workshop sought to share strategies, link movements across borders, and foster historical connections drawing on the insights of sanctuary leaders of the 1980s.[2]

The virtual roundtable I have curated here, based on my interviews and the workshop discussion, creates a conversation among activists who were not all able to physically meet in the same room—precisely due to the obstacles posed by borders, in some instances. This format offers a multivocal dialogue between activists from diverse backgrounds challenging state, supra-state, and colonial borders. The roundtable also features images of posters and graffiti that visually illustrate sanctuary activism in public spaces—on windows, walls, sidewalks, and in rallies. These artistic interventions attempt to transform the public sphere in relation to migration and belonging. These artworks support the growing sanctuary city and immigrant solidarity movement, across national borders, by making visible solidarity with those migrants disappeared through detention and deportation.

The roundtable does not offer a seamless narrative or comprehensive account of sanctuary activism, nor does it document the (shifting) migration policies in these different countries. Instead, it emphasizes the activists' voices and struggles against border imperialism and the ways they understand the concept of sanctuary, highlighting the tensions among their varied uses of this term. Their insights also allude to the ways migration-control policies of different states inform one another and how activist strategies travel across borders. Some activists, such as Rev. Fife and Rev. Michael Yoshii, belong to faith-based sanctuary movements upholding Christian principles of aiding the oppressed and "welcoming the stranger";[3] in the United States, sanctuary churches have provided refuge to Central Americans fleeing US proxy wars in the 1980s and denied asylum in the United States, which evolved into the New Sanctuary Movement in 2007.[4] Other activists—such as Abdullah, Matthews, and Stierl—are part of the global No Borders movement, a network of organizations in Europe that challenges state borders, demands freedom of movement, and organizes direct action. Most activists here engage with migrant solidarity activism based on antiracist, anticapitalist, and anticolonial principles that contest a liberal democratic approach to sanctuary, that is, one that seeks only to provide a safe haven to vulnerable immigrants without challenging the nexus among border regimes, Western imperialism, and neoliberal capitalism. My interest in learning from these activists emerged from my organizing with a Radical Sanctuary collective I cofounded at UC Davis in 2016 after Trump's election. Beyond resistance to deportations, we opposed white supremacy, fascism, neoliberal capitalism, heteropatriarchy, Zionism, and imperialism.

While I cannot delve into the specific historical, legal, and political details of each regional context, different policies and histories of migration shape the possibilities of sanctuary. Switzerland, a small nation-state with a very high percentage of noncitizens due to restrictive citizenship laws, has intensely profiled and deported "illegal aliens" since the 1990s, with the "foreigners police" (*Fremdenpolizei*) often targeting Black migrants.[5] There have been occupations of churches by activists, asylum seekers, and *sans-papiers* (undocumented) immigrants and an emergent "City for All" movement, based on the right to the city (for example, "We are all Zurich"), as I discuss below.[6] Across these contexts, migration and asylum are increasingly charged with rising right-wing populism, particularly in UK debates about Brexit. Further, the UK has its own border-control regime distinct from that of the EU. Since 2007, the UK "City of Sanctuary" movement has formed a national network of cities such as Sheffield and Cambridge that have passed city council motions supporting local refugee communities. This movement has organized solidarity activities promoting a "culture of hospitality" for noncitizens and challenged indefinite detention as part of Right to Remain's campaign, These Walls Must Fall.[7] Australia is a laboratory for immigrant detention, and Prime Minister John Howard's "Pacific Solution" made it a model of offshore incarceration in "remote island locations," like Indonesia and Nauru, to isolate and conceal migrants and refugees.[8] Activists like Singh have challenged Australia's "border imperialism" and observed that it is "built on the foundations of the White Australia policy, racism, and imprisonment," organizing campaigns with refugees and ex-detainees against policies of mandatory immigrant detention and refoulement.[9] Singh's insights crucially highlight how strategies for immigrant incarceration developed by states like Australia are adopted by other states.[10]

Different terms circulate in relation to sanctuary activism. For example, *sans-papiers* names undocumented migrants in Switzerland and France, and *solidarity city* describes sanctuary cities in Western Europe. "Welcome" culture often encapsulates the principles of sanctuary and solidarity with migrants in Europe. In the United States, too, no single definition of sanctuary exists, with sanctuary jurisdictions among municipalities, campuses, and congregations enacting a wide variety of meanings. In 2018, the Oakland mayor publicly defied the Trump administration's crackdown on undocumented immigrants, as had California. In response, the Justice Department sued the state, opposing the sanctuary laws that prohibit cooperation between federal immigration officials and local and state law enforcement, and the US attorney general condemned Oakland's "radical open borders agenda."[11]

The roundtable addresses three key themes: (1) the meaning of sanctuary in various campaigns that enact the right to freedom of movement across borders, in defiance of state laws, border policing, and imperial wars; (2) the binary of "good," or deserving, versus "bad," or unworthy migrants that characterizes the increasing institutionalization of migrant solidarity activism (for example, as demonstrated by the formal employment of sanctuary activists by nonprofit organizations); and (3) an abolitionist sanctuary model that goes beyond harboring undocumented immigrants and links border violence to carcerality, neoliberal capitalism, white supremacy, settler colonialism, and fascism.

Solidarity

Alyn Maria, US migrant solidarity activist, No More Deaths/No Más Muertes, Arizona—humanitarian organization that aims to end deaths, disappearances, and suffering in the US–Mexico border through direct aid and advocacy: We run a hotline and provide resources, such as water and medical care, for migrants crossing the [US–Mexico] border. We have a sanctuary camp on the border which was raided by border patrol agents, and they have apprehended border crossers. . . . The border has moved into the interior of the US, and they are testing practices on the US–Mexico border of collaboration between immigration agents and police.[12]

Sagnicthe Salazar, community organizer, Xicana Moratorium Coalition, Third World Resistance Network, Oakland, California: Our basic definition of sanctuary is providing safety in an imperial state where no place or person is safe. We want to reimagine sanctuary beyond the migrant rights movement. . . . There is a particular role for activists who are in the belly of the beast to address the impetus for forced migration from overseas. . . . We need to acknowledge that there are people who are not able to physically be at the workshop today [in San Francisco] due to racist border policies, such as Osama [Abdullah, who was denied a US visa].

Osama Abdullah, Syrian migrant and activist based in Zurich; volunteer with Alarm Phone/Watch the Med, a phone hotline run by European and North African activists supporting migrants crossing the Mediterranean and remotely assisting rescue operations (participating in the San Francisco workshop via Skype): I've been involved with the Alarm Phone (AP) since 2015. I help with translations into Arabic and with my knowledge of the Turkish-Greek border crossing context. My brother crossed to Greece when he fled Syria, also many of my friends. The AP plays a major role in supporting migrants—calling coast guards, sending out alarms on social media, providing language translation. Our team started with five people in Switzerland, and now we're thirteen. There is no hierarchy. People step in when they can. Our work comes from a moral compass; we want to change the situation and be active. In 2015, migrants collectively crashed the borders of the EU. We helped people directly then, but we never claimed to be a humanitarian organization. Our aim was to create a political movement based on solidarity.

We are part of an amazing network of organizations providing support and solidarity. For example, it includes the No Borders campaign in Greece and activists working on the ground who go to the borders and [migrant] camps, provide consultation for migrants, and give them advice on options and routes for travel. The situation keeps changing. I am also part of a new project, Moving Europe, which is a small group of activists, and Welcome to Europe, which does research on the [migration and asylum] laws in different countries in Europe and makes them accessible to people entering Europe, monitoring the situation at borders, human rights

Figure 1. Refugee
solidarity flier posted in
public spaces in the Bay
Area after Trump's
election. Designed by
Jewish Voice for Peace.

violations, police practices. It is based on the principles of the right to information
and the right to freedom of movement. Our solidarity network is based on antiracist
principles: the belief that the laws are discriminatory.[13] We believe in the right to
shelter, the right to food, the right to documentation. We help people in flight—this
might be considered a form of sanctuary for people in need; for example, someone at
sea who's in distress. The concept of sanctuary is based on working to keep one
another safe at borders and challenge exclusion. It is inspired by the Underground
Railroad. . . . There are ordinary people traveling around Greece or Germany who
give migrants a ride. There are churches, especially in Germany, that offer asylum
and advocate for asylum seekers, and also in Switzerland where they have housed
families.

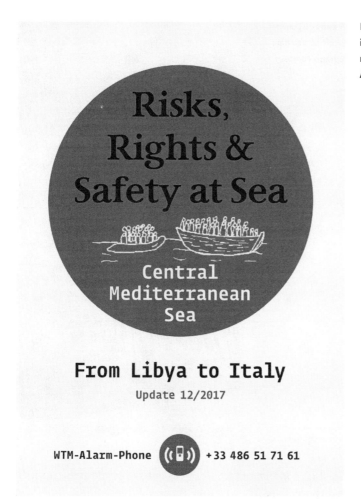

Figure 2. Alarm Phone informational flier for migrants. Courtesy the Alarm Phone.

Rev. Mike Yoshii, pastor and faith-based activist, Buena Vista United Methodist Church,[14] Alameda, California: We are involved with sanctuary work at different levels. There is an East Bay sanctuary network. We belong to the Methodist Church's national immigration task force, whose chair [Bishop Minerva Carcano] has an explicit focus on sanctuary; and there is the western jurisdiction of churches. . . . We are part of a statewide network of churches across denominations and faith groups, the Interfaith Movement for Human Integrity. Last April [2017], Buena Vista declared it was a sanctuary church. The city of Alameda has declared it is a sanctuary city.

Our church was always a sanctuary space. The congregation is historically Japanese and Asian American. It was founded in 1898 to serve immigrants from Japan facing racism. This is not today's definition of sanctuary. But in World War II, Japanese Americans who could not get housing lived in the church. . . . Not all

Figure 3. Welcome banner, Our Lady of Lourdes Church, depicting Mary and Joseph as travelers seeking shelter, Oakland. Photograph courtesy author.

churches are involved in justice making, but for us, it's core to living with our faith in action. It is based on the theology of supporting those who are oppressed and marginalized—also a spiritual sense of sanctuary.

Rev. John Fife, foundational US interfaith sanctuary activist and cofounder of No More Deaths/No Más Muertes, Arizona[15]**:** In the 1980s, Central American refugees arrived on the border of the US. There were detention facilities on the Southwest border, and legal aid clinics could not help Salvadorans to get asylum. With the help of a Catholic priest in Mexico, we smuggled people across the border into the church. We contacted congregations across the US and the movement for sanctuary started. This was a specific notion of sanctuary. We were testing: Could faith communities be centers of nonviolent direct action? The government did not want to indict us, though we were infiltrated by the FBI and had to deal with surveillance and entrapment. They indicted eighteen of us but the movement doubled during this time with support generated through public media. . . . We also sued the US government for violating refugee asylum laws. . . .

Faith communities can be effective sites of public resistance because the state doesn't know how to deal with faith institutions. Faith institutions are cross-border, transnational institutions. But we need layers of organizing to resist attacks on our communities: in cities, universities, with labor. We need civil disobedience against the "civil initiatives" in order to protect people against the abuses of the government. . . . Sanctuary provided the context from which refugees could speak.

Rev. Yoshii, Buena Vista United Methodist Church: Churches were a key element in the sanctuary movement because they provide a physical space; the identity of the church is a deterrent to state intrusion, it is a space of moral authority, and so you can leverage the space and identity of the church for building the movement. Tactically, it creates a public debate vis-à-vis the state.

Fabrice Mangold, Olivia Jost, and Jana Haeberlein, Swiss and German migrant solidarity activists, Anlaufstelle für San-Papiers (Bureau for Undocumented Migrants),[16] Basel, Switzerland

F: Some immigrants who wanted asylum and sans-papiers occupied churches in Switzerland and sought sanctuary, as well as solidarity activists.[17] The demand at the time was for regularization of immigrants without papers. . . . "Kirchenasyl" (church asylum), which makes a church the sanctuary, . . . has no legal basis [in Switzerland], but it is a kind of tradition. Two years ago, the police raided a church in Basel, where some activists tried a revival of this tradition, and deported all the people who slept there.

O: In 2008, refugees from Afghanistan, Iraq, Eritrea, and other countries who did not get asylum also sought refuge in churches. Around 2001, the No One Is Illegal movement was launched in Germany;[18] Swiss activist groups draw on organizing models in Germany and France. The French region in Switzerland is more progressive; there are more labor unions and more activism. It has been challenging for the migrant rights movement to sustain itself in Switzerland. . . . Switzerland is very small, very controlled, and it is difficult for undocumented migrants to escape control.

F: Unfortunately, there is no city or canton in Switzerland that would officially support undocumented people, which makes it difficult to start using the concept [sanctuary]. . . . Historically, there is a strong resistance to immigration in Switzerland and xenophobia and racism have long been a part of Swiss politics. Since September 11, 2001, there has been rising Islamophobia and racism here. It is difficult for migrants to get jobs due to racism; there is more profiling of Black people on the streets. There was the [mosque] minaret order passed in 2009.[19] Citizenship in Switzerland is based on the principle of jus sanguinis (blood), not on jus soli, so antiracist principles are important in migrant rights. Our principles are that of no borders and we use human rights.

J: For me, the term "sanctuary" has a decidedly North American connotation. It is close to what in German is called *"Bleiberecht"*—right to stay—but seems to be used here much more in reference to actions and political positions you find in North American cities and that activists here would like to achieve, too, at some point in the future. . . .

Figure 4. Antiracist flier, Basel, Switzerland.
Photograph by author.

There seems to be some overlap with the term "urban citizenship" in demands to introduce a so-called city card in Zurich, for example, though the implications are different, because people here are obliged to carry an official identification document with them at all times; a solidarity card here just does not have the same power as in other places.[20] Urban citizenship refers to claims to the city/town made by migrants and nonmigrants alike, to equal participation and access to resources and rights. But the gap between sans-papiers and other marginalized people in Switzerland with citizenship rights seems to be much greater here than in the US, because even though there is poverty and there are homeless people here, the state still cares for everyone much more.

Lisa Matthews, British migrant rights activist, Right to Remain, London, UK: Many cities, such as Sheffield and Bristol, have passed symbolic statements of sanctuary.[21] In the UK, deportation is used to describe those migrants with criminal sentences while "removal" is the term used to describe routine deportations. . . . There have been charter flights flying people back to Afghanistan, Sri Lanka, or Ghana. Some people refused to be deported on these commercial flights. There are also instances of pilots refusing to carry deportees against their will. There's a long history of direct action resisting flights for at least ten years.[22] Activists would book seats on their flights in order to prevent deportations. They managed to shut down a deportation from Stansted Airport. There have also been anti-raid actions in the UK and across Europe. . . . There are a lot of asylum seekers in Glasgow, and the "Glasgow Grannies" on housing estates had an alarm phone to allow people to

Figure 5. Right to Remain postcard against immigrant detention.

escape and resist officials. They actually managed to stop some dawn raids and blocked vans from leaving [with immigrants]. This has also happened in South London; for example, in Brixton people have chased out vans. There is an anti-raid network on Twitter. . . . I think this is the closest action to sanctuary activism in the UK. There have also been huge protests outside immigrant detention centers, and activists have blocked coaches leaving detention centers with Sri Lankan refugees being deported.

We were previously called the National Anti-Deportation Campaign but we had a major shift in our framework since 2013 to supporting grassroots groups and providing them with tools, building their [organizing] capacity. Earlier, the focus was only on the ultimate experience of deportation, but after prevention of deportation, we realized that life was still very precarious, and meaningless for many. So now we are called the Right to Remain. We developed a toolkit [about rights and options in the UK immigration and asylum system],[23] because we realized that after migrants and asylum seekers arrive here, they may face removal. Many are from Syria (about 85 percent of whom are granted asylum) and Iraq (only 10 percent are granted asylum). There is an appalling disparity in the granting of asylum, and there is very low acceptance of Afghan asylum seekers.

Lara Kiswani, Palestinian activist; Executive Director, Arab Resource and Organizing Center (AROC), San Francisco;[24] organizer with Third World

Resistance Network, Bay Area: Sanctuary is a form of community self-defense. The attacks on immigrant communities are also attacks on community organizing. So we need to defend communities and also defend our movements under Trump. There has been a criminalization of dissent. We need to organize defense at meetings, at protests, against digital surveillance and entrapment of young Arab males on electronic media. We need to consider the intersections of fascism and Zionism. For example, Arab and Muslim communities and refugees are dealing with forced migration due to wars. The same countries targeted for war are also the countries listed in the travel bans. AROC tries to lift up these contradictions and show solidarity with other communities also experiencing immigration exclusion.

There has been a politicizing of Arab communities here after Trump's ban and the attacks on immigrants. Many of them came out to SFO [airport] for the travel ban protests. . . . Thousands of people have signed up to volunteer for the rapid response network in the Bay Area [to support undocumented migrants facing ICE raids]. Currently there is greater awareness and publicity of deportations, but after 9/11 there was less visibility of deportations of Muslims and Arabs, greater fear, and those who were targeted felt more isolated. Now we're reaching out to them in their neighborhoods and workplaces.

Charandev Singh, activist and paralegal, RISE (Refugees, Survivors, and Ex-detainees), Melbourne, Australia: RISE is a refugee-led organization that promotes a radical notion of solidarity based on indigenous sovereignty.[25] . . . Australia is a major laboratory for border control, and it is a site of extreme carcerality. Aboriginal people [in Australia] are the most incarcerated indigenous people on the planet.[26] . . . There is indefinite detention of immigrants and asylum seekers in Australia which is arbitrary and mandatory, in theory, till death. This also includes detention of stateless people. There is total privatization of immigrant detention and a normalization of this carceral infrastructure. Carceral colonialism in the Pacific includes offshore prison camps run by Australia in Nauru and Papua New Guinea. . . . Over two thousand people have died crossing the sea [to Australia].[27] Since 2001, Australia has had a military blockade in the North Sea to deter migrants and stop people leaving to seek asylum. Australia has deported refugees to war zones and supports militias in other countries who obstruct asylum seekers.

Maurice Stierl, German scholar-activist, Watch the Med/Alarm Phone (AP), Frankfurt, Germany: There are similar forms of policing of migration across national borders at what are now global frontiers. . . . In 2015, 1 million people crossed the Mediterranean. . . . Now we see the closing of land routes for migration, increased deportations, a strengthening of Frontex [the EU border control agency], and a delegitimization of activists and humanitarian NGOs who support migrants. But the legacy of the long summer of migration in 2015 is that new communities formed in Europe, and new structures of solidarity resisting detention and deportation and the criminalization of migrants. The AP was founded in 2014 and is a form of flight help.

We also should note that migrant communities are already providing sanctuary as they facilitate unauthorized movement. . . . Some AP members are former migrants who crossed borders. We are committed to freedom of movement and creating safe spaces for precarious people on the move. . . . There has also been a shift to the right in Europe with greater xenophobia and a division between "economic migrants" and "refugees." We need to move beyond humanitarian approaches and hierarchies of care.

"Good" vs "Bad" Migrants and Refugees
Fabrice, Olivia, Jana, Claudia; Anlaufstelle für San-Papiers

F: Switzerland is good at splitting up migrants into different categories: the "good" refugees vs. the "bad" refugees. . . . There is a double divide, first, between "expats" (highly qualified, welcomed migrants) and other migrants, basically refugees. In the latter category, there is a divide between real refugees and "adventurers," who just seek work or a better life. There is a very strong tendency to put as many people in the adventurer category, no matter why these people came or what is threatening them in the countries they left. . . . Switzerland is one of the most conservative countries in Europe (let's say, central and western Europe) when it comes to migration politics and is also at the forefront with new "migration management strategies."[28] . . . Because of the sharing of data across the EU, many are trapped due to the collaboration between [EU] states. The only thing the EU states can agree on is having [migrant detention] camps in North Africa! Frontex is exporting borders. They have also created "hot spots" inside EU borders so they can check asylum seekers and send them back from there.

O: There is an image of "good" migrants who are hard working. People begin to define themselves via these categories and internalize them. We want to challenge these binaries, but it can be hard in organizing not to fall into these categories. Illegal immigrants are not as organized; they just want permits. A lot of our work is focused on people who work and want permits, so we end up supporting these immigrants too. The core issue is freedom of movement. . . . But some migrants do not agree with the political framework of activists. Some No Borders activists are dismissive of migrants who don't believe in "no borders, no nations," and some migrants are nationalist, so in some cases there can be contradictions between activists and migrants.

J: I myself really believe in the double-barreled approach of the Anlaufstelle: to try to change the current social order towards a plural society in which people may lead their lives self-determined and independent of their residence status. It takes political action and argumentation to fight for these aims. At the same time, sans-papiers remain in dire straits . . . so we also need to provide some direct help to them. No one is illegal. . . . Since the divide between welcomed "expats" [professionals working in pharmaceutical and biotech companies in Basel] and less educated refugees, asylum seekers and sans-papiers is so clear-cut, since there is no social consensus that sans-papiers have a right to stay here, it is hard to act politically, to lobby in public and make our points as Anlaufstelle clear. We always have to keep in mind that many people here—even in one of the most left cities in German-speaking Switzerland—don't favor sans-papiers staying here, and that limits our possibilities of action.

C: There is a hierarchy among immigrants of those who work and refugees who don't work. In Europe, in general there is more focus on refugees, on people on the move, and not so much focus on undocumented migrants, as opposed to the US.

Lisa, Right to Remain: The sanctuary model here—much of which is based on church activism—is generally about welcoming only asylum seekers (the "good" migrants). Many provide aid. But this act of welcome is often apolitical. Some nonprofit organizations also reinforce this state-sanctioned binary of the "good" vs. "bad" migrants and refugees . . . only advocating for those who are not criminalized.

Immigration is viewed in such a negative way in the major news media. In the Brexit referendum, immigration was a cipher for other things, such as deindustrialization, impoverishment. . . . There is racial scapegoating. But the polarization has galvanized people to come to protests and boosted the movement. After Brexit, there was a campaign called Day without Immigrants, drawing on the campaigns organized by Cosecha in the US [which called for a boycott and strike after Trump's election]. We have drawn on the US movement-building model, such as the Dreamers movement.

Sagniethe, Xicana Moratorium Coalition: There are divisions in Oakland and tensions between Black and Brown folks and between immigrant groups . . . for example, only 67 percent of [undocumented] youth benefited from the DREAM Act. There is a binary of "good" and "bad" immigrants. . . . We want to create unity among Brown folks and challenge antiblackness. Oakland Sin Fronteras is [a community organization] based on organizing against state violence, prisons, walls, [travel] bans, and policing. We show how police terror is linked to ICE [Immigration and Customs Enforcement] and challenge internal divisions within our communities as well as the criminalization of youth and youth cultures.

Charandev, RISE: We need to remember that US and Western imperialism has played a role as wars and occupations are driving migration. It is summed up in the slogan, "We are here because you were there." . . . We need to be careful not to create states of exception: sanctuary for some but not for others, or cages for some but not others. We need a radical challenge to carcerality. Australia is a prison nation, and an international crucible for incarceration.

Sanctuary and Abolitionism

Alyn, No More Deaths/No Más Muertes: International anti-immigrant policies are focused on the repression of social movements and political struggles. Can a sanctuary framework extend beyond "rights"?

Sagnichte, Xicana Moratorium Coalition: Schools are a place of education and also of sanctuary. We do workshops for educators with the Immigration Liberation Movement and . . . train teachers and support students in crisis. We need to reenvision the notion of safety. We're educating families about a form of safety rooted in their neighborhoods and training first responders so they don't have to call the police. . . . We want to end reliance on outsiders to the community. We're also working with local business owners to support the community given the high level of policing [in East Oakland], surveillance, and deaths of youth. We have to do trainings block by block, school by school. We hold block parties where we can discuss organizing with the community. We involve gang-involved youth in community organizing and community art projects for decolonization, such as murals. The principle is self-determination.

Charandev, RISE: Aboriginal activism focused on refugee solidarity challenges the Australian state's settler jurisdiction and exclusive control of national borders. Activists have created aboriginal passports and entered detention centers to welcome refugees and refuse settler logics. The work of RISE is based on an expansive notion of sanctuary that centers aboriginal sovereignty. This is a notion of radical sanctuary—radical in the sense of "deeply rooted."

Border imperialism and carceral colonization are rooted in the colonization of indigenous people and repression of indigenous resistance. Centrally, we need abolitionist resistance. Aboriginal peoples in Australia have been defying borders for 229 years! . . . Indigenous and aboriginal sovereignty are important in this debate. RISE has a Sovereignty and Sanctuary campaign. The question is: How do we challenge the forces of power from which people seek sanctuary? How do we focus on the contexts from which people flee, so they can stay?

Lara, AROC: The slogan for the Bay Area sanctuary movement has been "No Ban on Stolen Land" [in response to Trump's anti-Muslim/Arab/African travel bans].[29] We need to think about how these borders have emerged—they are colonial borders. . . . Sanctuary is a form of liberation and of self-defense of liberation movements.

Figure 6. Flier courtesy Arab Resource and Organizing Center, designed by Design Action Collective and AROC.

Rev. Yoshii, Buena Vista United Methodist Church: The question is also sanctuary from what? We need sanctuary from the manifestation of the military-security-industrial complex. The wall in Palestine is connected to the walls and fences on the US–Mexico border. We need sanctuary from the siege of policing and prisons. . . . Palestinians need sanctuary as a persecuted population. What is causing the refugee crisis in Palestine? There is a connection between Palestine and immigration. The military-industrial complex is connected to the [border] security complex. But these connections are not highlighted in relation to Palestine. For me, there's also a clear connection to the legacy of Japanese American incarceration. . . . We need to get to the root causes of militarism and racism.

We also support sanctuary for LGBT persons and disabled persons. That is part of our statement in support of sanctuary. We see the interconnectedness and intersectionality of these issues as part of a broader notion of sanctuary that includes advocacy and accompaniment [for undocumented immigrants] as well as the right to housing.

Sharif Zakout, AROC: People who live in the Mission [neighborhood of San Francisco] today are generally supportive of sanctuary, but aren't they also complicit in producing displacement via gentrification? What can we do to provide sanctuary in a city where people can't afford to live?[30] Immigrants are being pushed out to rural areas that are not liberal communities or sanctuary spaces. . . . The meaning of sanctuary is safeguarding people, and information.

Fabrice, Anlaufstelle für Sans-Papiers: I would say that most activists [in solidarity with sans-papiers] consider themselves part of a movement that sees migration in the context of capitalism and the laws trying to control migration in the conservative upsurge in Europe.

Maurice, Alarm Phone: As solidarity activists, we work at the sub-state level to create safe spaces for migrants. But we are also focused on the right to health care, the right to education. We want to highlight subterranean knowledges and practices—knowledge that is under the surface—to create networks of solidarity. . . . The AP is focused on the right to freedom of movement. We want to challenge the punishing of acts of flight, and we are seeing the criminalization of humanitarian NGOs and vessels in the Mediterranean. For us, movement is "motion" and *also* political struggle.

Figure 7. Graffiti, Basel, Switzerland. Photography by author.

Lisa, Right to Remain: Our work questions who has the right to say that you have the right to remain. We want people to navigate the [immigration and asylum] system and offer a broader critique. There is lots of organizing that is focused on reform of immigration detention, but the end goal for us is abolition.

Conclusion

Contesting a liberal notion of sanctuary that narrowly focuses on migrant rights and humanitarian aid, the radical perspective expressed by these left activists offers an abolitionist definition of sanctuary that challenges state violence, carcerality, wars, and settler colonization, as well as Zionism. The goal is not to reform oppressive state institutions, as stated by Lisa, Charandev, and activists from Critical Resistance who participated in the workshop; rather, the goal is to challenge their very existence. For example, during protests in the US in summer 2018 against the Trump administration's "zero-tolerance" policy of separating migrant children from their parents at the border, some activists raised the slogan "Abolish ICE" and temporarily shut down ICE facilities.[31] Jenna Loyd, Matt Mitchelson, and Andrew Burridge observe that "a key abolitionist tool" is "the analytic ability to understand how seemingly disconnected institutions of state violence—walls and cages—are interconnected." They argue, "freedom of movement and freedom to inhabit are necessarily connected."[32] Migrant solidarity activism cannot be disconnected from challenges to neoliberal capitalism, austerity measures, and broader anticapitalist struggles, as Sharif suggests in highlighting the right to housing as a key plank for radical sanctuary activism in gentrified cities. Solidarity activists build these cross-movement connections, though in some cases migrants and refugees may not necessarily share their left politics, as apparent in research on squatter movements in solidarity with migrants in Europe.[33]

Sanctuary can be based in official sites, such as publicly declared churches or local jurisdictions. But sanctuary is also created in unofficial spaces, such as migrant communities, as Maurice commented, and in everyday practices and activities. These constitute what Jonathan Darling and Vicki Squire call the "everyday enactments of sanctuary" that challenge "relations of privilege" in practices of providing residential sanctuary, where some offer safe harbor and others receive it.[34] Activists like Sagnicthe and Lara define sanctuary as community defense and movement defense. They thus link multiple attacks on the left—on migrant, Black, and Brown communities; on indigenous sovereignty; and on sanctuary activists by the state and fascist groups in different national contexts—and the need to defend all of these communities and movements *simultaneously*.

My interviews with activists in the UK and Europe also suggest that they had a particular understanding of sanctuary as a term imported from the US associated with formal sanctuary policies or actions that prevent deportation. Sanctuary as spatial refuge for undocumented immigrants in the Bay Area was operationalized most frequently (at the time of this research) in church spaces and by interfaith networks challenging federal laws that illegalize people, as Rev. Yoshii and Rev. Fife described. But some critics argue that refuge in a church is, in effect, a form of incarceration related to a larger carceral apparatus, including immigrant detention centers, refugee camps, offshore prisons, and enclosures by walls.[35] For others, like Elvira Arellano, a well-known sanctuary leader who sought sanctuary in a Chicago church, "Sanctuary is not a place where you hide," but a platform for publicly speaking "truth to the powerful."[36] Furthermore, sanctuary is imagined, and organized, by Alarm Phone activists like Osama and Maurice, not as a spatial concept based on territorial safe haven but as *sanctuary in motion*—a form of "flight help" that defies EU border control in the Mediterranean Sea. Just as the Central American sanctuary movement of the 1980s drew on the history of the Underground Railroad, reviving a tradition of fugitive solidarity across land borders, this sea-based sanctuary conceives of the ocean as a space of resistance and disobedience, challenging inhumane state policies that make racialized migrant lives expendable through drowning and death.

Sanctuary activism also includes access to information about migrant passages and migrant rights, the "subterranean knowledges" Maurice describes. This knowledge of resources for survival unknown to the state constitutes what might be called an epistemic disobedience of borders. Knowledge of border crossings is a weapon that helps the "informed migrant" to "overcome the rising walls of defense meant to block entry into Europe" and North America.[37] The "Welcome to Europe" booklets translated into different languages that I saw in European cities—such as the Anlaufstelle office in Basel—and the "Know Your Rights" cards distributed by activists in the US provide information to resist the global borders regime.[38]

The discussion with migrant solidarity activists also highlights their critique of a liberal conception of sanctuary, which is a point of ongoing debate in the sanctuary movement. In supporting immigrants who have been living in the US, the New Sanctuary Movement in some instances upholds the image of "good" migrants deserving of inclusion, as critiqued by Lisa in the UK context of faith-based sanctuary (see Paik 2017, 14).[39] The US sanctuary movement of the 1980s centered on solidarity with Central American refugees displaced by US imperial interventions, making this particular refugee figure the pivot for sanctuary, and explicitly linking political advocacy for Guatemalan and Salvadoran refugees with denouncing US interventions in Central America. That is, it was an anti-imperial movement, making connections with resistance to the Vietnam War.[40] In fact, US sanctuary cities emerged when Berkeley declared sanctuary for conscientious objectors in 1971, following the movement of church sanctuaries for war resisters in the late 1960s.[41]

Yet, these lessons from recent history have failed to translate into the current moment, in which the experiences of Syrian, Afghan, Yemeni, and (doubly displaced) Palestinian refugees remain largely absent in US mainstream discourse.

Trump's travel bans are glossed, including by activists, as a "Muslim ban," but this erases the ways in which they are specifically *racialized* acts of border exclusion that are *also* anti-Arab and anti-Black, a targeted "Arab/African/Muslim ban." Furthermore, though this is rarely mentioned, Israel has long banned Palestinian/Arab freedom of movement, with US state support. In addition, the US role in the catastrophic wars in Syria and Yemen is obscured in mainstream discourse about migrant rights, as is US violence in Central America (including in current discussions of the "refugee caravan" from Central America).

In contrast, the European "crisis" emblematized by the figure of the (Arab, African, or South Asian) refugee dominates debates about migration, even while a problematic hierarchy has been constructed privileging some as refugees deserving of asylum in Europe (Syrians) and devaluing others as supposedly "economic migrants" (Afghans, Africans). The enduring legacy of Western imperial interventions and the impact of disaster capitalism in the global South is here, too, evaded. Furthermore, the figure of the migrant/refugee is implicitly gendered—associated with Muslim, Arab, or Black males in Europe and criminalized Latinx males in the United States. A feminist critique exposes how the debate about migrant rights rests on ideas about deserving, heteropatriarchal families and biological kin networks.

The discourse about race, of course, varies widely across national contexts, yet it is important to consider the ways in which a US discourse about white supremacy can illuminate the white nationalist and right-wing populist backlash against migrants in Europe, many of whom are from formerly colonized nations. Concomitantly, a European left framework melding the principles of antifascism, antiracism, and anticapitalism can speak to the resurgence of these perspectives in US movements and the rise of the Antifa movement in the Trump era. The roundtable illuminates the ways in which the concept of sanctuary has traveled, across space and time as well over land and oceans, and evolved through persistent organizing, the journeys of people on the move, their struggles to stay, and their dreams of return.

Sunaina Maira is professor of Asian American studies and was co-director of the Mellon Research Initiative in Comparative Border Studies at University of California, Davis, in 2015–18. She is the author of several books including *Missing: Youth, Citizenship, and Empire after 9/11* and *The 9/11 Generation: Youth, Rights, and Solidarity in the War on Terror*. Maira has been involved with community organizations and antiwar and Palestine solidarity movements in the Bay Area and nationally.

Notes

I wish to thank the activists who participated in this project for their incredibly inspiring organizing, and Naomi Paik for her meticulous editorial work and thoughtful feedback, which was extremely helpful in producing this roundtable.

1. Critical Resistance, a foundational abolitionist organization, mobilizes to end the prison-industrial complex. See criticalresistance.org/about/.

2. The workshop, as well as my research interviews in Europe, were funded by a Public Engagement Fellowship from the UC Davis Humanities Institute awarded in 2017.

3. Orozco and Anderson, *Sanctuary in the Age of Trump*.

4. See Golden and McConnell, *Sanctuary*; Houston, "Sacred Squatting," 184.

5. No precise data on the percentage of undocumented migrants exists, but estimates approximate 25 percent of the population is comprised of noncitizens, including an increasing number of undocumented migrants. See Wicker, "Deportation," 225–29.

6. My research was with activists from Basel and Zurich, in the German-speaking region of Switzerland, which is viewed by these activists as more conservative than the French-speaking region.

7. Darling and Squire, "Everyday Enactments of Sanctuary," 192–93. See also www .righttoremain.org.uk/blog/these-walls-must-fall/.

8. Mountz, "Mapping Remote Detention," 97. This strategy of island incarceration also operates in Guam, a US territory; Lampedusa, an Italian island near Tunisia; and Lesbos, the Greek island that has become synonymous with the "refugee crisis" in Europe.

9. See riserefugee.org/sanctionaustralia/. The "White Australia" policy refers to several historical policies of the Australian government that excluded nonwhite immigrants.

10. Clearly, differences in citizen rights exist between states. Citizenship can be based on jus soli (citizenship rights based on birth in the nation-state, nearly unconditional in the US) as well as jus sanguinis (citizenship by descent). In Switzerland, jus soli is not available and migrants must wait for over a decade to apply for citizenship (one of the longest periods for naturalization globally), while in the UK and Australia, there is restricted jus soli, as generally in the EU. See Lippert and Rehaag, introduction.

11. "US Immigration Attacks Oakland Mayor for Warning of Raid That Arrested 150," *The Guardian*, February 28, 2018, www.theguardian.com/us-news/2018/feb/28/ice -immigration-raid-northern-california-oakland-mayor-warning; "Justice Department Sues California over Its 'Sanctuary' Immigration Laws," *The Guardian*, March 6, 2018, www .theguardian.com/us-news/2018/mar/06/california-sanctuary-cities-lawsuit-immigration -justice-department.

12. This expansion of the border refers to the apprehension of immigrants inside national borders and escalating ICE raids in the US interior and the increasing incarceration of immigrants, including children. The border extends to one hundred miles within any territorial US border, and with the Trump "Wall" Executive Order, all US territory is considered border space for unauthorized crossers.

13. AP activists challenge the EU's border and visa regimes and Frontex, the EU border control agency, which have increased policing migrants attempting to enter Europe via the Mediterranean, thereby forcing migrants to take longer and more dangerous and deadly routes. See alarmphone.org/en/category/reports/.

14. Rev. Yoshii is a progressive faith leader and activist in the Bay Area at Buena Vista United Methodist Church, which has social justice committees and community partnerships focused on immigrant rights, Palestine solidarity, disability awareness, LGBTQ issues, and housing advocacy, and is part of the East Bay Interfaith Immigration Coalition. The church has a long history of providing support and refuge to displaced and oppressed communities. See www.buenavistaumc.org/.

15. Rev. Fife cofounded the sanctuary movement of the 1980s to provide support to refugees fleeing US-supported death squads in Guatemala and El Salvador and to mobilize churches to help refugees crossing the border in defiance of federal law, as Central

American refugees were not considered eligible for asylum. He was the first pastor to declare that his church, Southside Presbyterian, would be a sanctuary for refugees. In 1986, Rev. Fife was convicted, along with other activists, of violating federal immigration law and served five years' probation. Golden and McConnell, *Sanctuary*, 46–47. See www.trackedinamerica.org/timeline/sanctuary/fife/.

16. Anlaufstelle für Sans-Papiers is a migrant solidarity organization in Basel and the first support service for undocumented migrants in German-speaking Switzerland, established in 2002. It supports migrants seeking residence and work permits and provides legal counseling, medical consultations, information, and advocacy.

17. Switzerland (while not a member of the EU) signed an agreement upholding the Schengen Agreement, which unified the external borders of the EU while officially abolishing internal border controls, which made it more difficult for those outside Europe to enter Switzerland after 2008. No precise data exists for Switzerland, but undocumented migrants from the global South have increased. See Wicker, "Deportation," 225–29.

18. The campaign No One Is Illegal (Kein Mensch ist illegal) was launched in 1997 to support undocumented migrants and resist deportations, and led to a global network of antiracist and faith-based asylum groups.

19. The right-wing, Islamophobic Swiss People's Party generated the referendum banning all minarets, though only four minarets existed in the country. Nick Cumming-Bruce and Steven Erlanger, "Swiss Ban Building of Minarets," *New York Times*, November 29, 2009, www.nytimes.com/2009/11/30/world/europe/30swiss.html.

20. Campaigns for "We are all Zurich" have created unofficial citizenship cards to pressure the local government based on the right to the city. See Bauder, *Migration*, 95–101.

21. See detention.org.uk/brighton-hove-and-cambridge-city-councils-say-these-walls-must-fall/.

22. See www.righttoremain.org.uk/blog/the-swedish-students-protest-was-brave-and-remarkable/.

23. See www.righttoremain.org.uk/toolkit/.

24. AROC is a grassroots social justice Arab American community organization that also provides legal and community services for Arab immigrant communities in the Bay Area. See araborganizing.org/.

25. RISE is the first and only refugee organization in Australia governed by refugees, asylum seekers and ex-detainees: riserefugee.org/.

26. One in four indigenous Australians were in prison in 2011, despite indigenous Australians being only 2.5 percent of the population, and the rate of indigenous incarceration has risen rapidly with mass incarceration, accompanied by more deaths in custody. "Aboriginal Crime and Punishment," December 15, 2011, Crikey, www.crikey.com.au/2011/12/15/aboriginal-prison-rate-continues-to-rise-is-neoliberalism-at-play/.

27. John Power, "Australians Demand End to Manus Island and Nauru Refugee Centres," *Al Jazeera*, March 25, 2018, www.aljazeera.com/news/2018/03/australians-demand-manus-island-nauru-refugee-centres-180325101723423.html.

28. Hans-Rudolf Wicker notes that Switzerland now has an uncommon "infrastructural strength," with a "foreigners police," as well as "panoptically designed surveillance and repression" of immigrants ("Deportation," 227–28). The Department of Migration and Security has built emergency shelters, or what activist Claudia Wilopo calls an "invisible

border or camp," for rejected asylum seekers outside cities as part of a strategy of "containment and control" (interview, March 24, 2018).

29. #NoBanOnStolenLand was introduced by indigenous activists at the 2017 US airport protests against Trump's travel ban targeting Muslims, Arabs, and Africans, that spread across the border to Canada. Lenard Monkman, "'No Ban on Stolen Land,' Say Indigenous Activists in US," February 2, 2017, www.cbc.ca/news/indigenous/indigenous -activists-immigration-ban-1.3960814.

30. Housing prices in the San Francisco Bay Area have skyrocketed in recent years, partly due to the influx of tech company employees from Silicon Valley, leading to a housing crisis. Districts like the historically Latinx Mission neighborhood have become highly gentrified and unaffordable, leading to intensified antigentrification struggles.

31. For example, Occupy ICE protesters in Portland blocked the entrance to the local ICE office and managed to shut it down temporarily, sparking similar protests in New York, Los Angeles, and other cities. Leah Sottile, "Portland ICE Protest Grows," *Washington Post*, June 27, 2018, www.washingtonpost.com/national/2018/06/27/portland-ice-protest -grows-demonstrators-seek-abolish-agency-amid-immigration-crisis/.

32. Loyd, Mitchelson, and Burridge, "Introduction," 9–10.

33. For example, radical activists might not believe in petitioning state institutions for papers, while migrants may want authorization to stay, and direct action or antinationalist politics may not always be shared by stateless refugees or undocumented migrants vulnerable to arrest and those involved in national liberation struggles; at the same time, there are unequal relationships between white solidarity activists and migrant squatters. See Mudu and Chattopadhyay, introduction. On the plight of Syrian refugees in the UK placed in substandard housing, see www.righttoremain.org.uk/blog/we-came-here-for-sanctuary -we-didnt-come-here-to-be-abused/.

34. Darling and Squire, Everyday Enactments of Sanctuary," 191. Grace Yukich ("US New Sanctuary Movement," 113) describes the range of activities beyond physical sanctuary in the New Sanctuary Movement as "radical accompaniment," such as "legal, spiritual, and financial support."

35. Mielke, "Objectifying the Border," 14–16.

36. Cited in Caminero-Santangelo, "Voice of the Voiceless," 102.

37. Wicker, "Deportation," 237.

38. The Welcome to Europe booklets contain information in different languages for migrants entering the EU about migration, asylum, detention, and deportation policies in different European countries as well as resources for medical care, work, and safety at sea; see http://w2eu.info/index.en.html. There are various iterations of the Know Your Rights fliers and wallet-size cards that are intended to provide undocumented immigrants (and allies) what their legal rights are in encounters with federal immigration officials, local law enforcement, and FBI agents. For example, see www.aclu.org/issues/immigrants-rights /know-your-rights-discrimination-against-immigrants-and-muslims?

39. Caminero-Santangelo, "Voice of the Voiceless," 97–98.

40. Golden and McConnell, *Sanctuary*.

41. The Berkeley City Council resolution refusing city cooperation with federal laws regarding military service became a model for the City of Refuge movement in solidarity with Central American refugees. It also provided a context for resistance after 9/11 in different communities to racial profiling of Arab and Muslim Americans. See Ridgeley, "The City as a Sanctuary," 219–22, 228.

References

Bauder, Harald. *Migration Borders Freedom*. New York: Routledge, 2017.

Caminero-Santangelo, Marta. "The Voice of the Voiceless: Religious Rhetoric, Undocumented Immigrants, and the New Sanctuary Movement in the United States." In *Sanctuary Practices in International Perspectives: Migration, Citizenship, and Social Movements*, edited by Randy K. Lippert and Sean Rehaag, 92–95. New York: Routledge, 2013.

Darling, Jonathan, and Vicki Squire. "Everyday Enactments of Sanctuary: The UK City of Sanctuary Movement." In *Sanctuary Practices in International Perspectives: Migration, Citizenship, and Social Movements*, edited by Randy K. Lippert and Sean Rehaag, 191–204. New York: Routledge, 2013.

Golden, Renny, and Michael McConnell. *Sanctuary: The New Underground Railroad*. Maryknoll, NY: Orbis Books, 1986.

Houston, Serin. "Sacred Squatting: Seeking Sanctuary in Religious Spaces." In *Migration, Squatting, and Radical Autonomy*, edited by Pierpaolo Mudu and Sutapa Chattopadhyay, 183–88. New York: Routledge, 2017.

Lippert, Randy K., and Sean Rehaag. Introduction to *Sanctuary Practices in International Perspectives: Migration, Citizenship, and Social Movements*, edited by Randy K. Lippert and Sean Rehaag, 1–12. New York: Routledge, 2013.

Loyd, Jenna, Matt Mitchelson, and Andrew Burridge. "Introduction: Borders, Prisons, and Abolitionist Visions." In *Beyond Walls and Cages: Prisons, Borders, and Global Crisis*, edited by Jenna Loyd, Matthew Mitchelson, and Andrew Burridge, 1–15. Athens: University of Georgia Press, 2012.

Mielke, Anelynda. "Objectifying the Border: Symbolism and Subaltern Experience of Borders in Palestine and Canada." *Borderlands* 16, no. 1 (2017): 1–25.

Mountz, Alison. "Mapping Remote Detention: Dis/location through Isolation." In *Beyond Walls and Cages: Prisons, Borders, and Global Crisis*, edited by Jenna Loyd, Matt Mitchelson, and Andrew Burridge, 91–104. Athens: University of Georgia Press, 2012.

Mudu, Pierpaolo, and Sutapa Chattopadhyay. Introduction to *Migration, Squatting, and Radical Autonomy*, edited by Pierpaolo Mudu and Sutapa Chattopadhyay, 1–32. New York: Routledge, 2017.

Orozco, Myrna, and Rev. Noel Anderson. *Sanctuary in the Age of Trump*. Interfaith Movement for Human Integrity, 2018. www.sanctuarynotdeportation.org/sanctuary-report-2018.html.

Paik, A. Naomi. "Abolitionist Futures and the US Sanctuary Movement." *Race and Class* 59, no. 2 (2017): 3–25.

Ridgeley, Jennifer. "The City as a Sanctuary in the United States." In *Sanctuary Practices in International Perspectives: Migration, Citizenship, and Social Movements*, edited by Randy K. Lippert and Sean Rehaag, 219–31. New York: Routledge, 2013.

Wicker, Hans-Rudolf. "Deportation at the Limits of 'Tolerance': The Juridical, Institutional, and Social Construction of 'Illegality' in Switzerland." In *The Deportation Regime: Sovereignty, Space, and the Freedom of Movement*, edited by Nicholas De Genova and Nathalie Peutz, 224–44. Durham: Duke University Press, 2008.

Yukich, Grace. "'I Didn't Know If This Was Sanctuary': Strategic Adaptation in the US New Sanctuary Movement." In *Sanctuary Practices in International Perspectives: Migration, Citizenship, and Social Movements*, edited by Randy K. Lippert and Sean Rehaag, 106–18. New York: Routledge, 2013.

Sanctuary in a Small Southern City

An Interview with Anton Flores-Maisonet

Kyle B. T. Lambelet

A day with Anton Flores-Maisonet is a day filled with interruptions. His phone constantly buzzes and beeps with calls and texts from folks seeking aid or solace. Immigrants in the small southern city of LaGrange, Georgia, know that Flores is someone to contact when they're in trouble, whether they need a driver to a meeting with a child's teacher, a counselor for a nephew in despair about his legal status, or an advocate for a mother picked up by ICE.

Flores did not set out to provide sanctuary. Invoking the privilege of sanctuary, we might assume, would require some measure of religious authority that could oppose the authority of the state. Flores's vocation has taken a different path. A former professor of social work at a church-related college, Flores got his start in radical politics protesting the United States' 2003 invasion of Iraq. He quickly realized that while the bureaucratic integration model of social work may allow for some critique of status quo politics, his calls for more fundamental changes placed him in a precarious relation to his institution. Though he made his protests using religious language and commitments that he thought were shared by his institution's denomination, Flores learned that such prophetic politics was beyond the pale.

Now, fifteen years later, Flores's full-time, largely unpaid work is with Casa Alterna, a hospitality house he helped to found that offers sanctuary and accompaniment to Georgia's immigrants. Casa Alterna offers accompaniment in a host of neighboring practices, some small and some large. In its early days, Alterna

Radical History Review

Issue 135 (October 2019)   DOI 10.1215/01636545-7607896

© 2019 by MARHO: The Radical Historians' Organization, Inc.

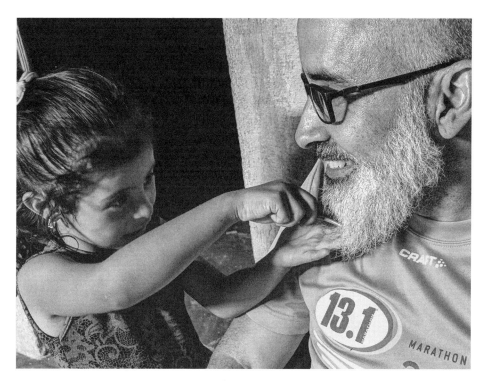

Figure 1. A child who identified Flores as "Santa Claus" combed his beard in Santa Teresa Llano Grande, Chiapas, Mexico. Photo courtesy of Bryan Babcock.

developed a cooperative housing model where immigrants could be free of unscrupulous slumlords, build equity, and find a stable and welcoming community at a time when such welcome was hard to find. After reading about a hunger strike of Salvadorans who were facing deportation, Flores learned that the second largest private detention center in the United States was in his backyard in Lumpkin, Georgia. In 2007 he held the first of many vigils demanding the closure of Stewart Detention Center and other detention facilities, including the successful campaign to close the North Georgia Detention Center. In 2010 Flores helped launch El Refugio, a house of hospitality and ministry of visitation, located one mile from Stewart. And by partnering with the School of the Americas Watch, an international network of advocates and activists began to widen the circle of those repelled by the cruel yet profitable incarceration of immigrants along with its connection to a wider structure of US-Latin American militarism.

Flores's political commitment to sanctuary has meant not merely public protest and organizing, but also providing sanctuary in his home by offering transitional housing to immigrants and even fostering a newborn child whose mother was incarcerated and, over a year later, deported. In 2017 Flores and his wife Charlotte moved into a cul-de-sac comprising mostly Guatemalan immigrants and continue to build relationships with the communities in Guatemala from which many of these neighbors originate. Casa Alterna offers some programs for and with their new neighbors, including academic tutoring, language exchange, accompaniment and interpretation, and a food cooperative; but the primary aim is to cultivate an interdependent neighborhood built upon community, trust, and political power.

Kyle Lambelet: *For folks unfamiliar with Casa Alterna, can you narrate for us what the day-to-day looks like?*

Anton Flores-Maisonet: Casa Alterna is a place where acts of mercy and justice are undergirded by the principal value of hospitality. In particular, the solidarity we seek is with immigrants from Latin America. Historically this has played itself out in different ways: by having a multinational, intentional community; by making home ownership a viable option for first-wave immigrant families, regardless of their status; by founding El Refugio in Lumpkin, Georgia; and by leading a campaign to close a for-profit deportation prison, Stewart Detention Center. Now, what it looks like since 2017 is that this house of hospitality exists in the midst of a first-wave immigrant neighborhood, almost entirely Guatemalan. We are a ministry of presence here. We want to make this little cul-de-sac a sanctuary, we want it to be a refuge, we want it to be a safe place, and that commitment has led us to do some direct things.

In response to a multiday ICE operation targeting our neighbors, we hosted the Georgia Latino Alliance for Human Rights for a defend-your-rights session.[1] And now neighbors are equipped with knowledge and resources like window postings that help protect our constitutional and human rights when immigration officials or law enforcement come knocking on our doors. That training was a result of some early-morning raids that we experienced in the fall of 2017. As folks left home for their first-shift jobs and as children were awaiting their school bus, right beside the children's bus stop, ICE waited in the dark in unmarked vehicles at the entrance of the cul-de-sac. As parents and their hired drivers left the street, the ICE agents would engage in racial profiling and would stop the drivers for bogus reasons. It just so happened that the drivers that were stopped were all Latinx but were also all legal permanent residents or US citizens. Each driver informed us that these plainclothes officers would not identify themselves but would ask the drivers and passengers to provide documentation. Some of the passengers were subsequently taken into ICE custody.

I was called on one particular morning and I was able to monitor and confront the ICE agents on their final apprehension. I was threatened with arrest for monitoring and photographing this incident from a public sidewalk. By the time I arrived, a neighbor with diabetes who was the passenger in a vehicle driven by a US citizen was in ICE custody. My neighbor was taken to an immigration detention center, but the driver and I decided we would file a complaint. I was deeply disturbed by ICE's new tactic. As a brown-skinned, US-born citizen, I needed to know that I can drive on my own street and on public roads without fear of being racially profiled by federal agents. A DHS official visited us from DC, and since then ICE has not returned to our neighborhood. I don't want to take credit for this; it was the courageous drivers who spoke out who deserve the credit. Together, we made our neighborhood a safer place for parents to leave for work and for children to catch the school bus. So, if we can think about sanctuary in this wide sense, then we aspire for our cul-de-sac to be a place of sanctuary.

KL: *Sanctuary is kind of a buzzword right now. There are several different entities that have taken on the term: sanctuary campuses, sanctuary cities. I'm interested to hear what sanctuary means in your context in LaGrange, Georgia.*

AFM: It seems to me that sanctuary means first and foremost housing someone who has an order of removal and publicly shielding them from that in a place of worship. When I hear the term sanctuary being used I think of it as an actual place where there is an act of moral or faithful resistance through offering lodging to a family that our government is seeking to remove from the United States. We have never done that publicly, we've never participated in that in the narrowest sense. I would do it if I really thought that it could somehow be a protection. But I suspect that ICE would treat our house of hospitality differently than, say, a church down the block. While this work is deeply rooted in our faith and our faith tradition, we're not an institutional church. I wouldn't expect that ICE would honor the sacred work we are engaged in.

That's why we've hesitated to use that word *sanctuary* when referring to us. Sanctuary is about a place where a person can live free from the fear of government intrusion and forced removal. I don't think we can completely offer that.

But, sanctuary is also a place where we honor God and affirm the inherent dignity of every person. Alterna has always been a place where the best thing we knew to do was to counteract fear with loving acts, and counteract dehumanization through personalizing who our neighbors are, and to give them names and faces. I don't think you can have sanctuary unless you no longer have fear and can encounter each other as fellow human beings created in the image of God. That's what we try to replicate wherever we are, in our former neighborhood, and now here in Historic Goose Holler.

When Charlotte and I decided to move into this neighborhood, others, including some of our immigrant friends, said we would regret living here. Folks used very dehumanizing language to talk about the people on this street. But, just as I suspected, the naysayers have been proven wrong by our new neighbors. What I have found are neighbors and friends with names and faces and stories. It is the immigrant neighbor who has welcomed us as the stranger. For in many ways, Charlotte and I are the stranger—for example the culture of our neighbors as first-generation immigrants and thus of our street is very different from our own as people coming from families with generational histories of citizenship. Living on this street is like living at a crossroads of cultures, American and Guatemalan. In a true sense, we are both welcoming the stranger and being welcomed as the stranger. I have the opportunity to welcome the other and serve as an ambassador or bridge between their home culture and that of the southeastern United States, and my neighbors have the opportunity to invite me into this micro-culture of a Guatemalan oasis of sorts.

KL: *It strikes me that in spite of your hesitancy to use the language of sanctuary in the narrow sense that many of the practices that you engage in are aimed at granting a kind of sanctuary. Maybe the terms that would be more familiar are practices of hospitality and resistance.*

AFM: In this sense I would say that everything we're doing is a form of sanctuary. When we started El Refugio, our house of hospitality near Stewart Detention Center, the idea was to not just engage in a political form of resistance but, as the name suggests, to provide a real space of refuge for the families of immigrants in detention.

Sanctuary is the idea that a person can find rest and safety. From what? Thinking about all the multiple layers by which an immigrant is persecuted, laws and policies continue to be some of the harshest tools used against immigrants. You can think about it in a federal sense in terms of immigration policy, but it trickles down. Local governments also have the power to enact anti-immigrant policies, even ones that are distinct from federal immigration law. For example, in our town where utilities are publicly owned, sometime after 9/11 the city implemented a policy that requires the provision of a social security number to obtain utilities services. Since its inception, the rationale for this policy has been refined to a financial one; having consumers' social security numbers on file is a means of ensuring that there is a mechanism by which to garnish someone's wages should they move out of town with an outstanding debt to the city of LaGrange. But, regardless of how often the reasoning gets modified, the spirit of the Privacy Act and of the Fair Housing Act is violated and those disproportionately impacted are Latinx immigrants, many of whom do not have a social security number.

For over fifteen years, immigrants have been summarily denied access to water, heat, and electricity. The result is that it reduced access to affordable housing, relegating immigrants to substandard housing and opening them up to other forms of exploitation by unscrupulous landlords. After years of trying to negotiate with the city—writing letters to the editor, organizing vigils, and even running for city council—we were finally able to partner with the National Immigration Law Center and the Southern Center for Human Rights to bring a lawsuit against the city of LaGrange. We were able to leverage our friendships to get plaintiffs who would be willing to say that they had been adversely affected by this policy.

The lawsuit is currently being appealed by our attorneys after a lower court dismissal, but there has already been a small victory; just the litigation itself has caused the city to unofficially change its practice. While the policy remains intact, if you refuse or decline to provide a social security number, they won't deny you services. Instead, they'll charge you the maximum deposit of $500. We are still not pleased with this as it is still not written policy. We remain committed to ensuring access to fair housing for all. After all, what better sanctuary is there than to live in the security and dignity of one's home.

KL: *Historically, the provision of sanctuary has relied on ecclesial authority, be that a religious institution or clergyperson, to create a space where fugitives can find protection often from unjust arrest. You're not a clergyperson. I guess the question is: Are there practices of sanctuary that you employ that aren't reliant on religious authority or the provision of institutional space? Does Casa Alterna practice aspects of sanctuary without sanction?*

AFM: I once heard the term "civil disobedience" restated as "divine obedience." Therefore, if one defines religious authority as obedience to a divine authority, we're being very faithful. But does the state recognize our authority as legitimate? Who knows? Perhaps this is a question of religious freedom in an era of harsh anti-immigrant policies and laws.

We have done sanctuary in ways that may be countercultural. Aside from being arrested for acts of civil disobedience outside an immigration detention center, we've expressed our commitment to divine obedience in a myriad of ways. We've cared for a newborn child whose parents were incarcerated and facing deportation. We've been given power of attorney for several children as preparation in case parents find themselves ensnared in our deportation pipeline. We've been a safe place where women with the additional vulnerability of unlawful presence in the United States can find safety as they muster the courage to leave an abusive relationship. As our name, Casa Alterna, hints at, sanctuary is an alternative to a world that is unsafe for the damned of this world.

Sometimes this is behind-the-scenes work, sometimes it's more public. In 2011, the legislature of Georgia passed House Bill 86. Deemed one of the harshest laws confronting immigrants in the US, HB86 amongst other things created harsh punishments for anyone who "harbored" unauthorized immigrants. This section of the law could have been so broadly interpreted that someone could potentially have

Figure 2. Anton Flores-Maisonet walking from El Sauce to La Libertad in Huehuetenango, Guatemala. Photo courtesy of Bryan Babcock.

been prosecuted for knowingly renting to or housing someone who was undocumentable, like many of the folks we have worked with through Casa Alterna. Motivated by the tenets of our faith, we publicly joined the lawsuit stating it would be a direct prohibition of our vocational call to love our neighbor and welcome the stranger.

One of our inspirations is the Catholic Worker movement and its vision of every congregation having a house of hospitality and every family a Christ room in which to welcome Jesus in the disguise of the stranger. The question for us then is, Who are we willing to host in our Christ room? And if Christ is in need of sanctuary, will we offer it? I think we would; I pray we would.

KL: *It strikes me—getting back to this idea of sanctuary drawing on religious authority—that rather than relying on religious authority, what you've relied on in the construction of sanctuary is a more democratic practice of empowering neighbors, acknowledging a common humanity, and offering protection from unwanted and oppressive, racist policies. You've resisted immigration control through empowerment of voice and agency on the block.*

AFM: Yes, while it remains deeply rooted in spiritual values, at Casa Alterna sanctuary is both creative and subversive. In the early days of Alterna one of the more creative and subversive initiatives we launched was a program called "Maneja en Paz" (Drive in Peace). This was a cooperative where anyone, licensed or unlicensable, could pay a $100-a-year membership. If any member were ever charged with driving without a license and without any disqualifying additional offenses, like DUI or excessive speeding, the cooperative would pay the first $700 of their fine. Maneja en Paz was creative and brilliant; it provided a tangible way for immigrants and allies to stand in solidarity and stand against exploitive, dehumanizing laws that criminalized folks driving to work, worship, or Walmart. Through a series of events, local authorities caught wind and said that this might be misconstrued as insurance fraud. I was angry at the system for arresting working poor immigrants for simply driving, but I was also afraid of possible sanctions that could be imposed against me for organizing Maneja en Paz. I consulted with a human rights attorney and she fueled my fear, but I also spoke with a human rights organizer and she encouraged me to go public with our cooperative. She believed it was the only way to make it a true act of civil disobedience, especially one that sought to provoke the conscience of the majority of uninformed Georgians. In the end, state laws became more repressive and we discontinued the cooperative, but not our unwavering commitment to immigrant justice. The practice of sanctuary as welcome and refuge can animate many forms of cooperative ventures.

KL: *It's the same tension that was at work between the Tucson branch and the Chicago branch of the sanctuary movement of the 1980s. How public should they go? Was the purpose one of accompaniment in which we are tailoring our political acts to the needs of migrants? Or is this a political movement where the larger policy shifts are the goal with an understanding that some local migrants may be exposed to a greater risk of deportation? I think your intuitions tend toward the primacy of relationships, more in the Tucson mode.*[2]

AFM: Yeah, and that internal debate or discussion still goes on today. There are churches that are doing sanctuary publicly. And then there are underground safe houses. We are always seeking to find ways to be faithful to the Gospel even if it means subverting the state. I'm pragmatic enough not just to do anything in the name of defiance. But we're always trying to creatively imagine alternatives to the state's exclusion of immigrants. Who else has thought of forming a little cooperative to pay for unjust tickets? If there's another model, I'd like to learn from it. Driving while Brown and being arrested or ticketed for driving unlicensable is not unique to LaGrange. Immigration detention confines approximately forty thousand per day across the United States. But in remote Lumpkin, Georgia, a small group of us dreamt of offering refuge, hospitality, and resistance. We were informed and inspired by other models, but subversion necessitates creativity. We're always trying to figure out creative ways to just remain faithful to the Gospel regardless of what the current policies are.

That's where the name *Alterna* comes from: an alterna-tive. A sanctuary is always an alternative reality to what the dominant systems are doing. You provide safety that does not exist outside your walls.

KL: *It takes us back again to this idea of sanctuary as a practice of reciprocity rather than a unidirectional, paternalistic provision of aid. Rather than, I create a sanctuary for you, it's a reciprocal giving and receiving of gifts that involves mutual recognition of common humanity.*

AFM: Yes, and at the same time I have to figure out, is there sanctuary for my own heart? One of the things I would admit and confess to is that decades of justice work comes at a cost. I carry my own wounds from struggling against systems of oppression. If I allow the toxicity of those wounds to fester in my heart it breeds an unhealthy form of anger. Not just anger at the system, but just a generalized anger where the recipients of that poison at times are the people closest to me, including myself. Therefore, sanctuary also means creating a space where one's own heart can also be healed. Is there a place for one's heart to find refuge in a world that is driven by fear and violence? That's probably the hardest battle: to find the sanctuary within that leads to creating spaces of sanctuary in the world. Some of the least peaceful people I know are peacemakers. And, at times, I am one of those people. How can one keep a radical edge and an engaged vision of what Charles Eisenstein calls "that more beautiful world our hearts know is possible," and yet keep a heart that has space for present moments of beauty, love, and joy?

KL: *What does that mean in your practice? How do you create sanctuary within?*

AFM: When I'm at my best, it's knowing how to keep a balance with technology; it's carving out time for solitude and silence. Those are my best practices. Prayer, meditation, mindfulness, solitude, and unplugging from the rat race. Presently, I regularly visit a spiritual director and practice contemplative prayer. In this moment of silent attention to God, because of some personal grief and loss, sometimes the best I can offer is my body but not my inner stillness. But I have to be okay and be gracious with myself. I remember asking a Benedictine monk once about his prayer practices. He lives in a community where they pray four times a day, including every day at four in the morning. I asked the monk if he ever had difficulty meditating and if he ever actually fell asleep during some prayers. His response back was very simple. "Yes, I fall asleep sometimes, but there's no better place to fall asleep than the lap of Jesus." What a lesson that was for me; a lesson in grace. So that's been me lately; even this morning during prayer, my mind was wandering on half a million things. And while that tells me something about my inner condition, it's ultimately a reminder to be gentle with myself because this world can be cruel enough on its own.

Kyle B. T. Lambelet teaches and researches at the intersection of political theology, religious ethics, and social change at Emory University. His current research explores the moral and political dimensions of nonviolent struggle. His forthcoming book *¡Presente! Nonviolent Politics and the Resurrection of the Dead* develops an extended case study of the movement to close the School of the Americas.

Anton Flores-Maisonet is cofounder of Casa Alterna, a hospitality house located in a West Georgia neighborhood of first-wave immigrants, primarily from Guatemala. Casa Alterna is committed to faithful acts of justice, mercy, and solidarity. Flores-Maisonet is also cofounder of El Refugio Ministry and Georgia Detention Watch. Casa Alterna has been named Organization of the Year by *Mundo Hispánico*, Atlanta's largest Spanish newspaper. You can follow Anton on Instagram and Twitter at @antonofalterna and Casa Alterna on Facebook at facebook.com/alternacommunity.

Notes

This interview was conducted on April 26, 2018.

1. The Georgia Latino Alliance for Human Rights (GLAHR) is an advocacy and base-building organization focused on empowering Latinx immigrants in Georgia. In their defend-your-rights sessions they educate immigrants on the legal rights they have when encountering law enforcement officials. For more information, visit www.glahr.org/.

2. For a brief introduction to the differences between the Tucson and Chicago approaches to sanctuary see Smith, *Resisting Reagan*, 61–70.

References

Smith, Christian. *Resisting Reagan: The U.S. Central America Peace Movement*. Chicago: University of Chicago Press, 1996.

From Sanctuary to Civil Disobedience

History and Praxis

Elliott Young

When a stranger sojourns with you in your land, you shall not do him wrong.
You shall treat the stranger who sojourns with you as the native among you,
and you shall love him as yourself, for you were strangers in the land of Egypt.
—Leviticus 19:33–34

The day after Trump was elected, I sent out an email to ten of my colleagues who study migration at universities and colleges across the country. I asked them, "What are we going to do when the deportation trains and mass immigrant detention camps start?" That thread quickly turned to suggestions for how we might help protect Deferred Action for Childhood Arrivals (DACA) students on our campuses. By that point students at Yale and Pomona had already begun circulating a petition to establish their campuses as sanctuaries from ICE. While we knew that Trump was unlikely to begin his anti-immigrant assault on DACA students because of the support they had garnered, we believed that we had a special responsibility to our students; our faculty status also gave us some capability to organize on our campuses.

I started a petition to declare Lewis & Clark College a sanctuary campus, which quickly drew more than 1,600 signatures. Faculty and students were generally on board. While some administrators supported the effort, others argued that declaring a sanctuary made a false promise to protect students since the college could not really prevent ICE from arresting students if they possessed a legal warrant. The movement for sanctuary campuses spread quickly across the country, with

Radical History Review
Issue 135 (October 2019)   DOI 10.1215/01636545-7607908
© 2019 by MARHO: The Radical Historians' Organization, Inc.

128 petitions and 29 colleges and universities, including presidents at neighboring Portland State University and Reed College, declaring their campuses sanctuaries by early December.[1] Lewis & Clark's president would eventually issue a statement indicating that the college would fight ICE to the full extent of the law, but declined to use the word *sanctuary*. The decentralized organizing that happened around sanctuary campuses worked alongside cities declaring themselves sanctuaries. In March, Portland's City Council passed a resolution declaring itself a sanctuary, a move that would later earn Mayor Ted Wheeler public attacks by Trump and Attorney General Jeff Sessions, along with a lawsuit by ICE that claims he has impeded their ability to perform their duties.[2]

With the sanctuary campus organizing in full swing, it became apparent that at a place like Lewis & Clark, where there were few if any DACA students, we needed to think more broadly about how to resist Trump's agenda. In the midst of this moment of political urgency, I ran into Kabir Heimsath, a colleague in the anthropology department. We discussed how ethnic studies, a program I directed at the time, could best respond to what we saw as a cataclysmic retrenchment in civil rights. Rather than just organize another series of talks, we felt the need to act. To paraphrase Marx, we needed to change the world, not merely interpret it.

Kabir came up with the idea of focusing on civil disobedience. The issue of creating a sanctuary campus had already raised the specter of civil disobedience. A group of law school students suggested announcing our intention to refuse to comply with ICE even if they arrived with lawful warrants; however, no campus was willing to take that next step. Instead, administrators were going to work to protect students through noncooperation with ICE as much as legally feasible. In practice, this meant not providing any information to ICE without a legal subpoena, and requiring ICE to present a legal warrant before allowing them on campus to arrest anyone. Although sanctuary campuses and cities have been misinterpreted as civil disobedience, that is, as breaking the law on purpose, all of the sanctuary schools and municipalities argue they are complying with the law. At stake in this distinction is whether schools or local governments should be required to cooperate with federal immigration enforcement. In Oregon, and other jurisdictions with sanctuary statutes, cooperating with ICE is a violation of the law.

Immediately after the election, Portland saw some of the most intense and long-lasting street protests in the country. Tens of thousands of people took to the streets, shutting down highways, obstructing traffic, and expressing our outrage over the election. For those few days, it felt like political change was happening in the street. Although there were a whole host of reasons to protest Trump, immigration was at the top of the list.

In a city that is politically progressive, at least in the context of the United States, it was hard to find local politicians at whom to vent the collective anger. Our local politicians oppose Trump. And yet, Portland was also home to a long history of racism and white supremacy, which continued in the form of police violence, especially against black, homeless, and mentally ill residents; dramatic displacement of communities through gentrification; and a general cluelessness about all things not white.[3] Nativism and white supremacy took the forms of constitutionally banning black people from coming to the state, and the Ku Klux Klan's anti-Semitism and anti-Catholicism in the 1920s. In the 1980s, neo-Nazi skinheads beat the Ethiopian Mulugeta Seraw to death with baseball bats and almost killed an Asian man in front of his wife and children.[4] In 1977, it was an incident of police racial profiling of a Chicano man who was singled out while dining in a restaurant in Independence, Oregon, that ultimately led the state to adopt its sanctuary law in 1987, with almost unanimous bipartisan support.[5] Although Oregon's state sanctuary law has served as a model for others and was widely viewed as positive, the nativist group Oregonians for Immigration Reform attempted and failed to abolish the law through a ballot initiative in the 2018 midterm elections. The initiative went down in flames with 64 percent of voters rejecting the antisanctuary measure.[6]

Sanctuary has a longer history stretching back to the medieval era in Europe, to the Underground Railroad for escaped slaves in the nineteenth-century US, and to those who harbored undocumented Central American refugees in the 1980s.[7] In the nineteenth century and 1980s cases, providing such sanctuary was an act of civil disobedience against unjust laws. It was at this moment of urgency, when civil disobedience seemed like one of the best strategies for confronting Trump, that we came up with the idea of organizing a semester-long workshop. The idea of the course was to explore historical examples from the United States and elsewhere of movements that used civil disobedience as a tactic, and to evaluate their successes and failures. In addition to the historical part, we also wanted to focus on praxis, where theory and practice meet.

With that as a framework, we came up with a series of possible topics and then looked for faculty, students, and activists from the community to facilitate each session. The sessions were held every Tuesday evening for a couple of hours. We also decided early on that we would not seek to offer credit for students in order to avoid pushback from faculty who might see this workshop as politically motivated and therefore not counting as academic credit. It also allowed us to free ourselves from the constraints of a regular class. There was no grading, reading was optional, and you could attend as many of the sessions as you desired. It felt liberating.

The workshop employed a Freirean pedagogy that sought to empower all participants rather than assuming that the facilitator/teacher had all of the answers. The hardest part in achieving the balance between presentation and democratic discussion was getting the professors to not take up the whole ninety-minute session. Ideally, we hoped for facilitators to provide some context and raise questions for half of the period, then break up into smaller discussion groups for half an hour, and to end with a larger group discussion for the last part of the period.

For the first session, more than fifty people crowded into a room meant for forty, including students, alumni, community activists and even some wives of Lewis & Clark College's board of trustees. There was a palpable feeling in the room that what we were doing was important. Over the course of the semester, attendance waxed and waned. There was one session with just a handful of participants, but the last workshop of the semester attracted a crowd of more than seventy-five.

The workshop addressed a broad range of topics, but it really began in the organizing around the idea of a sanctuary campus. Magalí Rabasa, a colleague in Hispanic Studies, joined me in facilitating the first session and co-coordinated the workshop the entire semester. Given our commitments to Latinx studies, we both were at the center of organizing for a sanctuary campus, while recognizing the need to address a broader swath of the college community. After the workshop ended, colleagues in the Graduate School of Education and other institutions asked me to describe its structure with the hope of replicating it in some form. The main issue in organizing such a weekly workshop is that it came on top of an already very busy work schedule. Finding time and energy for this work is not easy. If this kind of work could be stitched into one's regular faculty duties, and compensated, then it would be easier to sustain over a longer period than just one semester. Nonetheless, the experience of organizing a sanctuary campus at Lewis & Clark College and being part of a movement that spread with lightning speed across the country gave us hope for what was possible.

For the entire Civil Disobedience Workshop Syllabus, go to www .radicalhistoryreview.org/supplemental/issue135/young/.

February 9, Workshop Organizing: Latest Thoughts on Resistance

The first session was designed as an open discussion about the goals, visions, and structure of the workshop. We decided collectively that the workshop would emphasize creating a democratic space where all could participate. While continuity of participants was encouraged, recognizing other commitments and work obligations, we also decided that people could join in at any time and for any length of time. Note-takers were assigned at the start of each session so that those who couldn't attend would at least keep apprised of the conversation they missed. In addition to discussing the workshop format, we also talked about the most effective strategies of resistance in the wake of the election. It became clear from that first session that focusing on the readings was going to be difficult since only a few people had done the reading.

February 16, Philosophy and Civil Disobedience

The second session was facilitated by two philosophy professors, Joel Martinez and Jay Odenbaugh, along with a math instructor, Margot Black, who is also the founder of Portland Tenants United, the most radical of the tenants' groups in the city. They opened this session with a quote from Martin Luther King, Jr., who said to Alex Haley in 1965, "If you confront a man who has been cruelly misusing you, and say 'Punish me, if you will; I do not deserve it, but I will accept it, so that the world will know I am right and you are wrong,' then you wield a powerful and just weapon." The goal of civil disobedience, they argued, was to break the law in a very deliberate and public way in an effort to highlight a social injustice. The willingness to accept punishment, often meaning jail time or suffering physical assault, illustrates the moral conviction of the protestor.

February 23, Latin American and Latinx Struggles: Central American Solidarity and Zapatistas

This session, facilitated by Magalí Rabasa from Hispanic Studies and myself, provided a broad history of Central American solidarity movements in the 1980s, the Zapatista uprising in Chiapas in the mid-1990s, and more recent sanctuary movements to protect undocumented migrants today. Using a recent communiqué from the Zapatista Army of National Liberation (EZLN), "The Walls Above, the Cracks Below (and to the Left)," participants reflected on the Zapatista strategy of not seizing state power, but rather creating space for civil society to construct alternatives to the government. In the 1980s, faith leaders practiced this model of direct action beyond the limits of state sanction in openly defying US law by welcoming and harboring Central Americans fleeing violence. Although eight religious leaders of the sanctuary movement were ultimately tried and convicted in what became known as the Sanctuary Trials, the movement galvanized public opinion and revealed the brutality of US policies in Central America as well as exposing the politicized nature of US immigration and refugee law.[8] In 1990, as a result of the attention brought by the sanctuary movement, Congress passed temporary protected status legislation for Central American migrants.[9] Although the new sanctuary movement by colleges and universities, as well as cities, counties, and states, was not in defiance of the law, it was a public call to not cooperate with unjust immigrations laws.

March 2, Arab Spring

The facilitators, anthropologist Oren Kosansky and historian Sara Jay, opened the session by challenging the term "Arab Spring." By using this term, a reference to the Prague Spring, Western journalists tried to understand this movement by way of comparison to a European movement, and one that was abruptly crushed by Soviet military repression. Locally, the movement was understood as a revolution, a term studiously avoided by most Western commentators. One important point raised by this conversation was the need to understand the local context in which a movement emerges, and not simply try to fit it into a preexisting model.

March 9, Black Freedom Struggle: Civil Rights, Black Panthers, and Black Lives Matter

Historian Reiko Hillyer discussed the history of the 1960s civil rights movement, showing how hated Martin Luther King, Jr. was by a majority of Americans in his day. Although a sanitized and de-radicalized version of MLK Jr. has become a national icon in recent years, it is important to understand how leaders were viewed in their time. Founder of Portland's Resistance and third-year law student Gregory McKelvey talked about his own experience of being vilified for being a leader of very visible and effective street protests. Finally, Ameya Marie Okamoto, an eleventh-grade student at Catlin Gabel School showed her artwork featuring black youth killed by the police. Ameya's art was done in collaboration with Don't Shoot Portland, a Black Lives Matter group that has been working against police violence in Portland for a very long time.

March 16, Environmental Tactics of Resistance

This session highlighted local direct actions in defense of the environment. Arthur Bradford talked about his role in using tree sitting to protect a stand of sequoia trees in a residential community in Portland. International Affairs professor Elizabeth Bennett recounted her own tree-sitting effort to prevent the cutting down of large trees in her neighborhood.

April 6, Art and Activism

This session, led by Kaley Mason, a professor of music, and Jerry Harp, a professor of English, highlighted poetry and Indian music as a form of social resistance. The conversation turned to the question of whether today's social movements have a sound track in the same way that the 1960s generated a deep and memorable songbook of resistance, from Phil Ochs to Gil Scott Heron to Nina Simone.

April 13, Free Speech, Hate Groups, and the Public

We had already planned to end the workshop with a session on the question of free speech and hate groups when we found ourselves in the middle of just such a controversy on our campus. The International Affairs Symposium, an annual event organized by students and one faculty member, announced that they had invited Jessica Vaughan, policy director for the anti-immigrant group Center for Immigration Studies, for a debate about refugees. The Center for Immigration Studies (CIS) appears to be a mainstream Washington, DC, think tank, but it has links to far-right eugenicist John Tanton and regularly disseminates articles by Holocaust deniers and white supremacists. The Southern Poverty Law Center put CIS on its list of hate groups in the fall of 2016.[10] The student organizers extended the invitation to Vaughan well in advance of the election and the rebirth of the sanctuary movement, but by the time of the symposium we were in the thick of Trump's anti-immigrant agenda.

I wrote an article for *Huff Post* in which I questioned the judgment of students for inviting such an academically disreputable group to campus that regularly disseminates racist ideas.[11] The students maintained that they were not aware of the background of the CIS when they issued the invitation, but nonetheless they believed it would be useful to have Vaughan come to campus. The college decided to ban the public from attending the event over fears that people would protest or heckle the speaker. Portland's Resistance organized a protest outside, which was loud, but Vaughan was able to speak without interruption. Faculty and students vigorously questioned her in the question-and-answer period.[12]

Given the controversy generated by the CIS visit to campus, we decided that we would devote the workshop that week to the topic of free speech and hate groups, and to invite students, faculty, and community protestors to take part. In the packed room, faculty and students discussed whether there should be limits on free speech, and student symposium organizers expressed that they felt publicly shamed for inviting a hate group to campus. Gregory McKelvey argued that the slight discomfort of student organizers and others who had to walk by protestors paled in comparison to the pain of immigrants being deported and torn from their families. The student organizers who invited CIS to campus did not seem to feel that their invitation would negatively impact immigrant students or students whose families were facing the draconian policies advocated by CIS.

It was a fitting conclusion to the Civil Disobedience Workshop that at the very end of the semester, people responded to the presence of CIS on campus with a diversity of tactics. Some chose to simply attend the event and listen, others chose to attend the event and ask pointed questions, and still others decided that it was most effective to protest the speaker outside the hall. One group of activists from the city even banged on doors and set off fire alarms during the event. What became abundantly clear is that some felt that any protest that disrupted everyday tranquility was beyond the pale on a university campus. The history of all protest movements, however, is precisely to disrupt everyday life and highlight a social problem. It may mean you have to put up with more traffic, or that you have to pass by a group of loud protestors on your way in to listen to an anti-immigrant speaker, but that is a small price to pay given the importance of the struggle for social justice.

The sanctuary campus movement was the spark that led to the Civil Disobedience Workshop. Organizing around immigrant rights continued to be a flash point, even at the end of the semester when CIS to came to campus. However, what began as a movement around immigrant rights quickly connected to other struggles in the US and around the world. Although some criticized sanctuary as having no legal definition and therefore not really providing protection to undocumented immigrants, the ambiguity of the term allowed it to be redeployed in a variety of different contexts. A month before I testified in front of the Portland City Council in March 2017 to support the city's sanctuary resolution, the police had killed an unarmed black teenager, Quanice Hayes. The local Black Lives Matter (BLM) activists came to city council to disrupt the meeting and protest yet another killing of a black youth by police. Although there was some tension between the sanctuary folks who wanted the meeting to proceed and the BLM activists who wanted to shut down city council, many of us who testified made the point that we wanted sanctuary for everyone in Portland, not just immigrants, but black people, homeless people, and anyone targeted by state violence. "Sanctuary for All" is a way for us to link immigrant rights to all of our rights.[13] If they are taking away immigrant rights today, they will surely come after your rights tomorrow.

The new sanctuary that began as a movement of noncooperation had by the summer of 2018 become a movement of direct action against ICE. In June, a group of Portland activists surrounded the ICE detention facility in the city, shutting down its operations for two weeks and maintaining a camp outside for more than a month.[14] Citing his support for sanctuary, Portland's mayor declared that he would not use city police to remove the protestors. Federal officers eventually arrested protestors blocking the entrance to the detention center.[15] The Occupy ICE movement quickly spread to thirteen other cities with varying degrees of success.[16] However, it was the flexibility of the idea of sanctuary that allowed it to be interpreted by mayors and university presidents as being within the bounds of the law, at the same time as it could also inspire direct action civil disobedience by activists willing to put their bodies on the line to shut down (albeit temporarily) ICE operations. While some well-intentioned legal scholars argued against sanctuary on technical grounds that it couldn't actually protect immigrants, the capaciousness of the concept is politically effective.[17] Since the laws are so stacked against immigrants, the political struggle for their rights must always push beyond what is legal and fight for what is just.

Elliott Young is professor in the history department at Lewis & Clark College. Professor Young is the author of *Alien Nation: Chinese Migration in the Americas from the Coolie Era through WWII* (2014), *Catarino Garza's Revolution on the Texas-Mexico Border* (2004), and coeditor of *Continental Crossroads: Remapping US-Mexico Borderlands History* (2004). He is currently finishing a book on the history of immigrant incarceration in the United States.

Notes

1. Young, "On Sanctuary."
2. Floum, "City Council to Declare Portland a 'Sanctuary City'"; Friedman, "Trump Slams Portland Mayor."
3. Semuels, "The Racist History of Portland."
4. Denson, "1988 Story."
5. Wilson, "30 Years Later."
6. "Oregon Measure 105."
7. Young, "Sanctuary in the Trump Era."
8. Wiltfang and McAdam, "The Costs and Risks of Social Activism," 992.

9.   Gzesh, "Central Americans and Asylum Policy."
10. Piggott, "Anti-immigrant Center for Immigration Studies."
11. Young, "Safe Space for Hate Groups at Lewis & Clark College"; Lee, "Stephen Miller's Claim."
12. Campuzano, "Lewis & Clark Students, Faculty Push Back against Controversial Speaker."
13. Young, "Sanctuary for All in Portland."
14. "Occupy ICE PDX."
15. Friedman, "Portland Mayor to ICE Occupiers"; "ICE Resumes Normal Operation."
16. Campuzano, "Portland's Occupy ICE Movement Spreads to Other Cities."
17. Olivas, "Contronym and Controversy."

References

Campuzano, Eder. "Lewis & Clark Students, Faculty Push Back against Controversial Speaker as Protest Continues." *Oregonian*, April 11, 2017. www.oregonlive.com/portland/index.ssf /2017/04/jessica_vaughan_panel_lewis_cl.html.

Campuzano, Eder. "Portland's Occupy ICE Movement Spreads to Other Cities." *Oregonian*, June 23, 2018. www.oregonlive.com/expo/news/erry-2018/06/5e18f1cf119098/with_one_ week_down_in_portland.html.

Denson, Bryan. "1988 Story: Legacy of a Hate Crime: Mulugeta Seraw's Death a Decade Ago Avenged." *Oregonian*, November 12, 2014. www.oregonlive.com/portland/index.ssf/2014 /11/1998_story_legacy_of_a_hate_cr.html.

Floum, Jessica. "City Council to Declare Portland a 'Sanctuary City.'" *Oregonian*, March 21, 2017. www.oregonlive.com/politics/index.ssf/2017/03/city_council_to_declare_portla.html.

Friedman, Gordon R. "Portland Mayor to ICE Occupiers: Disband Now." *Oregonian*, June 23, 2018. www.oregonlive.com/portland/index.ssf/2018/07/portland_mayor_to_ice_occupier .html.

Friedman, Gordon R. "Trump Slams Portland Mayor for 'Shameful' Treatment of ICE Agents." *Oregonian*, August 20, 2018. www.oregonlive.com/portland/index.ssf/2018/08/trump_ slams_portland_mayor_for.html.

Gzesh, Susan. "Central Americans and Asylum Policy in the Reagan Era." *Migration Policy Institute*, April 1, 2006. www.migrationpolicy.org/article/central-americans-and-asylum -policy-reagan-era.

"ICE Resumes Normal Operation in Portland as Protest Continues." *KGW*, June 28, 2017. www .kgw.com/article/news/special-reports/at-the-border/ice-resumes-normal-operations-in -portland-as-protest-continues/283–568461821.

Lee, Michelle Ye Hee. "Stephen Miller's Claim That 72 from Banned Countries Were Implicated in 'Terroristic Activity.'" *Washington Post*, February 13, 2017. www .washingtonpost.com/news/fact-checker/wp/2017/02/13/stephen-millers-claim-that-72– from-banned-countries-were-implicated-in-terroristic-activity/?utm_term=.38975e577062.

"Occupy ICE PDX: A Timeline of the Portland Encampment." *Oregonian*, July 25, 2018. www .oregonlive.com/expo/news/erry-2018/07/62ee150670182/occupy-ice-pdx-a-timeline-of-t .html.

Olivas, Michael A. "Contronym and Controversy." *Inside Higher Ed*, November 29, 2016. www .insidehighered.com/views/2016/11/29/sanctuary-campuses-wont-provide-real-sanctuary -immigrant-students-essay.

"Oregon Measure 105." *BallotPedia*. ballotpedia.org/Oregon_Measure_105,_Repeal_ Sanctuary_State_Law_Initiative_(2018).

Piggott, Stephen. "Anti-immigrant Center for Immigration Studies Continues to Promote White Nationalists." *Southern Poverty Law Center*, November 7, 2016. https://www.splcenter.org /hatewatch/2016/11/07/anti-immigrant-center-immigration-studies-continues-promote -white-nationalists.

Semuels, Alana. "The Racist History of Portland, the Whitest City in America." *The Atlantic*, July 22, 2016. www.theatlantic.com/business/archive/2016/07/racist-history-portland /492035/.

Wilson, Conrad. "30 Years Later, Oregon's 'Sanctuary State' Serves as a Model for Others." *OPB*, April 17, 2107. www.opb.org/news/article/oregon-sanctuary-city-state-donald-trump -immigration/.

Wiltfang, Gregory L., and Doug McAdam. "The Costs and Risks of Social Activism: A Study of Sanctuary Movement Activism." *Social Forces* 69, no. 4 (1991): 987–1010.

Young, Elliott. "On Sanctuary: What Is in a Name?" *HuffPost*, December 2, 2016. publishing .huffpost.com/cms/post/583f8feae4b0b93e10f8df24.

Young, Elliott. "Safe Space for Hate Group at Lewis & Clark College." *HuffPost*, April 10, 2017. www.huffingtonpost.com/entry/safe-space-for-hate-group-at-lewis-clark-college_us_ 58ec03b0e4b0ea028d568c28.

Young, Elliott. "Sanctuary for All in Portland." *HuffPost*, March 23, 2017. www.huffingtonpost .com/entry/sanctuary-for-all-in-portland_us_58d3d2bae4b002482d6e6ec5.

Young, Elliott. "Sanctuary in the Trump Era." *NACLA*, February 3, 2017. nacla.org/news/2017 /02/07/sanctuary-trump-era.

Tiny Flying Houses and Other Forms of Resistance and Survival

Casitas voladoras y otras formas de resistencia y supervivencia

Rachel McIntire and Caleb Duarte

Human fragility is the reality of thin skin and brittle bones, housing hope and spirit and something primordial and yet divine. We make sanctuary, shelter, make-shift homes and temples to hold us, protect us, and ultimately support us as we develop into our full capacity as humans. The realities of human migration within a geopolitical context present challenges with each step—sometimes life threatening at particular borders, both those imagined and those formed by natural geological features. When considering the world we currently live in—replete with multiple, dynamic veins of migration—the impetus, means, and fragmentation of movement results in situations that require attention and care. Artist Caleb Duarte asserts, "My work deals with survival. Within this declaration, there is a shift made to what is essential—from that a break occurs from western assumptions of what is considered beauty, success, knowledge. The collective reimagines and contemporaneously reclaims body, mind, and spirit—again as an imperative to survival."

Within this historical imperative for personal and collective survival, the arts find a way to be both a force in shaping experience as well as a mirror reflecting actions and intentions. These opportunities of engagement present a window to review and revise in the present tense. In *The Archive and the Repertoire*, Diana

Radical History Review

Issue 135 (October 2019)   DOI 10.1215/01636545-7607920

© 2019 by MARHO: The Radical Historians' Organization, Inc.

Taylor explores how performance can transmit cultural memory and identity.[1] This underpinning idea of transmission exists as the foundation in Caleb Duarte's work, seeking to both guide and interrogate assumptions of distinct time and place. The objective of the artist as guide in this work serves to establish norms of understanding while building community that allows for the future art action to take hold— inviting unexpected outcomes in both material and form. The process is contemporaneously spontaneous and amorphous. The collective expression of disparate voices elevates the issue, allowing participation and often altering perception. Howard Zinn describes this transaction as transcendent in that the artist creates a space or event that transcends the immediate. In this unapologetic motion there might be beauty or even mayhem; most importantly, there is an intentional engagement of the collective.

I used to think that the role of Art was to challenge logic; to enact or impose a magical realism into society's notions of a shared reality. Like the DADAist after the war, the Impressionist, Expressionist, Povera artist or Surrealist. But now, within the chaos and absurdity of our current social political climate, and the paraded cruelty supported by many, I realize that Art must retreat into logic; into a sober sanity as a standard of reason, a reason guided by the displaced, the exiles, or by an indigenous knowledge of survival, resistance, and endurance.[2]

   Casitas voladoras is an example of one such work that engages the collective imagination within time and space. The project was imagined within the context of the Sanctuary Movement established by a coalition of faith-based organizations and individuals to support undocumented migrants who were fleeing unrest in Central America in the 1980s. The movement, currently recognized as the New Sanctuary Movement, emerged in direct response to the US foreign policy of that time and continues to protect immigrants in faith-based spaces. This policy backed dictators in the civil wars in Central America, causing thousands of refugees to flee for their safety.[3] The US government did not recognize them as political refugees and they were denied legal entry to the United States. The refusal of asylum seekers and the deportations that ensued led to uncertainty and insecurity on return to their countries of birth. The New Sanctuary Movement began in churches along the Mexican border, and has expanded to include more than 1,100 churches in forty-four states that support undocumented migrants.[4]

   Casitas voladoras is a performative collaboration that Duarte began with day laborers in San Francisco in 2008. The sculptural performance, in dialogue with the New Sanctuary Movement, included the construction of a miniature church that was carried through the city as an urgent art action. Participants, including undocumented migrants, artists and other members of the community took personal responsibility to create sanctuary outside of a church or NGO—an act of identifying and reclaiming safe space by undocumented people in a major US city.

The following year, Duarte and his father Francisco traveled to El Pital, Honduras. In the small river valley community, the Duartes' original intention was to collect oral histories and stories of migration for an independent publication entitled *Casitas voladoras*. Francisco Duarte, himself an immigrant from Mexico, was more than familiar with stories of immigration from throughout Latin America. The interviews and time with the community lent to the development of a trusting relationship with the community of El Pital. The community had previously worked with Caleb Duarte on several projects that had clear objectives, such as painting the school logo and helping to design the layout of the new library. As a result, a sense of trust was established, allowing Caleb to be honest and also playful when talking about the realities of migration in this rural Honduran town, where each family had at least one member in "el Norte." The conversations fueled the construction of tiny houses made from bamboo from the Cangrejal River and from bedsheets. The tiny houses were then carried by the children in a procession that sinuously wove through the community and across the river, finally resting in the large multi-use field in the center of town.

The work was not finished there. After a celebratory close in El Pital, Caleb moved north to California's Central Valley, where day laborers constructed more tiny houses, precariously balanced on long thin poles that reached to the sky. The next iteration created a full circle, with Duarte returning to San Francisco to work with undocumented immigrants from the state of Chiapas, Mexico. In this ultimate procession of theatrical protest, Duarte and the workers extended *Casitas voladoras* as a living, human-held structure using bedsheets and two-by-fours that caravanned with both real and implied weight through the busy streets of the Mission District, stopping traffic and drawing attention to the sculpture and the people carrying it.

Casitas voladoras exists as one example of performance in a continuum of responses honing a collective voice and vision. Through activation in these diverse venues the audience is invited, and at times forced through the act of bearing witness, to imagine how these structures and processions invite sanctuary. The playful houses held by those participating in informal, and often invisible, underground economies provide a new dialogue through the language of sculpture and performance in the context of a now protected hypervisibility. In this vision the nuance of organization, iteration, and production charge both cause and effect in the act that occurs.

Another example of such engagement occurred with *Entierro*, a performance that took place in a small autonomous Mayan community in Chiapas, Elambo Bajo. EDELO (En Donde Era La Onu / Where the United Nations Used to Be), a collective of artists and activists in Chiapas that Duarte cofounded, began working with children of Elambo Bajo. In the first phase of the project the EDELO artists asked community members to bury them in the earth. The artists in turn created a game with the community, wherein they would bury community members using the metaphor of planting a seed that would burst from the earth and emerge as a fruit-bearing tree. This game hinged on the concept of breaking away from a colonized mind-set, shifting to one focused on the earth and a cosmology centered on acknowledgment of the violent histories carried by our bodies.

Entierro traveled north to the Fresno Art Museum, set within the white-wall aesthetics of a museum with an art audience. In an attempt to present a similar energy and physical experience, Duarte asked a young Chicano tattoo artist to perform, trapped in a large rectangle of earth within a constricted circle for the duration of the opening. For three hours a tension was created in the viewers as they observed the young man with a stoic, sweat-stained face, held by the confines of earth on all sides. His actions drew out the weight of the experiential that is carried by our bodies, and that we hold as we negotiate a myriad of lived experiences.

Zapantera negra is yet another example of a far-reaching community art project that made visible the relationship between the Black Panther Party and Zapatista movements. In this project, which has continued in the form of a traveling exhibition and engagement, Emory Douglas, artist and former Minister of Culture for the Black Panther Party, partnered with EDELO to create a woven tapestry of historical understanding, employing the artistry of Zapatista embroideries. The exchange invited complicated conversations recognizing the political and social realities of groups seeking autonomy within their respective national contexts.

Dado el estado actual del mundo, el arte como entretenimiento trivial y pasivo ya no es sólo entretenimiento—en realidad, puede ser destructivo para nuestro futuro. EDELO se ocupa de presentar un espacio de exploración como una obra de arte en sí misma, regresando a la esencia de la creación.

(Given the state of the world, art becomes a trivial and passive practice if it is only practice—in reality, it can be destructive for our future if left passive. EDELO occupies the present tense of space in an exploration about ourselves returning to the essence of all creation.)
—EDELO Vision Statement

Duarte's work seeks to engage a diverse and often unsuspecting audience in finding the space to create dialogue about the possibilities of collective reimagining within the greater human experience. The work questions assumptions of privilege and the political and social systems that influence our lives. Within the work, fleeting moments and revelations often provide a glimpse into the capacity of humanity and the power of creativity to connect us with one another in dignity as we search for truth. The work continues to percolate with questions that examine the role of art and artist in making experiences accessible to diverse audiences in spaces intended for the production of art, and in public and private spaces. With the intention to situate divergent positions beside one another in mobile conversations, the generation of a new type of understanding is central to the effectiveness of the creative action. These transient efforts for truth continue to emerge from the cracks, made by the same hope for survival and justice that follows us throughout time.

CURATED SPACES provides a focus on contemporary artists whose work addresses social, historical, or political subject matter.

Caleb Duarte is best known for creating temporary installations using construction-type frameworks such as beds of dirt, cement, and objects suggesting basic shelter. His installations within institutional settings become sites for performance as interpretations of his community collaborations. Duarte has created public works and community performances at the World Social Forum in Mumbai, India; in Santiago de Cuba, Cuba; in El Pital, Honduras; and throughout Mexico and the United States. He has collaborated with autonomous indigenous Zapatista collectives, working youth, and Central American refugees. Duarte is professor of sculpture at Fresno City College, Fresno, California.

Artist and educator **Rachel McIntire's** interests are rooted in providing narrative-generating opportunities for individuals and groups. Rachel has played a fundamental role in developing art-based programs for youth throughout the Bay Area and internationally in Mexico, Honduras, Ecuador, and Tanzania. Recently, she has worked to create Divining Place, a dynamic artist-in-residence program connecting students with professional artists with the intention of creating space for a deep contemplative practice engaging contemporary social and environmental issues. Rachel serves as the K–12 Visual Art and Design Chair at Schools of the Sacred Heart in San Francisco.

Notes

1. Taylor, *The Archive and the Repertoire.*
2. Zinn, *Artists in Times of War.*
3. Rabben, *Sanctuary and Asylum.* See also Cunningham, *God and Caesar at the Rio Grande.*
4. Myrna Orozco, *New Report: Sanctuary in the Age of Trump*, https://www .sanctuarynotdeportation.org/sanctuary-report-2018.html (accessed November 11, 2018).

References

Cunningham, Hilary. *God and Caesar at the Rio Grande: Sanctuary and the Politics of Religion.* Minneapolis: University of Minnesota Press, 1995.

Rabben, Linda. *Sanctuary and Asylum: A Social and Political History.* Seattle: University of Washington Press, 2016.

Taylor, Diana. *The Archive and the Repertoire: Performing Cultural Memory in the Americas.* Durham, NC: Duke University Press, 2003.

Zinn, Howard. *Artists in Times of War.* New York: Penguin, 2003.

Figure 1. *Casitas voladoras*, 2009. Sculptural performance, 2008, El Pital, Honduras. Photo, Francisco Duarte.

Figure 2. *Casitas voladoras*, 2009. Sculptural performance, 2008, El Pital, Honduras. Video still, Caleb Duarte.

Figure 3. *Casitas voladoras*, 2009. Sculptural performance, 2008, El Pital, Honduras. Video still, Caleb Duarte.

Figure 4. *Casitas voladoras*, 2009. Community festival during sculptural performance, El Pital, Honduras. Video still, Caleb Duarte.

Figure 5. *New Temporary Sanctuary Movement*, 2008. Public intervention, San Francisco, California. Photo, Caleb Duarte.

Figure 6. *New Temporary Sanctuary Movement*, 2008. Public intervention, Red Poppy Art House, San Francisco, California. Photo, Caleb Duarte.

Figure 7. *Our Built City*, 2015. Two-month community collaboration, San Francisco, California. Photo, Mia Eve Rollow.

Figure 8. *Burial*, 2013. *Entierrro*, Community performance with the autonomous community of Elambo Bajo, Chiapas, Mexico. With EDELO (Where the United Nations Used to Be) and artist Mia Eve Rollow. Photo Caleb Duarte.

Figure 9. *Burial*, 2013. Institutional burial performance at the Fresno Art Museum, Fresno, California. Performer, Arturo Villanueva. Photo, Caleb Duarte.

Figure 10. *Zapantera negra*, 2016. Sculptural installation with Zapatista artists and Emory Douglas, Minister of Culture of the Black Panther Party. H Street Graduate Studios, Fresno State University. Photo, Caleb Duarte.

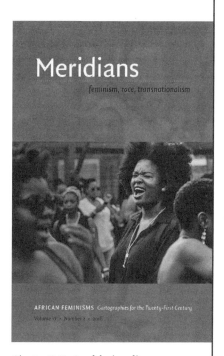

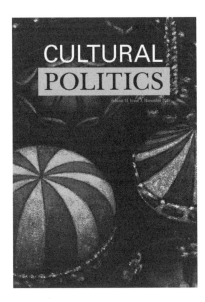